Homework

Homework

TEN STEPS TO FOOLPROOF PLANNING BEFORE BUILDING

PETER JESWALD

TEN SPEED PRESS
BERKELEY, CALIFORNIA

P.O. Box 7123
Berkeley, California 94710

A Kirsty Melville Book

Cover design by Ross Carron.
Book design by Margery Cantor.
Illustrations by Akiko Shurtleff.

Library of Congress Cataloging-in-Publication Data

Jeswald, Peter.
    Homework / Peter Jeswald
        p.   cm.
    Includes index.
    ISBN 0-89815-744-7
    1. House construction—Planning.   I. Title
    TH4812.J47 1995
    690′.837—dc20

Printed in Canada

1 2 3 4 5—99 98 97 96 95

Contents

ACKNOWLEDGMENTS

I would like to extend my sincerest thanks and deepest appreciation to the following people: Bob Abramms, who first encouraged me to commit my ideas to paper and provided early guidance and advice. David Vreeland, who has accompanied me to every one of my seminars, and with whom I have discussesd many of the issues addressed in this book. His knowledge and insight has been invaluable. Michal Fritz and Duncan Prahl were early advocates of the *Homework* concept and supported my efforts for the past three years. Phyllis Jeswald, my wife, patiently and tirelessly edited the first workbook version of *Homework*.

Many people graciously took time out of their busy lives to read portions of the manuscript or talk with me. Their comments and feedback were indispensible. These include Bruce Austin, Greenfield, Massachusetts, building inspector; Phil Lamere, Greenfield Savings Bank; Bob Phillips, United Savings Bank; Rick Arnold and Mike Guertin, U.S. Building Concepts; Ross Gorman, Cohn & Co. Insurance Agency; Richard Fitzgerald, Boston Society of Architects; Dan Mercer, National Association of Home Builders; and David Janoff, National Association of the Remodeling Industry. I would also like to thank all my former clients, seminar sponsors, and seminar attendees. Much of what I have learned, I learned from them.

The people at Ten Speed Press have been a pleasure to work with, providing strong, flexible leadership while soliciting and respecting my input. In particular, my editor, Lorena Jones, has expertly guided this rookie writer and refined this book with her considerable skills.

Introduction

While creating a home satisfies our romantic and nesting nature, it also has a practical side. Any building project, from a custom home to a modest renovation, is a complicated undertaking that requires the skills of many people and a vast array of information. The success or failure of any project is largely determined by three factors: the competence of the people involved, the quality of the information assembled, and the effectiveness with which that information is communicated. While it is important to hire the best and most skilled people you can find (we'll talk a lot in this book about what it means to be the "best"), that alone is not enough. It is equally important that you be well organized and that your project be well planned, so that all the participants have the right information to make the right decisions at the right time. People, information, and communication—these are the essential ingredients of a successful building project, and the subject of *Homework*.

It is vital that you understand the people/communication part of the process; a building project is as much about construction people as it is about construction materials and methods. In fact, the planning and construction processes are largely about establishing and maintaining good working relationships with all the people involved. This includes not only building industry professionals, but also the people in your personal life: your family and friends.

YOUR THREE TEAMS

Before you begin your *Homework*, let's get an overview of what lies ahead, take a brief look at some the people who will be involved, and see how these people will be a part of your project. Later we'll take a more detailed look at these people and the roles they play. To begin, it is helpful to think about the people you will be working with as members of three groups, or "teams." Each of these teams has certain primary responsibilities, and each is instrumental in making your project a reality. I call these teams: the Home Team, the Design Team, and the Construction Team.

The Home Team consists of the homeowner (you and your partner), your immediate family, other relatives, and friends who will provide direction and emotional support for the project. Additional team members might include a banker, insurance agent, real estate agent, real estate consultant, and lawyer. Their jobs are to provide the Home Team with the advice, information, and resources required for the successful completion of the planning and construction processes. The Home Team is, of course, the driving force behind a building project. Without it there's no reason for the project to move forward. Therefore, the Home Team's primary responsibilities are to identify and communicate the needs that are to be met (called a "program"), determine the financial feasibility of the project, hire the members of the other two teams, and oversee the preconstruction planning process.

The Design Team might include a designer, structural engineer, civil engineer, wetlands consultant, landscape architect, and interior designer. The Design Team's job is to work closely with the Home Team to identify its needs, help create a program, translate those needs into an appropriate, buildable, affordable design, and make sure that the design is built as it was intended. The Design Team is a crucial link between the imagery of your dreams and the reality of a finished home.

The Construction Team consists of a large number of construction tradespeople, including carpenters, roofers, electricians, and plumbers. In fact, building an average house requires the services of more than thirty different construction trades, not counting the dozens of material suppliers and manufacturers. The responsibility of the Construction Team is to take the design that was developed by the Design Team and transform it into a physical reality.

Although it is helpful to think of these three teams as distinct units, it's not quite that simple. The distinctions between the teams tend to get blurred because one person can be a member of more than one team. For example, you are a member of the Home Team, but during construction you might do some of the painting, which would make you a member of the Construction Team. Also, depending on the scope of your project, the builder might contribute significantly to the design process, making the builder an active member of the Design Team. Sometimes the distinctions between the teams get so blurred that it's difficult to clearly separate one team from another. But while it might be difficult to identify the different teams by the personnel, it is important to recognize the existence of each team and their responsibilities, and to know that these responsibilities must be carried out in order for your project to be successful.

To recap, a project is first conceived by the Home Team, then transcribed by the Design Team, and finally built by the Construction Team. In order for this sequence to proceed smoothly, each team must perform its tasks punctually. Ideally, each team will have a leader. The primary responsibilities of the people in the leadership roles are to assemble the team, organize and work effectively with the other team members, and communicate with the other team leaders to keep the project on course. Notice that I said *leadership roles*; this is a very important distinction, because that's exactly what they are. The leadership positions of the three teams are actually *roles* that need to be filled, and not necessarily by separate people. The leadership position for the Home Team is the Project Planner, for the Design Team the Project Designer, and for the Construction Team the Project Manager. It is also important to understand that any one role can be filled by many different people. On top of that, the same role may be occupied by more than one person at various stages of the design process. In Step 1, we'll take a closer look at some of the different people who can fill the leadership roles.

The planning and construction of your project should be a collaborative effort, with all three teams working harmoniously toward its successful completion. Even though many other people will have major parts to play, the ultimate responsibility for the success or failure of your project will fall on your shoulders. By following *Homework*'s ten-step process you will be able to skillfully fulfill that responsibility.

ONE FOR ALL

Homework is invaluable for everyone planning any type of residential building project. If you are planning a new home, whether a custom or manufactured home, this book is for you. If you're planning an addition or renovation, no matter how large or small, this book is for you. How can this be? Isn't new construction different than additions or renovations? Yes and no. Yes, because there are differences between the two general categories of construction, and no, because all residential projects have to go through the ten-step process outlined in this book. Certainly the emphasis put on individual steps will vary from project to project according to their type, size, and scope, but the essence of every step is contained in every project.

In writing this book I have used the custom, "stick built" house (defined in Step 1) as the benchmark project because a custom-built house most fully utilizes all of the ten steps. To address the areas where other types of projects differ from the custom home, I point them out when they arise and offer corresponding information in boxes with titles such as "Addition Alert" and "Manufactured Housing." I encourage everyone, no matter what their project, to read the entire book and pay particular attention to the sections that target their project.

CUSTOMIZE TO OPTIMIZE

While I encourage you follow these ten steps, don't follow them blindly or take them on faith. They are ten steps, not ten commandments. I have done my best to organize *Homework*'s ten steps to reflect what I believe is the most effective approach for the typical residential building project. Of course, almost everything varies from the theoretical norm, and your project will be no exception. With that in mind, you should tailor *Homework* to suit your needs, your situation, your means, and your goals. For starters, quickly read through the entire book before you begin extensive work on any one step. After all, it is unlikely that you are going to complete every worksheet, need every piece of information presented, or follow the exact presentation of the ten steps. Skimming the book will allow you to get an overall picture of the entire process, determine how you fit in, and then rearrange or modify the ten steps accordingly. Also, there are some steps ("Step 5: Hire the Professionals," for instance) that you might have to do more than once during the process. By reading ahead, you'll discover which steps these are and be prepared. Finally, there are some steps (such as "Step 8: Secure Your Financing") that require some advance work; there are issues that must be addressed ahead of time in order to successfully complete that step. As you read, note which steps need this kind of attention so that you won't lose any time.

OUTSIDE READING

Homework's main goal is to conserve some valuable resources: your time, your money, and your peace of mind. To be most effective, however, *Homework* should not stand alone. Many of the subjects covered in *Homework*, such as designing a house, buying land, and securing a loan, can be extremely complicated and involved. To cover these in depth is beyond the scope of *Homework*. Many good books and articles have been written on these topics, and I encourage you to read extensively on these subjects and to seek the help of industry professionals when appropriate. The Appendices contain a comprehensive listing of books, periodicals, and other valuable sources of information; use it!

STEREOTYPE a standardized mental picture…representing an oversimplified opinion, affective attitude, or uncritical judgment of a person, a race, an issue, or an event [as defined by *Merriam Webster's Collegiate Dictionary*].

The world around us is filled with stereotyped images, and the construction industry is no exception. Designers are stereotyped, builders are stereotyped, bankers are stereotyped, building inspectors are stereotyped, and yes, even homeowners are stereotyped. I wish I had the power to eliminate all stereotypes and the resulting prejudice, but that's just a little beyond my reach. I would, however, like to strike a smaller blow, and encourage you to eliminate stereotyping from your planning and construction process. You have nothing to lose and everything to gain. As I said earlier, the success or failure of any given project is largely determined by three factors: the competence of the people involved, the quality of the information assembled, and the effectiveness with which that information is communicated. If you allow stereotypical assumptions to cloud your thinking and influence your decisions, the raw material you need for success—competent people, good information, and effective communication—will be harder to attain. To help ensure the success of your project, do yourself and everyone else a favor: be thorough, be objective, and above all be rational in your process.

PROJECT PLANNER, LEADER OF THE HOME TEAM

Homework is about the preconstruction process, and preconstruction is about the various planning stages of a building project. Although the preconstruction process deals mostly with information you need to have before construction begins, much of what you learn can be utilized throughout the project. *Homework*'s purpose is to teach you how to become the leader of the Home Team—the most organized, efficient, and effective Project Planner that you can possibly be. As the Project Planner, you will:

- Discover what you need to know, when you need to know it, who to communicate it to, and how;

- Learn to make appropriate decisions at the appropriate time;

- Reduce your level of stress and anxiety, approach your project with an air of confidence, and actually enjoy yourself;

- Realize significant savings of both time and money while achieving a superior result and terrific sense of satisfaction.

And if you do your *Homework* this can happen. But the "if you do" part is crucial, because *Homework* is not just a planning guide, it's also a planning tool. Like any tool, *Homework* will only work if it is used. So please, don't read this book once and put it up on the shelf to be forgotten. Keep it with you, refer to it, write in it, use the worksheets, and learn from it. That's the only way your work will get done. So good luck, and get to it!

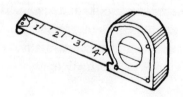

STEP 1 **Build Your Foundation**

You may think that you're ready to jump right in with both feet, but think again. Before you do, let's take a look at what you're getting into and what you'll need to survive the jump.

THE GOAL FOR STEP 1   To increase your awareness of the impact that a construction project can have on your life, and to learn some of the survival skills you will need to succeed.

The preconstruction planning process, like a well-built house, should begin with the construction of a solid foundation. A house that's supported by an inadequate foundation will develop serious problems over time, even if the rest of the structure is sound. The same is true of the planning process. It doesn't matter how well you execute the other steps in this book; if you don't take the time now to build a stable base from which to work, your efforts will most likely be less successful and less rewarding. Unfortunately, it's easy to ignore this important portion of the planning process. At one time or another, this part has been overlooked by nearly everyone involved in the planning process—designers, builders, and homeowners. We are all guilty. I'm not certain exactly why this is, but I have some theories. Perhaps in our eagerness to "get started," we choose to do tasks that feel more like "real work" and show tangible results. Maybe, under the influence of the ticking clock, we say to ourselves, "Oh, I can't do this now, I'll take care of it next week . . . maybe." I'll bet some of us fall prey to the familiar "I already know *that*" or "You can't teach an old dog new tricks" traps. It could be that we find this part of the process unfamiliar, or too uncomfortable to deal with. Or maybe, once we discover that this part will actually take time, we decide that it's really not worth *our* time or energy. So if you hear internal voices whispering reasons to leave this step and skip ahead, ignore them. The work in this step, while it will take time and may be difficult, is going to set the tone and determine the attitude with which you approach the entire planning and building process. The proper attitude will greatly enhance your prospects for a successful and enjoyable experience.

The building blocks of a solid foundation for the preconstruction planning process are good personal and good working relationships. It sounds simple enough on the surface; most of us take pride in the relationships we've developed with our family, friends, and community. But believe me, nothing will test those relationships like a residential construction project. You must maintain and strengthen your existing relationships, most notably those with your family, and be able to establish new relationships with the professionals you'll work with throughout the planning and construction process. The place to begin your work on relationships is right at home.

The first order of business is to make sure that you and your family are aware of the scope and potential impact of your upcoming project. Hold a family meeting and get everything out in the open. Does everyone in your family—and this means everyone, including your two year old—know what you're planning? No secrets are allowed here, because building a new home or making changes to the one you're living in affects every member of the family. I'm sure you've heard that "building your home will be the biggest investment of your life." But that's not necessarily true. Your children, if you have them, are the most precious, the most expensive, and the largest investment you will ever make. Special attention should be paid to children's feelings and needs during the course of planning and building a new house, addition, or renovation. To a young child who has spent all his or her years in the same house, the prospect of moving to a new one can be quite upsetting. An addition or renovation that makes substantial changes to the living environment can also be very unsettling, so be prepared for that. On the other hand, a brother and sister who share a bedroom would probably be overjoyed at the thought of finally having their own rooms. Be sure to listen to the tears as well as the cheers; there may be things to learn from both.

I recently worked on an addition/remodeling that illustrates these points. The family—husband, wife, a five-year-old son, and an eight-year-old daughter—lived in a small, two-bedroom house. As a result, the children shared a bedroom. The children were growing and so was the family's need for space. They wanted a new dining room, a master bedroom suite, a porch, an office, and, of course, a new bedroom that would create separate bedrooms for the children. The children were extremely excited at the prospect of their having their own rooms, and were also curious about how it was going to be done. They were made a part of the design process, and at every design meeting time was devoted to showing them the latest variations and listening to their comments and reactions. One of their most frequent questions was, "When can we move in?" During the course of construction, the children watched closely as their "new" house and *their* rooms took shape. They frequently talked with the builders and asked, "When will it be done? When can we move in?" Finally, the day came when the boy's new bedroom was ready. The parents expected a mad dash for the door, but were surprised when their son said, "I'm not ready to move yet." Their daughter, whose room was to be refurbished, wasn't ready for the change either. Sensitive to the situation, the parents allowed their children as much time as they needed. After a week or so, on a bright Saturday morning, the boy announced, "All right, I'm ready," and the move was made. In spite of the fact that both children had been part of the planning and construction, they still needed time to truly comprehend its meaning.

Other questions to be asked at this family meeting include:

- Is this a good time for the family to undertake a building project?
- How will the change impact individual family members—changing neighborhoods, losing friends, leaving social organizations?
- How will it impact family life—school, vacations, day-to-day activities, work?
- Given your current financial or job situation, does a major construction project make sense at this time?

- Will there have to be some belt-tightening and, if so, how will it be done?
- Do you have the time to commit to a building project?

Once again, be sure the entire family considers and responds to these questions. This family meeting should be the first of many held to address issues as they arise throughout the process. You should consider designating regular times for family meetings, adjusting the number held per week or per month as the situation warrants. This sharing of the decision-making processes will help foster a sense of cooperation and encourage your family to work enthusiastically together toward the successful completion of *their* project. Let's take a closer look at some of the issues that your family should be aware of.

SPEND, SPEND, SPEND

One issue that deserves more scrutiny is money. Let's be up front here: if you're planning a building project, you'd better be prepared to spend money—probably a lot of money. If that thought sends shivers of fear up and down your spine, it's not surprising. Many of us get glassy eyed at the thought of spending a few hundred dollars. The project you're considering will probably cost you tens or hundreds of *thousands* of dollars—more money than you are likely to spend on any one thing in your lifetime. Scary? You bet. Painful? Perhaps, but you can learn ways to lessen the pain and make your financial decisions with a clear head. First, however, you must acknowledge the fact that spending money is inevitable—hey, it can even be fun. Then, if you do your *Homework* conscientiously, you'll learn how much money you can afford to spend, how to spend less of it, and how to get the most out of the money you do spend. In the end, writing those checks might not be so painful.

If you think that money is all you'll spend, think again. No matter how you do it, a building project is extremely time-consuming. This appetite for time seems to be indiscriminate, ignoring your desire to "not get very involved," and affecting large and small projects alike. Residential construction seems to be one of those activities that will use up all the time you give it, and then some. It's just a fact of construction life. No matter how much time you think you will have to devote to your project, double it once and maybe twice. In my opinion that's not necessarily a bad thing; you should give, and give happily, as much time as you can to your project. To succeed—to do the best you can—you need to allow time for your thoughts and objectives to grow and mature. You need time for exploration, time for reflection, and time to enjoy this process. One of my pet peeves is that clients often come to me and say, "Peter, we'd like you to design our project, but we want to have it yesterday." Maybe it's a symptom of our instant society: instant coffee, instant cereal, instant gratification. "Instant" is out of place here; it leaves you no time to savor the experience. Cramming your *Homework* is not a good idea.

To acknowledge the importance of your commitment, set aside a period of time each day, no matter how little, to devote to your project. I find that work doesn't seem so overwhelming if I can keep current and do a little every day. Sometimes, however, you will need large blocks of time to get tasks done. If you have vacation time or sick days coming, consider using them for your project. Of course, not everything runs on a schedule. Be prepared for those times, farther into the process, when you'll have to drop everything if an emergency or crisis arises.

DECISIONS, DECISIONS, DECISIONS

What type of material for the living room, dining room, bedroom, and bathroom floors? What color for the living room, dining room, bedroom, and bathroom walls? Do you really have to pick a color for the roof? What style of cabinets for the kitchen? Are you *really* going to live here during the construction? You'll suddenly find yourself having to make thousands of decisions—enough decisions to make your head spin and your stomach turn. But don't despair; here's some advice on how to deal with those symptoms.

1 Get help. You shouldn't have to make all the decisions by yourself. You should, of course, enlist the help of your family and friends, but there will be times when you should seek advice from appropriate professionals. Don't be "too proud" to ask for help when you get stuck; if you don't ask, and continue to thrash about, you might find yourself sinking in quicksand.

2 Be judicious. Decision-making is a process of weighing the alternatives; often there is no clear-cut, perfect answer—only the best alternative chosen from a list of pros and cons. In the end, you must compare the options and tally the score to make the choice that's right for you.

3 Be pragmatic. Sometimes decisions that seem so critical at the moment, and over which you agonize for days, really aren't all that crucial in retrospect. In fact you could have lived happily with any number of possibilities. Be careful with this one, though, and try to separate the *crucial, important,* and *routine* decisions.

4 Be realistic. Acknowledge that nobody's perfect; no matter how well prepared you are, no matter how hard you try, some mistakes are going to be made. You're going to make some mistakes, and the people you hire are going to make some mistakes. When this happens, assigning blame is not helpful or productive. Seldom does the responsibility for a mistake fall on one person's shoulders. The most effective approach is to forgive the parties involved, correct the mistake as soon as possible, and try to determine how to avoid similar mistakes in the future. Strangely enough, you might find it hardest to forgive yourself, but cut yourself some slack.

EXPECT THE UNEXPECTED

Throughout the planning and construction process, complications such as plan revisions, underground rock ledge ("bedrock" that has to be blasted out), rotten beams, and four weeks of rain are occasional visitors; no matter how well you've prepared, there's a good chance some of them will drop in on you. You should learn to take these unexpected events in stride, and understand that they're just "par for the course."

SET UP A SUPPORT SYSTEM

By this I don't mean a structural support system, but rather an emotional support system for you and your partner. The stress and strain associated with planning and then building is probably unlike anything you've experienced before. The pressures of working and making decisions together, spending vast sums of money, and dealing every day with the unfamiliar will severely test the best of relationships. In fact, if your relationship is currently on shaky ground, you should seriously consider rebuilding it before building anything else. I'll bet you know at least one couple who have had difficulties during a construction project; frankly, divorce is not uncommon. Thankfully, most couples survive, and you probably will, too, but you won't avoid the pressures. Accordingly, you should consider taking some steps to help you deal with the pressures:

- Tell a close friend or two about your plans to build. Ask them if they would be available, "just in case," to offer a shoulder to cry on, to listen to you complain about your partner, or to hear you scream bloody murder about that stubborn designer.

- Find times to get away from it all, to be alone and recharge your batteries. Take a walk, watch a good comedy, treat yourself to lunch, or do something special to unwind and reward yourself for all the hard work you're doing.

- Before you get too far into the process, talk openly with your partner about the friction and conflicts that will probably occur between you, and affirm that no matter what is said in the heat of the battle, you still love each other. You might even write each other love letters and place them in envelopes marked, "To be opened at an appropriate time."

- Consider the possibility that, in spite of the fact that you *know* you love each other, there might be a chance that you could use some professional help. It wouldn't hurt, before things get too involved, to choose a family counselor you could call on to help you through any particularly rough times.

- Be patient and compassionate. I will use the word "process" many times in this book, because that's exactly what this is: a process, a gradual unfolding. At times, for example when you have to make fifty decisions in fifty minutes, it might seem anything but gradual. If you can be patient with decision-making, patient with the people you hire, and, most of all, patient with yourself, you will go a long way toward keeping your peace of mind.

ANOTHER WORLD, A DIFFERENT LANGUAGE

Now it's time to turn our attention away from your familiar environment to another world—the world of residential construction. This world has the power to evoke a wide range of feelings—excitement, fear, dread, awe. For the uninitiated, entering the construction world can feel like walking into the middle of an Abbot and Costello routine, in which everybody knows "who's on first" except you. Before you can successfully navigate in this new world, you have to know more about the people who inhabit it and the language that they speak.

During the past several years, as I've traveled around the northeast presenting my home-planning workshops, I've been surprised by the number of people who are confused about which professional to hire for a particular job. Questions that arise often include, "Who should I hire to design my project—an architect, a building designer, or a builder?" and, "Do I need to hire a general contractor, or can a carpenter do the job?" It became clear that people often don't have a handle on who does what in the construction industry. I believe the root of the problem is twofold: first, more than one type of professional is often capable of doing the same job, and second, many jobs are actually a composite of several different jobs which, when taken together, form *roles*. As I explained earlier, these roles can not only be filled by more than one professional, but the same role can be, and frequently is, filled by more than one person during the course of a building project. It's a little like using several actors to play the same part in different acts of the same play. In order to make sense of the construction world, you need to understand the differences among the various professionals, and recognize the roles they play. In Step 5, we'll take a closer look at both, but for now I'd like to offer the following "job descriptions."

DESIGNERS

In the broadest sense of the word, a designer is a person who takes a concept and transforms it into a understandable form—typically by means of a drawing or model—that effectively communicates that idea to other people. Anybody who's planned a dog house or a bird house has been a designer. My daughter was a designer when, at the age of six, she drew a plan of a tree house, complete with door, drawbridge, pyramid roof, and the edict: "No boys allowed." I actually built the tree house as designed, with one minor revision: no drawbridge. You will step into the designer's role when, in Step 2 of this book, you explore the possibilities of your project. In fact, at one time or another, we have probably all been designers. However, some time during the planning process you may need the assistance of someone more skilled than yourself, someone with professional experience.

DESIGN PROFESSIONALS

What is a design professional? For our purposes I'm going to offer this definition: *A design professional is anyone—and I mean anyone, regardless of his or her training, qualifications, or skill— who gets paid to provide design services.* That pretty much opens the door for anybody; there's no telling who's going to walk in and ask for a job. Don't worry; in Step 5 you'll not only learn how to evaluate all the professionals you might encounter, but also how to choose the one who's right for you. For now, you only need to know that there are many kinds of design professionals associated with residential construction. They include, but are not limited to, architects, building designers, kitchen designers, bath designers, interior designers, landscape architects, and lighting designers. I also include engineers, such as civil, structural, and mechanical, under the umbrella of design professional. And, to answer the question posed above, yes, builders can often act as design professionals. Most of these design professionals work on one easily defined, specific part of a building project. It's clear that kitchen designers design kitchens, landscape designers design the terrain around a building, and lighting designers design the way buildings and their surroundings are illuminated. But what do we mean, and who are we talking about, when we speak of "the designer"?

WHO IS "THE DESIGNER"?

"The designer" is a frequently misunderstood, misused term. To help clarify, I offer yet another simple definition: "*The designer*" *is any design professional who "designs" a building by arranging the spaces to meet the requirement of the owner's program.* Three types of professionals who frequently act as designers are architects, building designers, and builders. In Step 5, we'll take an in-depth look at these design professionals, the services they offer, the differences among them, and how to choose the appropriate ones for your job. Therefore, when someone says "my designer" they might mean "my architect" or "my building designer." When I say "designer," I'm speaking in general terms about any one of several design professionals that may do the designer's job, and when I say "building designer," I'm speaking about a specific type of professional.

THE ROLE OF THE PROJECT DESIGNER

Typically, a designer offers a wide range of services, from short-term consultation to total involvement in a project from the preliminary design stages through to the end of construction. When a designer is hired on a "full-service" basis, he or she takes care of the many tasks that are required to shepherd a building from initial concept to completed structure. But what about those times when the designer is hired as a "consultant" and provides minimal service? What becomes of the tasks that they would have performed under a full-service contract? Do they simply disappear? No, of course not. But who does them?

In the Introduction, I described the three planning/building teams and the role of their leaders, and indicated that the Project Designer is the leader of the Design Team. When a designer provides all the design services, from start to finish, they act as the Project Designer. On the other hand, when the designer is hired to provide less than full services, other people must pick up the slack. Frequently, the homeowner performs some of the tasks required early in the process, and then the builder takes on the Project Designer's role later. In this scenario, three people—the homeowner, the designer, and the builder—will fill the role of the Project Designer. What's important to understand is that there are a number of tasks that must be performed during the design process, and these tasks make up the responsibilities of the Project Designer. If the designer isn't hired to do them all, some other person or persons must. Later in this step, I'll list the tasks that comprise the Project Designer's job description.

WHAT IS A BUILDER?

"Builder" is another term that is frequently misunderstood and causes a lot of confusion, and frankly I'm not always certain what I mean when I use the word. The problem is that the term is just too broad to be clear. To illustrate this point, I'd like you to take a little quiz. A builder is: (a) a carpenter, (b) the carpenter's boss, (c) the carpenter's boss's boss, (d) all of the above, or (e) sometimes a, b, c, and d? The answer is e. Confused? To understand how this is possible, we need to travel a somewhat roundabout route, so bear with me. First, we need to understand another word: contractor.

THE CONTRACTOR

Contractor is yet another confusing term, and to get some help clarifying it, I turned to my trusty dictionary, which offers: "*contractor 1: one that contracts or is party to a contract.*" Not much help, I thought, so I read on: "*a: one that contracts to perform work.*" Now we're getting somewhere, so I continued: "*b: one that contracts to erect buildings*." Huh? That's fine for contractors who erect buildings, but what about all the other people who contract to perform other work? Aren't they contractors too? Well, despite what my dictionary says, I think they are, and I'd like to finish what my dictionary started.

To make the word *contractor* meaningful in the construction world, it must be used in conjunction with an adjective that describes the kind of work the contractor does. There are many different types of contractors involved in residential construction: foundation contractors, framing contractors, roofing contractors, siding contractors, plumbing contractors, electrical contractors, heating/ventilating/air-conditioning contractors, and drywall contractors. The list goes on and on. Nowadays you can even hire a contractor to install shelving in your closets. Name a piece of the building, and you've named a contractor. Now, let's get back to my dictionary.

BUILDING CONTRACTOR

"*Contractor b: one that contracts to erect buildings.*" What my dictionary is describing here is a *building contractor*, but what exactly does this mean? A lot of work goes into erecting a building; how much of it is the responsibility of the building contractor? In an attempt to clarify the issue, I'll again offer my own definition: *A building contractor is the person who, at the very least, is responsible for constructing the shell of a building.* The shell of a building consists of the framing members—joists, studs, and rafters—and the sheathing (these are defined later in this step) that make up the floors, walls, and roof of a building. I said "at the very least" because most building contractors have the skills or employees—typically called carpenters—to construct other parts of a building. Other work performed by building contractors includes installing the windows, siding, roofing, exterior trim, and interior trim (hanging doors and putting up window and door casings, and baseboards). Often, however, a building contractor hires other contractors to work on a building; when this happens, the building contractor's job extends to management and entails much more than constructing the shell of the building. This is where much of the confusion around the term "builder" lies. First, in general usage, the term "building contractor" gets shortened to "builder" and, second, the "builder" is then thought of as a manager. Let's take a closer look at the manager's role that the building contractor sometimes assumes.

THE PROJECT MANAGER'S ROLE

As we saw above, there are any number of different contractors that can be employed to complete a single building. That's all fine and good, but who gathers these individual contractors and gets them to work as a team to finish a building? This complex job falls on the shoulders of the leader of the Construction Team: the Project Manger. I define the Project Manager as *the person or persons responsible for pricing the job, hiring all of the contractors necessary to complete a building* (*who are typically called subcontractors*), *and overseeing construction from start to finish.* Notice that I said person or persons; if you recall from the Introduction, the Project Manager fills the leadership *role* of the Construction Team. Like the Project Designer, this role can be filled by several people, and depending who is filling that role, the Project Manager may or may not actually do any physical work on the building.

As I hinted above, the building contractor can, and often does, fill the role of the Project Manager. To do this, a Building Contractor will hire subcontractors to perform the work he or she can't or don't want to do, quote a price for the project, and make sure the job is completed in an orderly fashion. This is perhaps the most common arrangement and when I use the term "builder" in this book, I am referring to a building contractor who is also filling the role of the Project Manager.

And now to explain the answer to the multiple-choice question posed at the beginning of this section. As you saw, a builder can wear many hats. If the "builder" is a one- or two-person outfit, the builder will probably also be one of the carpenters on the job. If the "builder" is a slightly larger company, the roles may be more specialized and the owner of the company—the builder—could be the carpenter's boss. In much larger construction companies, with two, three, or more crews and two, three, or more supervisors, the "builder" is the supervisor's boss. So, who the builder is depends on what type of building company you've hired.

But what if the Building Contractor you hire doesn't want to act as the Project Manager, or what if you would like someone else to do that job? Who else can do this managerial work, often called "general contracting"? There are two options: you could hire a General Contractor (GC) or a Construction Manager (CM). The major difference between the builder and a GC and CM is that the latter two are strictly managers, not construction workers. In Step 5, we'll take a closer look at the differences between these two "management positions," but for now you should be aware of the fact no matter who you hire to build your project, somebody will have to act as the Project Manager. It might be your Building Contractor, a General Contractor, a Construction Manager, yourself, or a combination of two or more, but the work of the Project Manager has to be done.

SPEAKING IN TONGUES

Now that you understand some of the important roles that construction people fill and the tasks they perform, you need to learn a little about the language they speak. Soon, whether you like it or not, *you'll* be forced to try to communicate using that language. Of course, it's impractical and unnecessary for you to learn all of the technical language used by every person and trade in the construction industry. You should try to learn as much as you can, though, and as you move through the process, you'll have to decide exactly how much of the language you want to learn. You can check the Appendices for helpful reading material, and I also recommend that early in the process you try to get out and observe the construction industry at work. There are certain terms that are used by almost everyone in the construction industry and learning them will make your life much easier. The following is a list of what I would call "universal" terms—some of the most common and widely used terms in the construction language.

Here's a chart to help you visualize and understand the Design and Construction Team leadership roles, the professionals who fill them, and the jobs they do.

DESIGN TEAM

LEADER'S ROLE: PROJECT DESIGNER.

Professionals who can fill the role: architect, building designer, building contractor, general contractor, and construction manager.

Jobs that need to be done:

• Helping to establish a budget to guide the design process.

• Shepherding the design process, including creating a program, generating preliminary design schemes, finalizing the design, and preparing the construction documents.

• Soliciting bids, analyzing the figures, and revising the construction documents if necessary to meet the budget.

• Providing assistance and advice on hiring the builder.

• Verifying that the project is built according to the construction documents.

• Determining when the project has been completed and final payment to the builder is to be made.

• Acting as an advocate on behalf of the homeowner when problems arise during construction.

CONSTRUCTION TEAM

LEADER'S ROLE: PROJECT MANAGER.

Professionals who can fill the role: building contractor, general contractor, or construction manager.
Jobs that need to be done:

• Gathering price quotes from subcontractors.

• Hiring and scheduling subcontractors.

• Obtaining permits and approvals.

• Overseeing the quality of the subcontractors' work.

• Paying the subcontractors.

• Acting as a mediator between the subs and the homeowner.

• Overseeing the completion of the job and obtaining the certificate of occupancy.

THE PLANS

As we are finding out, the world of construction is filled with ambiguities, and you can add "the plans" to that list. As it's commonly used by both professionals and non-professionals, the term "plans" has more than one meaning. It can mean a single floor plan for a building; when bundled together with other drawings, it can denote a complete set of drawings that illustrate how an entire building is to be built; and it can mean anything in between. "Plans" are also referred to by different names: blueprints, prints, working drawings, and construction drawings are some examples. "Blueprint" is an archaic term, its name derived from a now-outdated process used for copying drawings. This process showed the drawing as white lines on a blue background. The process that replaced it, called diazo printing, shows blue, black, or brown lines on a white background. More recently, large-format photocopies—18″ × 24″ and 24″ × 36″—are also being used to reproduce original drawings.

Several terms are used in relation to "the plans":

SCALE   For practical reasons, architectural drawings are all drawn "to scale," or proportionally smaller than the actual project. The scale used varies depending on the type of drawing and what is being communicated. The most commonly used scale is the "¼" scale, which means that ¼ inch on paper is equal to 1 foot of actual size.

SITE PLAN   A drawing that shows the topography of a piece of land and the location of the building project on that land. The data shown on a site plan usually includes the boundaries, grade elevations (the slopes and contours of the land, not to be confused with the "elevation" drawings described below), compass directions, site conditions (such as trees, streams, wetlands, and rock ledge), and proposed improvements (such as buildings, driveway, septic system, and well). Site plans are typically drawn at a small scale, such as 1 inch equals 20 or 40 feet.

PLOT PLAN   A simplified version of the site plan that usually only shows the boundaries, compass directions, and location of any improvements.

FLOOR PLANS   Drawings or diagrams that show the arrangement and relationship of the rooms or spaces for each floor of a building. This most common type of architectural drawing assumes that the point of view is from directly above the drawing, and that the building shown is "cut off" 4 feet up from the floor. In addition to the rooms, other features such as doors, windows, counters, and cabinets are typically shown. Floor plans are typically drawn at a scale of ¼ inch equals 1 foot.

FRAMING PLANS   Drawings that indicate the proper placement of a building's structural members. Examples are the floor framing plan and roof framing plan which show the locations of the floor joists, rafters, and structural beams.

OTHER PLANS   There are many other types of plans that may be required for the construction of a building. Some of these include foundation plans, electrical plans, plumbing plans, HVAC (heating/ventilating/air-conditioning) plans, and roof plans.

ELEVATION DRAWINGS   "Elevations" are two-dimensional drawings that represent the walls and other vertical or sloping surfaces of buildings. Elevations can be drawn of the outside (called exterior elevations) and the inside (called interior elevations) of buildings. Elevation drawings show such features as windows, doors, roof lines, siding materials, cabinetry, and shelving. Because these drawings are two-dimensional, they are sometimes difficult to interpret. To fully describe complicated buildings, perspective drawings or a scale model might be required.

BUILDING SECTIONS   "Sections" are drawings that represent cuts through a building; they illustrate the vertical relationship of the various spaces and structural elements of the building. To understand what's revealed with a section drawing, cut an apple from top to bottom. The apple core would then be shown in "section." These drawings are very helpful in visualizing and communicating how a building fits together.

DETAILS   Detail drawings are done to illustrate precisely how a particular item is to be constructed. Details are typically drawn at larger scales than floor plans, from ¾-inch to 3-inch or sometimes even full scale. This enables each separate piece of the item to be clearly shown. Detail drawings are often done for cabinets, trim work, and structural connections.

SCHEDULES   Schedules are lists of items that are to be installed in a building, and usually contain information about the quantity, size, style, color, and manufacturer. Items that are typically found in schedules are windows, doors, flooring materials, and cabinets.

SHOP DRAWINGS   These drawings, based on a building's plans and specifications, are prepared by manufacturers or fabricators. Custom cabinetry, complicated trim work, and built-in furniture are examples of items that might require shop drawings.

PERSPECTIVE DRAWINGS   Perspective drawings, also called perspectives, are two-dimensional representations of a three-dimensional view of a building. If a perspective is correctly done, it will look like a line drawing of a photograph. Because perspectives can show a true "picture" of a building, they are more effective in communicating what a proposed building will look like.

SCALE MODEL   A scale model is a three-dimensional, physical construction of a proposed building. Models are built at small scales: ¼-, 3⁄16-, or ⅛-inch scales. Because models are actual physical objects, they can show all the aspects of a proposed building, from all angles. Sometimes models are made to open up and reveal the interior spaces as well.

CAD   This is short for Computer Aided Design. The power of the personal computer can be utilized by designers to assist with the design process and the production of construction documents. While they don't actually "help design" a building, computers are quickly becoming an important, almost indispensable, design tool. There are many computer programs available. Some are quite costly and complicated to use, and others are relatively inexpensive and easy to learn. If you own a computer, you may wish to see if some of the low-end CAD software packages interest you.

CONSTRUCTION DRAWINGS   This is the complete set of drawings, including plans, elevations, sections, details, and schedules. Together these drawings graphically show how—and with what materials—a proposed structure is to be built. Another name for these drawings is "working drawings."

SPECIFICATIONS   Detailed written descriptions of the methods and materials to be used for the construction of a building. The specifications typically supplement the construction drawings and can be printed as a separate document or included on the construction drawings, or a combination of both.

CONSTRUCTION DOCUMENTS   The construction drawings and the specifications taken together make up the construction documents. The importance of a complete and accurate set of construction documents cannot be overemphasized. They are a tangible expression of your wishes and expectations. They are vitally important to the builder, and a requirement of the building inspector and your lending agent. Construction documents are sometimes called "contract documents" because they usually become part of a contract entered into with a builder.

PROGRAM   A program is a collection of data, jointly prepared in the beginning of the process by the designer and homeowner, that delineates all the requirements of a building project. (Additional material such as drawings and photographs can be included in the program.) A program is much more than a "wish list," and should communicate the ideas, dreams, and needs of a client. A program should not merely be a list of "rooms" that are to be stitched together on a piece of paper. It should also include pertinent information about the building site and local codes and regulations. A good program is essential to producing an appropriate building.

PLANS SERVICE   A business that sells pre-designed or "stock" house plans. The plans are typically prepared by designers and can be purchased with a complete set of construction documents.

THE BUILT WORLD

The following terms are basic to understanding the components of a building and how they're put together. During the course of the planning and building process you will encounter thousands more. If you thoroughly understand these, you should be able to add to your vocabulary relatively easily.

CONSTRUCTION TERMINOLOGY

ON CENTER OR O.C.   The distance between the centers of two consecutive, equally spaced members. This usually refers to the spacing of structural members such as floor joists, wall studs, and rafters. Typical spacings are 16″ o.c. and 24″ o.c.

LEVEL   Perfectly horizontal. Floors, window sills, and countertops are examples of things that should be level when properly constructed.

LOAD   The amount of force exerted on a structural member or system such as a beam, joist, post, floor, wall, or roof. The total load is typically a combination of the dead load (the weight of the materials themselves) and the live load (the weight of the building's occupants, furnishings, snow, and wind).

MATERIALS TAKE OFF OR "TAKE OFF"   The compilation of a list of building materials required to construct a particular part of a building. For instance, a framing contractor will do a take off of the materials, such as lumber and nails, needed to put up the frame of a house.

PLUMB   Perfectly vertical, perpendicular to the horizontal. Walls and posts should be plumb when properly constructed. Some parts of a building, such as door frames and window openings, must be both level and plumb.

PITCH   The slope of a roof or drain pipe. For example, roof pitches are usually described by the number of inches of rise (vertical distance) per number of inches of run (horizontal distance). An "8-in-12" roof slopes at a rate of 8 inches of rise for every 12 inches of run. A "12-in-12" roof slopes at a rate of 12 inches of rise for every 12 inches of run, which equals 45 degrees.

SPAN   The horizontal distance between two vertical structural supports. As a general rule, as the span increases so must the size, or carrying capacity, of the structural member bridging the span.

STRUCTURAL COMPONENTS

BEAM   A horizontal structural member, typically wood or steel, that usually supports joists or rafters. Beams can be similar in depth to joists, but they are typically 4 inches wide or more.

HEADER   A small "beam" that spans window and door openings and supports floor and roof loads.

JOISTS   The horizontal structural members that support floors or ceilings. Depending on the structural requirements, their size varies from 2″ × 6″ to 2″ × 12″ solid lumber. Other types of "engineered" members—floor trusses and plywood "I" beams—are also used as floor joists and can be deeper.

POST   A vertical structural member—usually wood, steel, or concrete—that supports a concentrated load, typically from a beam. A wooden post is usually a 4″ × 4″, as a minimum size.

RAFTERS   The structural members that support the roof of a building. Rafters typically rest on the tops of exterior walls, and their "tails" form the roof overhangs. Depending on the span and load, rafters vary in size from 2″ × 6″ to 2″ × 12″.

ROOF TRUSSES   Manufactured structural members that combine rafters, ceiling joists, and intermediate web members, to form the roof and ceiling of a building. Trusses typically are prefabricated and engineered to use smaller-sized members than rafters, while spanning the same distances and carrying equivalent loads.

SHEATHING   Materials such as boards, plywood, flake board, or OSB (oriented strand board) that are used to cover the exterior of the wall and roof framing members.

STUDS   The vertical structural framing members in a wall. Depending on their use, wood studs can be 2 × 4s, 2 × 6s, or (rarely) 2 × 8s.

TYPES OF HOUSING CONSTRUCTION

CUSTOM OR "STICK-BUILT" HOME   A home that is constructed at the building site from individual framing members such as studs, joists, and rafters.

MANUFACTURED HOME   More commonly referred to as a "mobile home." These are constructed to meet different standards (Federal Construction Safety Standards) than other systems-built homes and are required to be built on non-removable steel chassis.

SYSTEMS-BUILT OR FACTORY-BUILT HOME   A home that is constructed, to some degree, in a factory and shipped to the building site to be assembled. Using CAD, systems-built homes can be made in nearly every style and size. There are three broad categories of systems-built homes: log, modular, and panelized.

• **LOG HOME**   A home that is built by stacking individual, solid-wood logs one on top of each other to create walls. The logs are pre-cut in a factory and shipped to the job site for assembly. The most popular woods are pine and cedar, but oak and maple can also be used.

• **MODULAR HOME**   A home that is built by joining two or more modules together. These modules, or "mods," are three-dimensional units produced in a factory, shipped to the job site, stacked together, and finished by a local builder.

• **PANELIZED HOME**   A home that is made from factory-built components, typically wall and roof panels, that are shipped to the job site and assembled in combination with standard, stick-built, construction techniques. The actual construction methods used to create the panels varies from conventional framing to "stress skin" panels of rigid foam insulation.

THE REGULATIONS

Laws, regulations, and codes—be they federal, state, or local—are going to have a major effect on your project. Their applicability and enforcement varies tremendously from jurisdiction to jurisdiction. You will do yourself a great service by researching and understanding the ones that affect you.

BUILDING CODES   The legal minimum requirements established or adopted by a local government or jurisdiction, such as a state or municipality, that govern the design and construction of buildings.

BUILDING LOT   A building lot is a piece of "real property," or land, that is approved under the local regulations—typically the zoning by-laws or the building codes—for use as a building site for a house. A building lot can be a 50-foot-wide by 200-foot-long city lot, or a 300-acre parcel in the country, as long as it meets the requirements.

CERTIFICATE OF OCCUPANCY OR C.O.   A written statement issued by the building inspection department certifying that a house or addition has been built in accordance with all pertinent building codes and regulations, and may be occupied by the owner. Legally, you cannot occupy a building, and many lending agencies will not release the final disbursement sum, until the C.O. has been issued.

CHANGE ORDER   A change order is a *written* revision or alteration to the construction documents, typically made after a construction contract has been signed. Change orders should state the nature of the change, how much the change will cost, and how it will affect the construction timetable. All changes, even minor ones, should be made in the form of written change orders.

CONTRACT   A legally enforceable agreement between two or more competent parties stating their intention to do, or not to do, certain things in return for consideration (money). Contracts do not have to be lengthy or complicated, but they must be complete. They are covered in depth in Step 5.

ZONING BY-LAWS OR ORDINANCES   Rules and regulations established by local governmental agencies that augment the building codes and regulate the use of buildings and land. They define such things as minimum building lot size, maximum height of buildings, and the minimum setback and side yard requirements.

SETBACK   The minimum distance that is allowed between a street or public way and a building. Setbacks are often a limiting design factor when planning an addition.

SIDE YARD   The minimum distance that is allowed between the sides of a building and the adjoining property lines. Again, side yard requirements can often impact the design of additions.

A final word of caution: as with any language, the construction language is subject to regional dialects and variations. Be sure to make allowance for local nuances.

WORKING WITH PROFESSIONALS

Now that you've been introduced to the people and the language they use, it's time for you to learn some guidelines that will promote effective communication and good relationships with them. I would like to begin with a simple, yet extremely powerful, principle: the Golden Rule.

THE GOLDEN RULE

Whatever you want others to do for you, you should do for others. This simple statement, as ordinary as it might appear, is the binding principle that expresses the core of human relationships and can be seen as the root of all other rules. If you were to follow only this premise throughout the planning process, you would be well on your way to establishing successful relationships.

BE HONEST

This almost goes without saying, but you should be honest in your dealings with people. I believe that honesty begets honesty, and is its own reward. The test for you might come some evening when you're reviewing a recent bill, and discover that a contractor has made a mistake and undercharged you. What do you do? You might be tempted to ignore it and pay the incorrect total, in effect stealing from the contractor. Will you get away with it? Probably not, because even if your conscience lets you off the hook, chances are that the contractor will catch the error during a later review, and then how will you feel?

LISTEN

Listen carefully and openly to the advice and feedback that you are given by professionals. If something you've said is being questioned, try to avoid getting defensive. The chances are that years of experience have gone into that advice, and that a lot of the experience has come through learning from mistakes. It's a lot less painful to learn from others' mistakes, so you would be smart to at least listen to what's being offered. At the same time, however, you should avoid following any advice blindly. Apply your own common sense to the situation, and perhaps get a second opinion before making any decisions.

SHOOT STRAIGHT

Be forthright in your responses and constructive with your criticism. Basically, this means let people know what you think, but say it in a way that can be heard. For instance, if you disagree with or just don't want to follow someone's advice, you could say, "I'm sorry, but I'm just not going to do it, and I don't think it's a very good idea," but you run the risk of alienating that person. A better approach would be to acknowledge the value of the advice by noting situations when it could be implemented, and then explain why you don't believe the advice is right for you. The person will feel appreciated, and your lines of communication will remain clear.

STAY COOL

Be under control emotionally, and don't fly off the handle. Planning and building a home or addition can be stressful, and there will be times—no matter how hard you try to avoid them—when you will feel like throwing a temper tantrum. Don't do it! Very little gets accomplished by yelling, cursing, and name-calling. During these situations, try to have the presence of mind to ask for a time out. If you're talking on the phone, ask nicely if you can call back; if you're face to face with your antagonist, ask to be excused and then find a way to clear your head. Take a walk, run, talk with a friend, or pound some pillows if you must, but don't resume your conversation until you've worked off some steam and can think and talk clearly again.

GET THE FACTS

Don't act on assumptions or jump to conclusions. You need the facts before you react to anything. You are not a mindreader, so check out your assumptions by asking questions, doing some research, and getting the answers in written form.

BE DECISIVE

When you've made a decision, stick to it. Constantly changing your mind can undermine the morale and affect the support of the people you're working with. Of course you'll change your mind sometimes, but try to avoid changing your mind without a good reason. A good reason might be that you've discovered some new information that impacts your decision, or that your situation has changed. Firm decisions are best made by getting all the information you can, discussing the issues thoroughly, and taking enough time for the decision to "age."

Along the way, decisions that were made jointly will be changed and those that were put off until later will have to be made on the spot. On these occasions, one person should be given the decision-making authority.

THE PRINCIPLES

Before we go on to Step 2, I'd like to share a few more thoughts. The following principles have broad application, so use them to help focus your thoughts and guide your actions as you do the tasks required of you at each step along the way.

THE PRINCIPLE OF THREES

During the preconstruction process you're going to shop, shop, shop. Yes, you're going to shop for material goods, choosing myriad building materials as the design of your project nears completion, but you're also going to shop for professional and business services. You will "make these purchases" by hiring the people and choosing the businesses with which you want to work. To be a smart shopper, you must be a comparison shopper, and to be a comparison shopper, you must follow the Principle of Threes: *No matter what you are choosing, buying, or hiring, pick from at least three possibilities.* That means if you're interviewing designers, interview at least three; if you're choosing a bank, pick from at least three; and if you're getting a price quote on *anything*, get at least three. Comparison shopping takes time, so plan ahead.

THE PRINCIPLE OF THE WRITTEN WORD

Simply translated, this principle means: *put it in writing, get it in writing.* I have frequently made the point that the planning and building processes are largely about establishing and maintaining good relationships and clear communication. This is true, but *verbal* communications are often not enough. It's just too easy for the spoken word to be vague, misunderstood, or just plain forgotten. To be certain that intentions get communicated clearly, they must also be communicated in written form. Not everything needs to be written down, but every *important* thing should be. Formal agreements must be written in the form of contracts, the design of a building must be written in the form of construction documents, and revisions to the construction documents must be written in the form of change orders. These are just a few examples; it's up to you to use your common sense, identify issues that are important to you, and apply the Principle of the Written Word where you see fit.

THE PRINCIPLE OF COMPREHENSION

I'll be honest with you: no matter how well you do your homework, no matter how many hours you spend researching, studying, and absorbing, you will not learn everything there is to know about the preconstruction process. And even if you could, you'd forget some of it. After all, you're human. This means that, more than once, you're going to encounter something you don't understand, and you may whisper to yourself, "I have absolutely no clue what's going on here." When this happens, you might try to cover up your confusion by vigorously nodding your head up and down and agreeing to what you don't know. Stop! Don't do it! Instead, apply the Principle of Comprehension: *ask questions, ask some more questions, and keep on asking until you understand the situation.* Before you sign a contract, understand what you're signing; before you take out a loan, understand the terms; and before you agree to a change in the design of your project, understand what the effects of the change will be. There is no need to be embarrassed about your lack of knowledge, unless you make decisions based on that ignorance.

THE PRINCIPLE OF SOONER, NOT LATER

This principle has been promoted in the United States since the days of Benjamin Franklin, and still it's seldom heeded: *Don't put off until tomorrow what you can do today.* In the construction world, the procrastination virus can run rampant, and I'll admit that the avoidance bug bites me far more times than I'd like. After all, there are so many decisions to be made and so many things to be done that sometimes it feels like you've just got to have more time. Yes, sometimes you do need more time, and when that's really true, take it. But watch out: the procrastination bug may sneak up on you. Your best defense is to set up a schedule that lists the decisions you have to make and deadlines you have to meet.

THE PRINCIPLE OF ASKING FOR WHAT YOU WANT

"There's no harm in asking" goes the old saying. You should heed this advice while planning and building your project. Over the years I have had many clients who were hesitant to request certain design elements—an unusually shaped room or intricate window grouping—for fear that the features would be too costly or difficult to include. Sometimes clients will ask me, almost as an afterthought, if I could change the location of a wall "just a little" so they'll be able to accommodate something like an antique dresser. If it's possible, I am always glad to oblige and happy that they asked. I'd much rather move the wall on paper, than see the carpenters move it. I often wonder how many clients didn't ask such questions. After all, the whole purpose of your project is for you to get what you want. It would be a shame if you fell short of your goal just because you were too shy or embarrassed to ask for what you want. Sometimes you might not even be sure what it is you want, but something feels unresolved. Other times you might have to be a little, but appropriately, pushy. The point of this principle is *you can't get what you don't ask for*. There really is no harm in asking, and the worst that will happen is that you'll be told no.

THE PRINCIPLE OF PAY NOW, SAVE LATER

This principle, too, can trace its roots to Benjamin Franklin and his admonition to not be "penny wise and pound foolish." We all want to save money but often in order to save money you have to spend it. For example, sometimes clients will question the need for a complete set of construction documents—after all, they're not free. I begin by pointing out all the tasks that require good construction documents, all the potential errors and problems these documents can help avoid, and all the people who will use them during the course of the project. And then I ask, "Would you rather pay one person *now* to figure how to build your house, or three or four people (the construction workers) *later*." One usually wins out.

THE PRINCIPLE OF ACKNOWLEDGMENT

During the course of planning and building, you will receive the help of many people. It's important to acknowledge their help with a thank you. A phone call, a note, or photos of the completed project are ways you can show your appreciation.

You have now created a solid base for your planning process and it's time to move on to Step 2.

STEP 2 **Explore the Possibilities**

Now that you've completed the initial preparations, you're ready to step out and begin to experience the world you learned about in Step 1. After all, that was just the beginning and there's a lot more you need to learn.

THE GOAL FOR STEP 2   To open your eyes, heart, and mind to the world of possibilities.

This step does not include hiring a designer, or buying land, or anything outside of yourself. Instead, it involves exploring, pushing the limits of your thoughts, your dreams, and your wishes. Planning your home begins with you and the people you live with.

What does exploration mean to you? There are probably as many responses to that question as there are readers of this book, and that's as it should be. Just as no two people are exactly alike, no two building projects are exactly alike. There are many events and situations that set your project apart. Your unique personality and needs will greatly influence the way you go about exploring the possibilities. And as you explore, it will be helpful to keep something in mind: you are exploring territory that—while it's been covered many times by others—is quite likely new to you. It doesn't matter that in 1994 there were 1,198,000 single-family housing starts in the United States. As far as you're concerned, there is a whole new world that you need to learn about, explore, and—most of all—enjoy. So go ahead, loosen up, and prepare to have a good time. That's what Step 2 is all about. It's about generating enthusiasm, discovering the unknown, and having fun. Now is the time for believing that anything and everything is possible. Now is the time for long conversations with your family and friends, while sitting around the kitchen table doodling on napkins. Now is the time for pretending that you have all the money in the world. That's right; for now I want you to disregard what I said in Step 1, and ignore money. Thinking about money—how much you'll need, where you're going to get it, and how you're going to spend it—is no way to have fun. So, please, put away any thoughts of money. And while you're at it, put away your graph paper, ruler, and calculator. Your intention here is to survey the options with broad, all-encompassing strokes. Those tools are far too precise, and thoughts of money far too limiting, to occupy your mind just yet. Their time will come. Right now, you have more important, pleasant things to attend to.

BEGIN AT HOME

The place to begin your exploration is right at home with your immediate family. Make it clear that the thoughts and ideas of every family member need to be voiced, and that their opinions are important. Remember what I said in Step 1: it's extremely important that everyone in the family be fully aware of, and committed to, the project you are about to undertake. Everyone's involvement will increase the level of enthusiasm and broaden the base of thinking and ideas that will shape the project. Encourage everyone to be on the lookout for ideas, and to be thinking about what they would like to include in the project. And, as in Step 1, when I say everyone, I mean everyone—even the youngest children. Children offer fresh, usually uncensored perspectives on life, and as a result will most likely have valuable contributions to make to the planning process. This is an effective way to respect their place in your heart and your life, and to demonstrate that they are full partners in the planning process.

Once things are up and running on the homefront, it's time to broaden the scope of your exploration. Begin to talk about your project with your extended family, friends, and co-workers. Hopefully they know you well enough to give you some informed, yet objective, feedback. Ask them for their opinions, and listen carefully to their suggestions. Don't be shy, embarrassed, or defensive. After all, if your ideas turn out to be totally off the wall, wouldn't you rather hear it from someone close to you? If you're fortunate, you'll come across a friend who has done a project similar to the one you're contemplating. They'll probably be more than happy to share their experiences with you: what worked and what didn't, what they liked and what they didn't, and what was successful and what wasn't. In addition to all the valuable suggestions you're likely to get, seeking the opinions of friends at this time has an additional benefit: it eliminates the "second guesser." You know who I mean. That uncle, perhaps, who upon viewing the completed floor plans says, "Yes, that's an interesting approach, but I did it this way and things worked out much better than this is going to." Early in the planning process, input from family and friends is more likely to be a help than a hindrance. So be brave, call up your uncle, and tell him about your plans.

CURL UP WITH A GOOD BOOK

Reading is one of the main activities you should engage in during the course of Step 2, and throughout the whole planning process. Read, read, read, and then read some more. Even though you may not have been involved in a construction project before, millions of other people have. As a result, there is a wealth of material available concerning residential construction. These experiences have been written about and documented through drawings and photographs, and you should take full advantage of everything available to you. There is no need to begin in a vacuum and, besides, nothing will stimulate family discussion quite like a gorgeous color photo layout in a glossy magazine.

At your local library and bookstores you'll discover numerous books and periodicals on building-related subjects. Some of the publications you might find useful include books on home planning and design, magazines on the general subject of houses, and magazines and books containing "stock" plans. You're probably familiar with many of the major national home magazines; they provide a lot of valuable information. You should also consider reading some professional and/or trade magazines; although some of the material may be too technical for you, you'll probably find some articles of value, as well as a refreshing insider's perspective. (For a list of recommended books and periodicals see the Appendices). Local newspapers usually have a weekly "home" section, as well as fall and spring "home improvement" supplements. If the newspapers you read feature a "house of the week," pull them out and save them; I have plans for them later. These sections usually contain stories of local interest as well as articles on a wide range of appropriate subjects. Invariably, at every home planning workshop I give, a member of the audience mentions an important piece of information that they found in a book, magazine, or newspaper. As part of reaching out to your friends and co-workers, ask them if they have any publications you could borrow. Friends who have done a building project may have plans and sample building materials to show you.

Insider's Tip

In addition to professional magazines, there are books, pamphlets, and brochures written for professionals that you might find of interest. You can request a catalogue or listing from various professional organizations, review what's available, and buy those that interest you. This is a great way to get information from the insiders. See the Appendices for a list of names, addresses, and phone numbers of trade and professional organizations.

After you've surveyed what's available, select the publications that are most relevant to you and buy the books and magazines you haven't been able to borrow. If you're beginning your planning far enough in advance, you might want to subscribe to some of the magazines that appeal to you. Begin to collect information that catches your eye by cutting out or photocopying the articles or photos of interest. Be sure to note the name of the publication and what you found important about the photos or articles you keep; this information will come in handy, and represents only the tip of what will most likely become a large iceberg. Later in this step, I'll give you some guidelines for organizing this information so that you won't sink under its growing weight.

While I believe that it's important to expose yourself to as much information as possible, I would like to offer a word of caution here. You will probably be better served if you use the information you find in books and magazines to help stimulate the formulation of your own ideas, rather than trying to find your "dream house." While there is nothing wrong with borrowing or re-interpreting ideas, trying to create an exact copy of something may lead you into trouble. It's a little bit like trying to find "Mr. or Ms. Right"—that perfect person with whom you'd like to spend your life. As we all know, nobody's perfect and, similarly, there is no "perfect" house—only one that suits you best. Careful thought is the enemy of ordinary results, so take the time to care, discover what it is you want, and find the personal touches that will make your project truly yours.

ON DISPLAY

Other excellent places to find information are home shows, showrooms, and local, county, and state fairs. In addition to a wide array of design and building basics, the latest in home innovations and technology are usually on display at home shows and fairs. Builders, designers, and other industry professionals who exhibit at these shows typically have portfolios of their work for you to review. Lumber yards, plumbing supply houses, and other material suppliers almost always have showrooms packed with materials and equipment for you to look at. I know of one Rhode Island lumber yard that has a "home-planning center," complete with everything someone planning a building project could need: hundreds of magazines to borrow and cut up, thousands of house plans to study and purchase, and shelves filled with everything from building code handbooks to builder's portfolios for you to peruse. This resource center is a treasure chest of information for the home builder—and, remarkably, you will not meet any sales people, and the services are free. Call up the local, independently owned lumber yards in your area and find out if they offer similar services. If they do, your job is going to be much easier.

As you make the rounds of home shows, fairs, and showrooms, you should pick up all the pertinent literature you can find and add it to your growing collection. If available, you might also pick up estimated costs of the items and services you encounter, but please don't look at them too carefully now. Remember: for the time being, you're pretending that money is no object. So put all those cost figures into a folder marked "$$" and leave them alone until later.

There is, however, another very important task you should be undertaking now. You should begin to have some one-on-one interactions with the construction industry professionals you encounter. At this point in the planning process, you're probably not ready to engage in an in-depth discussion about your project. So for now just have some informal conversations with the builders, designers, and systems-built representatives you meet, to get a feel for what they are like. Pick up a business card at each booth, and make some brief notes on the back about your impressions of the conversations. This is a good opportunity to get a first-hand look at the people in the construction industry and to meet a lot of professionals in a short period of time.

Addition and Renovation Alert

If you're considering an addition or renovation, you have some extra work to do. You have to determine whether or not your project is worth doing. While there are no pat answers about what makes a project worth doing, there are three major areas that you should address before you alter your existing home: financial, practical, and personal concerns.

FINANCIAL CONCERNS center around recouping your investment. You will need to answer questions like:
- How long do you plan to stay in your current home?
- How will your project affect the value of your home?
- Are other houses in the neighborhood being improved, or is the neighborhood in a state of decline?
- Will your project make your house substantially larger or different than the others in the neighborhood?
- What kind of project makes sense as a financial "investment," and will you be able to recoup your investment when you sell?

The answers to these questions depend a lot on local building trends, property values, and economic conditions, so you should seek the advice of a real estate agent or real estate consultant to help you determine the answers.

PRACTICAL CONCERNS have to do with the physical and design limitations of your current property and home.
- Will the layout of your current house allow you to design the addition or changes that will meet your needs?
- Does your property have enough space, in the right places, to permit the type of project you need to do?
- Will building codes or local zoning ordinances cause a problem?

You could research the regulations yourself to get answers to some of your questions, but unless you know for certain that your house can be altered to meet your needs, you should probably hire a designer (The Principle of Pay Now, Save Later). For a relatively small fee, a designer can assess your situation and determine whether these practical concerns will severly limit your project.

PERSONAL CONCERNS are much more subjective, and there are no "right" answers to the questions you must ask.
- Have you searched for other existing homes, or thought of building a new home, to meet your needs?
- Are your needs likely to change soon, requiring more alterations in the near future?
- Do you like the neighborhood? Can you imagine yourself ever leaving?
- Do you want to do your project no matter what?

These questions will probably have to be answered through a series of family meetings. It's been my experience that personal concerns carry a lot of weight, and will even override the financial issues. In fact, perhaps recognizing that there is no perfect solution, people are often willing to work within fairly rigid practical constraints.

ORGANIZE YOUR INFORMATION

The process of exploring the possibilities could very well take a year or more, and in that time you could amass a mountain of printed materials and other information. This information will not be very helpful to you if it's poorly organized. In fact, if you're not careful, you could find yourself wondering what possessed you to cut out even one lousy magazine article as you search in vain for that picture of your dream dining room. To help you avoid dumping it all in the recycling bin, here are a few organizational hints:

- Suggest that your family members keep a notebook or log to jot down their ideas, thoughts, and any pertinent information they may stumble across during the course of the day. I know from my own experience that some of my best ideas come to me at the most unlikely times. I also know that if I don't write them down, they can vanish just as fast as they came.

• Organize the printed material you gather as you gather it. To do this, you must have a system in place before you start collecting. There is more than one way to do this, so give some thought to the way that would work best for you—"banker's boxes" with hanging files, manila folders, or 3-ring binders and pocket folders. Whatever method you choose, be sure to label the categories you set up (such as kitchens, baths, siding, roofing, windows, lighting, etc.) and cross-reference the material as you see fit. You might find it helpful to pick up an office supply catalog (see Appendices) for additional ideas.

• Start a Rolodex with the names of the professionals and businesses that you encounter throughout your project. In addition to their names, address, and phone numbers, you should include other data that you think is important. For example: how you learned about them, the names of other people in their office, whether they are a one- or two-person business, perhaps the names of their spouses and children, and your first impressions of them. Remember those business cards I suggested that you pick up as you make the rounds of home shows? Add them to your Rolodex, and alphabetize all the cards for easy access.

Well, there you have it. You're fully prepared to become an information magnet. Be sure to cover as much territory as you can and take as much time as you need.

Insider's Tip

Earlier in this step I asked you to put away any drawing tools you might have in your possession. A designer would never begin exploring and generating ideas using mechanically drafted, "hardline" drawings, and neither should you. All too often, those hard lines can draw you into a trap that will cage the flow of creativity. If you would like to do some sketching at this time, by all means do. But please, make the drawings rough sketches and don't try to create a finished plan. To help you, I suggest the following:

• Use "tissue" tracing paper for your sketches. It's cheap, so you can use it freely. It also allows you to "build" your ideas one on the other by tracing over a previous sketch. "Tissue trace" comes in both yellow and white, in widths from 12" to 36", and is available at art supply stores. I prefer white because it photocopies more easily, and I find the 12" width a good choice.

• Use a soft lead pencil (HB or F). This is a must when using tissue trace, otherwise you'll tear the paper. Even when using other paper, a soft lead is important because its softness "loosens up" and frees the sketcher's arm and thoughts.

• Draw "bubble" diagrams that get your general ideas across without worrying precision. A bubble diagram should be a collection of ovals that represent various spaces and their relationships. Again, do not attempt to accurately draw a house or room.

• Draw small. If you were to sketch a house—and I'm not sure you should be doing that now—it should fit on a napkin. The reason for drawing small is that it will let you ignore the details and concentrate on other, broader issues that are more important at this time.

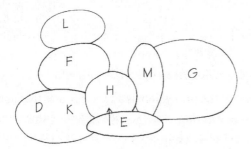

This is the progression I follow during the schematic design phase explained in Step 7. First, I use " bubble diagrams" to loosely define the possible relationships of the proposed spaces.

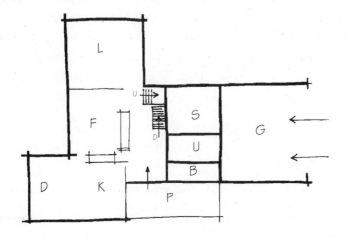

Next, I shape the bubbles into approximately sized rooms and spaces.

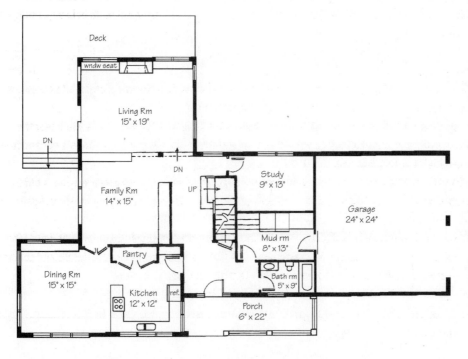

Then, after I've drafted a rough, but to-scale plan, I sketch a free-hand plan, tracing over the drafted plan and using broad-tipped markers for the walls and fine markers for the smaller elements. This approach allows me to quickly produce more than one option. The resulting plan is reasonably accurate and easy to understand. The shortcomings of these preliminary schemes are addressed as the design process continues.

BRAINSTORMING

So far, I've given you a number of ways to look outside of yourself for information and ideas. To round out your exploration of the possibilities, you need a tool to help you look inside yourself and discover your ideas, define your needs, and determine your goals. That help comes in the form of a brainstorming session.

Brainstorming is a technique that encourages free thinking, the generation of new ideas, and the resolution of problems. The most important principle of brainstorming is that the process of generating ideas is totally separate from the process of evaluating them. This is different from the standard "debate" format that we are more familiar with. In debate format, a proposal is criticized shortly after it is put forth. This may be a great way to win arguments, but it's a lousy way to generate ideas and find solutions. To guard against allowing debate to contaminate the brainstorming process, a session structure should be agreed upon.

A brainstorming session is separated into two distinct phases: the generation phase and the evaluation phase. During the generation phase, the guidelines are:

1 All criticism of any ideas is withheld until the evaluation phase. In my workshops, I ask participants to describe their brainstorming experiences. Does brainstorming work? "Yes," is the emphatic response. What's the most difficult part? "Getting started." Why? "Because everyone's afraid of being criticized, of saying something stupid."

2 Wild or even silly ideas are welcomed, indeed encouraged. In the generation phase, there are no "bad" or "stupid" ideas. Believe this, and the brainstorming process can really work.

3 Quantity of ideas is encouraged. Just let them keep coming.

4 Brainstormers are encouraged to combine or improve on the ideas suggested by others. Now is no time for petty jealousy.

5 The brainstorming group should act as a whole, and not break up into smaller groups. When it comes to brainstorming with your family, there is no such thing as too many cooks.

In order for a brainstorming session to work, these guidelines should be closely followed. You should choose a session leader whose job is to make sure that the brainstorming format is adhered to. Also, either tape record the session or assign someone to take notes. There is no set time limit, but when the group stops generating new ideas it's time to move on to the evaluation phase.

During the evaluation phase the list of ideas is reviewed and edited. The goals are to:

1 Pick out the ideas that are obviously useful.

2 Extract helpful thoughts and idea "pieces" from otherwise useless or ridiculous ideas.

3 Note any ideas that might warrant some more investigation and find out more about them.

Brainstorming works, and you can use it to help make decisions and solve problems throughout the planning and construction of your project. If you're planning an addition or renovation, you might find brainstorming particularly helpful in the early stages. There is usually more than one reason for considering an addition or remodeling project, and there is almost always more than one way to get the job done. Brainstorming can help you discover alternative solutions that you may not have been aware of.

Attention Systems-Built Homes or Plans Service Buyers!

Perhaps those of you who are planning to build a systems-built home or get your plans from a plans service are sitting back smugly in your chair and saying, "I don't need to do all this work. That's why I made the choice I did." Well, I strongly disagree with you. In fact, in some ways you need to do the work in Step 2 more than the others. Here's why:

• The design constraints and flexibility limits that are often inherent in the products and services offered by systems-built homes and plans service companies suggest that before you choose a particular company, you need to have a very accurate idea of what you want. You and the company should be a good match right from the start. The best way to assure that is to follow through with Step 2.

• One of the most attractive features of systems-built homes and plans services is the time savings they offer. In the case of a modular home, the house can "go up" almost in the blink of an eye. The disadvantage of this kind of time savings is that you have a shorter period of time within which to make decisions. Again, you need to know up front what it is you want, and Step 2 will help you do that.

• Many of the systems-built homes and plans service companies originate in one geographic area, but offer their products and services throughout the country. One company's products may be better suited to your area than another. By thoroughly exploring the possibilities, you are more likely to pick the right one.

Perhaps some of you are saying, "Systems-built homes? Don't know much about them." That's just the point of Step 2. There are many possible solutions to the housing puzzle, including custom homes and systems-built homes. Your job is to discover and consider as many as you can, and maybe you'll invent some new alternatives.

THE RECAP

Exploring the possibilities should be an experience that is savored and enjoyed. According to a recent study, most people take a long time—anywhere from one to four years or longer, from initial concept to groundbreaking—to think about building a new home or addition. I think that's just fine; time spent here is not wasted. If you don't have the luxury of that much time, that's okay. By following the suggestions in this step you can make efficient use of the time you do have, and most likely fully enjoy yourself. So when you have read the rest of the book, come back to this step, do the work, and complete the worksheets.

Brainstorming Worksheet

Record the information generated in the brainstorming session here. Remember, anything goes and you should be broad and inclusive. Some topics for this brainstorming session might be:

- What are some of the possible alternatives (realistic or not) to building? How about buying a boat, moving into a cave, or just rearranging the furniture?

- If I had an endless supply of money, what would I build?

- If I could change my house in any way I could imagine, how would I make it perfect?

So, choose some topics and let it rip!

TOPIC:

_____

_____

_____

_____

_____

_____

_____

TOPIC:

_____

_____

_____

_____

_____

_____

_____

_____

_____

_____

TOPIC:

_____

_____

_____

_____

_____

_____

_____

_____

_____

_____

Brainstorming Evaluation Worksheet

Evaluate the ideas that you have generated and record the results below. Remember, you want to pick out the ideas that are obviously useful, separate helpful thoughts from frivolous ones, and identify ideas that might need more elaboration.

USEFUL IDEAS:

_____

_____

_____

_____

_____

_____

_____

_____

HELPFUL THOUGHTS:

_____

_____

_____

_____

_____

_____

_____

_____

_____

IDEAS THAT REQUIRE MORE INFORMATION:

_____

_____

_____

_____

_____

_____

_____

_____

_____

STEP 3 **Establish Your Budget**

Step 3 will be your first, but certainly not your last, reality check. Many of us would like to avoid talking about money altogether if we could, but we can't—especially when it comes to a building project. So you'll just have to grin and bear it.

THE GOAL FOR STEP 3   To determine a preliminary, yet realistic, budget for the construction of your project.

Just a few pages back, I was telling you to throw caution to the wind, ignore reality, and pretend that you had all the money in the world. However, as I said at the time, I had some good reasons for asking you to do that, and now I have some good reasons for asking you to think about money and establish your budget. First of all there is the simple truth that, for most people, money is the dominant factor that will shape their project. Money does this by putting limits on the size, complexity, and level of finish that you can afford.

Second, even if you could afford to spend lots of money on your project, you might not want to spend all that you can. I'm sure you can come up with a long list of items, other than your building project, on which you'd like to spend money. So beware the building project that turns into a monster and devours all of your disposable income; you probably don't want to dispose of it all in one place. You need to make a conscious choice about the amount of money you want to allot to your housing needs. If you're planning an addition, there are a number of other practical reasons, some of which we touched on in Step 2 and will further examine in Step 4, why it might make financial sense to limit the amount you spend.

Third, if you don't establish a budget now, you might squander your money on ideas and designs you can't afford no matter how much you want them. The president of the Rhode Island lumber yard that I mentioned in Step 2 told a workshop audience that, far too many times, he sees people choose a design, pay for a set of plans, and hire a builder, only to discover that what they want is far beyond their financial reach. The result: a disappointed homeowner who has either to pay for expensive revisions or, in the worst case, begin all over again. So please, take the time now to establish your budget; it's a wise, dividend-paying investment.

Fourth, during the course of establishing your budget, you will get a clear picture of your financial situation. This is important, because some of what you learn may not be good news. Excessive long-term debt or a bad credit report are two things that will compromise your ability to obtain financing for your project. However, by discovering these facts before applying for a loan, you will have time to remedy the situation and avoid costly delays or rejections.

Finally, remember The Principle of Sooner, Not Later? You know that you're going to have to deal with the money issue sooner or later, so you might as well do it sooner. If you're planning to borrow money to pay for your project, the lending agency will require you to establish a budget anyway. Of course, at that time you'll have to be more accurate, and your budget will take the form of your construction loan and permanent mortgage loan.

HOW MUCH HOUSE CAN YOU AFFORD?

Now, what should your budget be? Your budget should be an accurate estimate of the amount of money you believe that you can afford, and will have available to pay for your building project. By "estimate," I mean just that: an estimate, not a precise and final computation. As you will learn later on, there are many factors, some of which you can control and some you can't, that will ultimately determine what you actually spend on your project. However, now is not the time to be thinking about them.

By doing some simple mathematics, you can learn how much money you can afford to spend, but deciding how much money you will have available is more subjective and might be more difficult. You probably have some savings stashed away. Those savings could be in several forms—"rainy day" or emergency funds, retirement savings, or college savings for your children. You might find it tempting to say, "Oh, if we run short, we can always 'borrow' a little from the kids' accounts." In some cases this might make sense, but before making such a decision you should consult your accountant or financial advisor. In any event, for purposes of establishing your budget, do not include any money that you're not certain you'll have available to spend.

Even though I place great importance on establishing a budget, it is not my intention to have this budget ruin all the fun. Just as you have to guard against that money-gobbling monster I mentioned earlier, you cannot let your budget become another breed of monster, blocking the flow of thoughts and ideas and swallowing up your creative juices. Rather, use your budget as a tool to help you assess your situation and guide your progress.

FINDING THE FUNDS

Where will the money come from? The first thing you need to do is investigate the most likely sources of funds, such as your personal accounts and lending agencies. Your personal accounts might include savings accounts, certificates of deposit, and other liquid investments such as stocks and bonds. You could include gifts from relatives, but most lending agencies have policies limiting the application of such gifts toward loan down payments, so it might be best to consider these gifts as a cushion.

Let's face it: if your project is of any size, and your financial situation is typical, there won't be enough money in your personal accounts to cover the cost of your project. You will need turn to a lending agency to obtain the remainder. There are many types of lending agencies and loans to choose from, and you will learn more about them in Step 8. Although each type of lending agency may offer different types of loans, each with its own set of loan qualifications and limits (the factors that determine how much you will be able to borrow), their general policies and limits are similar. So for now, to keep things simple, let's consider one type of lending agency and loan to use as the basis for establishing your budget. Let's look at a typical construction loan that might be offered by a mutual savings bank. Mutual savings banks are state-chartered lending agencies. That is, each bank must follow the rules and regulations of the state in which it is chartered or licensed.

When considering a loan application, lenders refer to the 4 "Cs" of credit: Capacity (can you repay the debt?); Credit history (will you repay the debt?); Capital (do you have enough "up front" money?); and Collateral (will the lender be fully protected if you fail to repay the loan?). The 4 "Cs" are translated in four standards that you must meet in order to qualify for a loan; they will also determine the size of the loan you will be able obtain. These four factors are income qualification, credit history, debt qualification, and appraisal qualification.

INCOME QUALIFICATION

Income qualification answers half of the capacity question, "Can you repay the loan?" and is expressed as a percentage of your gross monthly income (before-tax income on the I.R.S. 1040 form). To ensure your ability to repay, the lender wants to be certain that your monthly housing expenses, which include the mortgage payment, property taxes, and home owner's insurance, do not exceed a stated percentage of your gross monthly income. Currently, the figure 28% is commonly used. This means that to qualify for a particular loan amount, your anticipated monthly housing expenses cannot be more than 28% of your gross monthly income. For example, let's say your gross monthly income is $4,589 ($55,068/year). Considering only the income qualification, and estimating property taxes and insurance at $1,800 and $420, respectively, per year, your monthly housing expense limit would be $1,285 and your mortgage payments could be as high as $1,100/mo. ($4,589 x 28% = $1,285 − $150 property taxes = $1,135 − $35 insurance = $1,100). You would qualify to borrow $180,000 at 6% interest for 30 years (see Appendices for Mortgage Payment Charts). I intentionally chose a low interest rate to encourage you to do your own calculations. However, borrowing this amount means that you have borrowed the maximum you can, leaving little room for error or emergencies. You probably would not want to do that. We'll address the issue of leaving yourself a cushion later, when we go through the sample budget calculation.

YOUR CREDIT HISTORY

Once the income question has been addressed, the bank will turn to your credit history to answer the question, "Will they repay the loan?" The bank will order a credit report, which contains information about any loans you currently have, your loan repayment history, and any past legal actions taken against you. Unfortunately, it is not uncommon for credit reports to be inaccurate and to contain information that's misleading, outdated, or just plain wrong. If a bank finds your credit history to be unacceptable, it won't issue you a loan, even if you meet all the other qualifications, until the problems are resolved. Here's where doing your homework in advance can really pay off; you have the opportunity to correct an inaccurate credit report or improve an unsatisfactory credit history.

First you must obtain a copy of your credit report. (See the Appendices for a list of credit reporting agencies.) When you receive the report, look it over carefully. If you find any errors, get them corrected. If you have any unresolved disputes, make sure that the report contains your side of the story. If you are currently having credit problems, resolve them before applying for a loan. If your credit problems are in the past, it is possible to remove them from your report. By law, most unfavorable credit information should be removed from a credit report after seven years; any record of bankruptcy should be removed after ten.

What if you don't have a credit history, either good or bad? Lenders want to see a track record of debts owed and repaid. If you hope to borrow money from a lending agency, you need to establish a credit history. If you don't have time to establish a traditional credit history with credit card purchases, car loans, or student loans, you might be able to establish a "non-traditional" credit history. One way to do this is to document your monthly rent payments to landlords and your monthly payments to utility companies for electricity, gas, oil, water, and telephone. Contact a local lending agency to see what they would accept.

DEBT QUALIFICATION

With your credit history taken care of, it's time to address the second half of the question, "Can you repay the loan?" Your ability to repay is also dependent on the total amount of your long-term debt. Long-term debt is any debt that will take longer than 10 months to repay. It includes, in addition to the construction loan you will seek, such debts as existing mortgages, car loans, credit card balances, alimony, or child support payments. Debt qualification, like income qualification, is expressed as a percentage of your gross monthly income. The current typical debt limit is 36%, and as a second test the bank will calculate the size of the loan you qualify for within these limits. First the bank determines what the maximum loan amount would be by multiplying your monthly income by 36% ($4,589 × 36% = $1,652). The $1,652 figure represents the *total* monthly debt allowance, including your mortgage payment, that you can carry. Let's assume that your additional debt—car payments for instance—is $527 per month. To calculate the monthly mortgage amount you qualify for under the debt limit, first subtract your additional debt from your debt allowance ($1,652 − $527 = $1,125). Next deduct the other housing expenses and get the maximum monthly mortgage payment of $940 ($1,125 − $150 property taxes = $975 − $35 house insurance = $940). In this case you would only qualify for a loan of about $160,000 at 6% interest for 30 years, not the $180,000 loan that was calculated in the income qualification portion. A bank will typically lend the lower amount for which you qualify.

This example points out another good reason for establishing your budget now. If the additional debt figure was $367 instead of $527, you would have qualified for the $180,000 as under the income limits ($1,652 − $367 = $1,285 − $150 = $1,135 − $35 = $1,100). The effect of what bankers call "excess" debt ($527 − $367 = $160) was to reduce the loan amount by $20,000. If, when calculating the amount of your long-term debt, you discover excessive debt that will significantly reduce the amount of the loan you will qualify for, you could consider reducing your long-term debt before applying for a loan.

Addition Alert

APPRAISAL QUALIFICATION

After you've met the income, credit history, and debt qualifications, the appraisal qualification is the last thing that a bank will consider. The bank wants answers to the last two questions: "Will the lender be fully protected if you fail to repay the loan?" and "Do you have enough 'up front' money?" To protect itself against potential loan repayment failure, the bank will use your property to secure the loan. Then, in the event of a loan foreclosure, the bank will sell the property to recoup its investment. But how does the bank know that if the property is sold, the sale price will cover the amount of the loan? To assure this, the bank determines the value of the property by having its value determined by a professional appraiser. Using a combination of methods, the appraiser will arrive at a total value for your property. The total value is the value of the land plus the value of the improvements. In the case of new construction, the improvements are the house.

Addition Alert

If you are planning a substantial addition or renovation, you should know the *current* appraised value of your property. As a case in point, several years ago I was retained by a professional family to work with them on a house they had recently purchased. The couple loved the house and, because it was situated on such an unusual and breathtaking site, they bought it in spite of the fact that it was much too small for their growing family. The design of the house readily lent itself to expansion, and my job was to help create a master plan to meet their current and future needs. Those needs were fairly extensive: a new master bedroom/bathroom wing, a totally renovated and enlarged kitchen, a family room addition, two renovated bathrooms, and a conversion of the space above the garage into two bedrooms and a play area. While they knew that they wouldn't be able to accomplish all of this immediately, they did want to do the above-garage conversion and kitchen renovation right away. After we developed a master plan that met their program, I developed more detailed plans for the kitchen and garage conversion. Before I completed the construction documents and cost estimates, the owners went shopping for a loan. What they learned came as a big shock and disappointment. Although they passed the income, credit history, and debt qualifications with flying colors, their property did not meet the appraisal qualification for the amount of the loan they were seeking. None of the lenders they interviewed would lend them the money they wanted. How could this be?

It turns out that the couple had bought their house at the peak of the market. In the year since then, property values in the area had plummeted to the point that the couple's property did not meet the loan-to-value qualifying ratio and the banks refused to make them a loan. As a result, the couple had to scale back their immediate plans and, using their own money, build only the garage conversion. In the long term, it's still not clear whether the value of the property will ever warrant completion of the master plan.

The lesson to be learned is this: before you spend much time, effort, and money planning an addition to your house, make sure you know the current appraised value of your house (you can hire an appraiser yourself), and understand how that figure effects your borrowing power.

The final question the bank wants an answer to is: "Do you have enough 'up front' money?" This means that a bank will not make a loan that is equal to the property's full appraised value, but only a portion of it. The amount of money a bank will lend against the value of the property is expressed as a percentage and is called the Loan-to-Value Ratio. Typically the maximum amount a bank will lend for a new house is 80%, and for an addition 75%, of the appraised value of the entire property (in some situations these amounts can be higher [see Step 8]). Another way to look at it is that the bank wants you to have a 20% to 25% vested interest, or "equity," in the property. This equity may take the form of a cash down payment or land that you own outright. To understand what this means, let's continue with the previous example and assume that you would like to borrow the $160,000 that you calculated you could afford, and that the house of your dreams, excluding the land, is appraised to cost exactly that amount.

If you're planning a new home, let's assume you own the building lot outright, and its appraised value is $30,000. When this figure is added to the $160,000 amount you are willing to spend on your house, the result, $190,000, is the *total* value of the property. If the bank's Loan-to-Value Ratio is 80%, you would qualify for a loan of $152,000. This is $8,000 less than your hypothetical house is going to cost. If you still wanted to build a $160,000 house, you'd have to come up with the additional $8,000 yourself.

Appraising Additions

If you're planning an addition or remodeling, let's assume that you currently have a mortgage on your house, and that the project you're contemplating is valued at $30,000. From a recent appraisal, you know that your house is currently valued at $160,000. The total value of the property when your hypothetical project is completed would be $190,000. Remember, for this example you're going to refinance your house, in other words, pay off your existing loan and take out new one. If the bank's Loan-to-Value Ratio is 75% for additions, the amount of your loan would be $142,500 ($190,000 x 75% = $142,500). Now, let's assume that you have $120,000 left to pay on your current mortgage, which would leave you $22,500 of equity to apply to your proposed project ($142,500 - $120,000 = $22,500). In this case, to complete your project, you would have to provide $7,500 in cash to pay for your $30,000 project ($22,500 + $7,500 = $30,000).

Okay, so much for the hypothetical. It's time to work with real numbers. Move on to the following worksheets, collect the data you need, and do some math. Take your time with this and make sure you understand what you're doing. Remember, you want a realistic figure, but not a precise one. Sharpen those pencils!

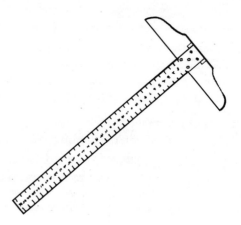

Establishing a Budget Worksheet—Example

The following worksheet has been prepared using the example previously described. Turn back to the example and follow along with the calculations, making sure that you understand them all. When you understand the example, move on to the next worksheet and use your own figures to complete it. It's a good idea to verify all the qualification figures given in this book with a phone call to a local lending agency.

Qualification	% Figure
Income	28%
Debt	36%
Appraisal	80%

Now, let's pull together the hypothetical data (we'll assume they're your figures), crunch some numbers, and see what it means to establish a budget.

As indicated before, the place to begin is the income qualification. To determine your monthly income, take your gross income before taxes and divide by 12.

1 INCOME QUALIFICATION

Monthly Income:

Borrower #1	$2589
Borrower #2	$2000

Other Income:

Alimony	0
Child Support	0
Other	0
Other	0
Monthly Income	$4,589
Multiply by qualification limit %	28%

Maximum monthly housing expense	$1,285
Less property taxes and house insurance	– $185
Maximum monthly mortgage payment	$1,100

2 CREDIT HISTORY

For the purposes of this workbook, we'll assume that you have a good credit history and rating. But remember, at this time you should learn what your actual credit history is by taking the precautions that were recommended earlier in this step.

3 DEBT QUALIFICATION

Let's take a look at the size of the mortgage you qualify for under the debt qualification limit. Remember, if you are planning an addition or remodeling, and have a current mortgage on your existing home, for the purposes of these calculations we will assume that you are going to refinance, in effect wiping out your current mortgage and starting from scratch. Therefore, do not include your current mortgage in this debt figure.

3a Debt Qualification Amount:

Gross monthly income (from 1, above)	$4,589
Multiply by debt limit %	x 36%
Maximum monthly debt allowance	$1,652

Now you need to calculate the amount of your other monthly debts, excluding your mortgage payment.

3b Total Monthly Debt:

Car payments	$527
Alimony	0
Credit card payments	0
Student loans	0
Other	0
Other	0
Additional monthly debt	$527

3c   To determine the amount of your monthly mortgage payments, deduct your additional debt and your housing expense from your maximum monthly debt allowance.

Maximum monthly debt allowance	$1,652
Less additional monthly debt	–$527
Less housing expense	–$185
Maximum monthly mortgage payment	$940

A bank will typically lend you the lesser amount that you qualified for under the income and debt qualification limits. Using the lesser figure, you can calculate the size of the loan you will be able to obtain.

3d   Amount of loan you qualify for:

Lesser amount from 1 or 3c, above	$940
Interest rate *	6%
Length of the loan	30 years
Amount of the loan **	$160,000

4   APPRAISAL QUALIFICATION

Now let's take a look at how the appraisal qualification and required equity amount will affect your loan.

4a   Total appraised value of the property:

Value of land	$30,000
The amount you want to borrow for a new house or the value of your existing house	$160,00
Value of addition or renovations	0
Total value of property	$190,000

4b   Amount of loan that agency will provide:

Total value of property (from 4a, above)	$190,000
Multiply by Loan-to-Value Ratio (in %)	x 80%
Amount of loan bank will make	$152,000

* Current interest rates can usually be found in local newspaper advertisements or financial pages.

** You can determine the amount of loan you qualify for by consulting the mortgage tables in the Appendices.

4c   Amount of down payment and/or equity required of you:

Total value (from 4a, above) $190,000

Less amount of loan (from 4b, above) .... –$152,000

Amount of down payment and/or equity $38,000

The next piece of the budget puzzle is to find out where your down payment and/or equity will come from. As we have seen, your equity can come from such things as your building lot, if you own it outright, the difference between what you still owe on your current house mortgage and how much you can borrow against your house now, or a cash payment. If your current equity doesn't meet the equity or down payment requirements, the balance is usually an additional cash payment. The cash will probably have to come from your personal accounts—checking, savings, investments or other liquid assets. Remember, these should be funds that you can afford to allocate to your construction project, not those you have set aside for emergencies or other obligations like your children's education. Let's see how what you have stacks up against what the bank will require.

5   FUNDS FROM YOUR PERSONAL SOURCES

Equity sources:

Land $30,000

Equity in your home 0

Other 0

Personal accounts:

Checking 0

Savings $8,000

(Stocks, bonds, C.D.'s) 0

Other: 0

Other: 0

Total equity available $38,000

6   By adding together your loan amount and any cash equity you're going to include, you can calculate the amount of money you will have available to spend.

Loan amount (from 4b, above)	$152,000
Cash equity (from 5, above)	$8,000
Total funds available	$160,000

7   ESTABLISH YOUR BUDGET

You have now calculated how much money you will have available to spend, but this is not the budget for your project. In reality, you won't have all this money to spend on the design and construction of your project. To establish your budget, the fees and expenses associated with obtaining and servicing a loan must be deducted.

First let's deduct the fees, or closing costs, that occur when you first obtain a loan. Typically these costs are between 2% and 4% of the amount of the loan. You could either pick a percentage, multiply it by the loan amount, and deduct that figure from the money available or, to get a more accurate estimate, you could contact a local lending agency and deduct the actual fees they charge.

7a   Closing Costs

Amount of loan (from 4b, above)	$152,000
Less total fees	– 3%
Subtotal	$147,440
Plus cash equity	+$8,000
Budget	$155,440

When you are certain that you understand how the worksheet calculations were completed, move onto the blank worksheet and use your own figures.

Establish Your Budget Worksheet

Now that you've run through the calculations using the figures given in the example, it's time to use your own numbers. If you can't readily find some of the information you need, you can plug in an estimate. But as a word of caution, use conservative numbers. As always, it's a good idea to verify all the qualification figures given in this book with a phone call to a local lending agency.

Qualification	% Figure
Income	_____
Debt	_____
Appraisal	_____

Now, let's pull together the real data and establish your budget.

As indicated before, the place to begin is the income qualification. To determine your monthly income, take your gross income before taxes and divide by 12.

1   INCOME QUALIFICATION

Monthly Income:

Borrower #1 _____

Borrower #2 _____

Other Income:

Alimony _____

Child Support _____

Other _____

Other _____

Monthly Income _____

Multiply by qualification limit % _____

Maximum monthly housing expense _____

Less property taxes and house insurance .... _____

Maximum monthly mortgage payment .... _____

2 CREDIT HISTORY

For the purposes of this workbook, we'll assume that you have a good credit history and rating. But remember, at this time you should learn what your actual credit history is by taking the precautions that were recommended earlier in this step.

3 DEBT QUALIFICATION

Let's take a look at the size of the mortgage you qualify for under the debt qualification limit. Remember, if you are planning an addition or remodeling, and have a current mortgage on your existing home, for the purposes of these calculations we will assume that you are going to refinance, in effect wiping out your current mortgage and starting from scratch. Therefore, do not include your current mortgage in this debt figure.

3a　Debt Qualification Amount:

Gross monthly income (from 1, above) .... _____

Multiply by debt limit % .... ✕ _____

Maximum monthly debt allowances .... _____

Now you need to calculate the amount of your other monthly debts, excluding your mortgage payment.

3b　Total Monthly Debt:

Car payments .... _____

Alimony .... _____

Credit card payments .... _____

Student loans .... _____

Other .... _____

Other .... _____

Additional monthly debt .... _____

3c To determine the amount of your monthly mortgage payments, deduct your additional debt and your housing expense from your maximum monthly debt allowance.

Maximum monthly debt allowance .... _____

Less additional monthly debt .... – _____

Less housing expense .... – _____

Maximum monthly mortgage payment .... _____

A bank will typically lend you the lesser amount that you qualified for under the income and debt qualification limits. Using the lesser figure, you can calculate the size of the loan you will be able to obtain.

3d Amount of loan you qualify for:

Lesser amount from 1 or 3c, above .... _____

Interest rate * .... _____

Length of the loan .... _____

Amount of the loan ** .... _____

4 APPRAISAL QUALIFICATION
Now let's take a look at how the appraisal qualification and required equity amount will affect your loan.

4a Total appraised value of the property:

Value of land .... _____

The amount you want to borrow for a new
house or the value of your existing house .... _____

Value of addition or renovations .... _____

Total value of property .... _____

* Current interest rates can usually be found in local newspaper advertisements or financial pages.
** You can determine the amount of loan you qualify for by consulting the mortgage tables in the Appendices.

4b Amount of loan that agency will provide:

Total value of property (from 4a, above) .... _____

Multiply by Loan-to-Value Ratio (in %) .... × _____

Amount of loan bank will make .... _____

4c Amount of down payment and/or equity required of you:

Total value (from 4a, above) .... _____

Less amount of loan (from 4b, above) .... − _____

Amount of down payment and/or equity .... _____

The next piece of the budget puzzle is to find out where your down payment and/or equity will come from. As we have seen, your equity can come from such things as your building lot, if you own it outright, the difference between what you still owe on your current house mortgage and how much you can borrow against your house now, or a cash payment. If your current equity doesn't meet the equity or down payment requirements, the balance is usually an additional cash payment. The cash will probably have to come from your personal accounts—checking, savings, investments, or other liquid assets. Remember, these should be funds that you can afford to allocate to your construction project, not those you have set aside for emergencies or other obligations like your children's education. Let's see how what you have stacks up against what the bank will require.

5 FUNDS FROM YOUR PERSONAL SOURCES

Equity sources:

Land .... _____

Equity in your home .... _____

Other .... _____

Personal accounts:

Checking .... _____

Savings .... _____

Stocks, bonds, C.D.'s .... _____

Other:

_____ .... _____

_____ .... _____

Total equity available .... _____

6   By adding together your loan amount and any cash equity you're going to include, you can calculate the amount of money you will have available to spend.

Loan amount (from 4b, above) .... _____

Cash equity (from 5, above) .... _____

Total funds available .... _____

7   ESTABLISH YOUR BUDGET

You have now calculated how much money you will have available to spend, but this is not the budget for your project. In reality, you won't have all this money to spend on the design and construction of your project. To establish your budget, the fees and expenses associated with obtaining and servicing a loan must be deducted.

First let's deduct the fees, or closing costs, that occur when you first obtain a loan. Typically these costs are between 2% and 4% of the amount of the loan. You could either pick a percentage, multiply it by the loan amount, and deduct that figure from the money available or, to get a more accurate estimate, you could contact a local lending agency and deduct the actual fees they charge.

Closing Costs:

Amount of loan (from 4b, above) .... _____

Less total fees .... − _____

Subtotal .... _____

Plus cash equity .... + _____

Budget .... _____

Well, this is your budget, and then again it's not, because I have one final suggestion to make. It seems that no matter how carefully the calculations are done or how tightly the budget belt is pulled, building projects cost more than initially estimated. There are many reasons for this, and we'll touch on some of them later and discuss how to avoid them. For now, you should take precautions against the unpleasant effects of cost overruns by including a cushion in your budget. That way your project won't come in over budget even if it costs more than originally estimated. In fact, some banks anticipate cost overruns and require that you take out a loan that is larger than the project's estimated cost—10% of the budget figure is often added to the total budget to cover cost overruns.

9   YOUR CUSHIONED BUDGET:

Your budget (from 8b, above) .... _____

Multiply by .... __x 90%__

Your cushioned budget .... _____

I promise, that's the last budget calculation for this step.

As I have said, I strongly believe that you should take time early in the planning process to establish your budget. I also believe that it is important for you to do the actual work of gathering the data and doing the calculations. It's a lot of work, but this is a good time to remember two principles: The Principle of Sooner, Not Later, and The Principle of Comprehension. Fully understanding what constitutes a budget and how the loan process works are critically important to the success of your project, not to mention the possibility of realizing substantial savings of time and money. So I urge you again, take the time now to establish your budget.

If you'd like some help with this process, or want another perspective, you might contact a local lending agency and have them pre-qualify you. The pre-qualification process is very similar to the work you've done to establish your budget, and is a service offered free by most lending agencies. There are some good reasons for becoming pre-qualified. First, the loan offcer will be able to help you through the process and answer questions about your unique situation. Second, you will use the "hard," or real, numbers supplied to you by the lending agent to do your calculations and probably be able to get a more accurate estimate. And third, and I think very importantly, you will begin to get a feel for what it's like to work with a lending agency. With your budget in hand you can continue the planning process, knowing that you have a firm grip on the financial realities.

STEP 4 *Identify What's Realistic*

Now that Step 3 is done, you're ready to move on to more pleasant tasks. In Step 4, you'll to continue to explore the possibilities, narrow the choices a bit and begin to determine the probability of getting what you want. It sounds mutually exclusive, but it's not.

THE GOAL FOR STEP 4   To describe and define your building ideas and objectives more fully, and prepare yourself to effectively communicate them to designers, builders, or other industry professionals—the people who will help turn your dreams into reality.

The first thing you should do is revisit your files and evaluate all the ideas and information that you've been collecting. As I said earlier, many people take a year or more to explore the possibilities; if this is true of you, you've probably got quite a collection. You could consider lightening the load a little—after all, a lot of things can change in a year. Perhaps the cabinets that were your heart's desire last year turn your stomach now, or the house style that once took your breath away leaves you flat. Even if you've only been at this a relatively short period of time, what looked good to you yesterday may have lost some of its luster overnight. That doesn't necessarily mean that you're a fickle trend-surfer. It's perfectly natural for your desires, tastes, and goals to change and mature as you become more familiar with the available options. That's why it's not a good idea to begin exploring the possibilities two weeks before you break ground. Also, by re-evaluating things from time to time, you will keep the number of choices under control; when the time does come to make those final decisions, your task should be somewhat easier. So go ahead, reorganize your files if they need it, weed out some of the old, and make room for the new. That's right, the new; your exploration of the possibilities did not end with Step 2, and it will continue in one form or another throughout the entire planning process. So enjoy your continued searching, collecting, and evaluating.

Up until now, you've kept most of your exploration efforts close to home—talking with family and friends, reading books and magazines, and searching your thoughts for your dreams and wishes. And from time to time you've probably been a drive-by voyeur, nearly leaving the road as you crane your neck to get a good look at a particular house behind the hemlocks. Perhaps you've strolled through a special neighborhood, basking in the glow of all those wonderful houses and dreaming of the day when one like *that* one will be yours. If you have, great. If you haven't, get ready. But before you do, some preparation is required. You need to equip yourself with the appropriate tools and information to get the most out of this next phase.

A big part of determining what's realistic is learning approximately how much house or addition your budget is going to buy. I'm going to show you a way that you can do this before you meet with any professionals. It is based on the "cost-per-square-foot" concept of estimating residential building projects. The cost-per-square-foot is a method widely used by designers, appraisers, real estate brokers, bankers, builders, and other industry professionals to get a rough approximation of the cost of a building. Designers typically use this method in the early stages of the design process to help guide the design as it develops and keep it in the budget ballpark. And that's how you should use it, as a "ballparking" tool to measure your construction dreams and see if they have any basis in your financial reality. The reason cost-per-square-foot should only be used as a rough guide is that there are many, many influences other than size—such as site considerations, complexity of design, local labor costs, and level of finish—that determine the actual cost of a project, and it's impossible to account for them accurately using such a general method. A more accurate determination can only happen much later in the process.

The first thing you need to know is how to calculate square footage. Square footage is the area of a surface—in this case, the area of a house. A "square foot" is a square that measures

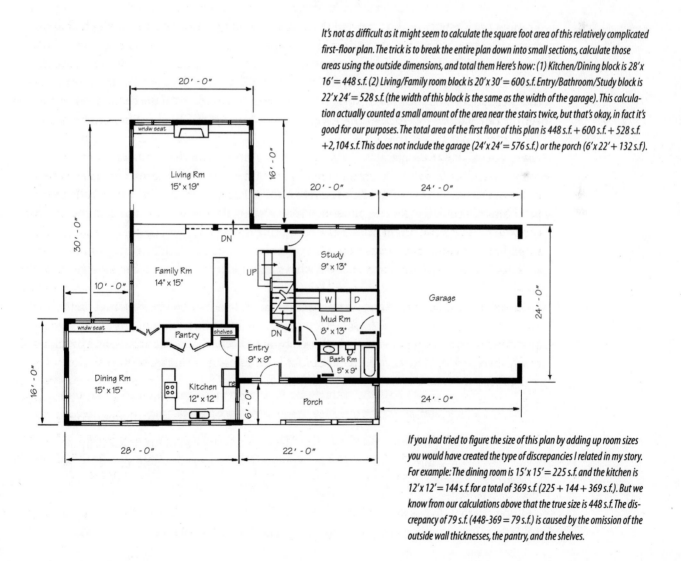

It's not as difficult as it might seem to calculate the square foot area of this relatively complicated first-floor plan. The trick is to break the entire plan down into small sections, calculate those areas using the outside dimensions, and total them. Here's how: (1) Kitchen/Dining block is 28' x 16' = 448 s.f. (2) Living/Family room block is 20' x 30' = 600 s.f. Entry/Bathroom/Study block is 22' x 24' = 528 s.f. (the width of this block is the same as the width of the garage). This calculation actually counted a small amount of the area near the stairs twice, but that's okay, in fact it's good for our purposes. The total area of the first floor of this plan is 448 s.f. + 600 s.f. + 528 s.f. + 2,104 s.f. This does not include the garage (24' x 24' = 576 s.f.) or the porch (6' x 22' + 132 s.f.).

If you had tried to figure the size of this plan by adding up room sizes you would have created the type of discrepancies I related in my story. For example: The dining room is 15' x 15' = 225 s.f. and the kitchen is 12' x 12' = 144 s.f. for a total of 369 s.f. (225 + 144 + 369 s.f.). But we know from our calculations above that the true size is 448 s.f. The discrepancy of 79 s.f. (448-369 = 79 s.f.) is caused by the omission of the outside wall thicknesses, the pantry, and the shelves.

1 foot by 1 foot. A square having sides 2 feet long has an area of 4 square feet ($2' \times 2' = 4$ s.f.). The area of a rectangular house is derived by multiplying the width by the length. For instance, if you were planning a two-story house that was 24 feet wide by 40 feet long, the house would contain 1,920 square feet ($24' \times 40' \times 2'$ stories = 1,920 s.f.). To account for more complicated shapes, such as wings, ells, and bump-outs, you would add their individual areas to the main body of the house. When encountering complicated shapes, for instance octagonal bays, it's a good idea to figure their area as if they were rectangles. The resulting larger areas help to offset the additional cost of constructing those complicated shapes.

WHAT'S INCLUDED?

One of the most commonly asked questions concerning square footage is "What's included in the square foot figure?" To illustrate this point, I'd like to share a story with you. I was talking with a friend, who is a locally well-known and respected builder, and he began to vent his frustration in dealing with a potential client. The client was working with a designer on plans for a very large house, and wisely wanted to get some feedback from this builder about the potential cost of the house. My friend used the cost-per-square-foot method to give the client a ballpark estimate. After the builder submitted the estimate, he got a call from the client complaining about the high figure and reported that, according to the designer, the builder had used an incorrect square foot figure. The builder said he would check his calculations and call the client back. After all, the house was quite large and fairly complicated, and he could have made an error. He checked his figures several times, yet still came up with the same total square footage. At this point, the builder suggested that he, the designer, and the client meet and go over the calculations together. At this meeting the reason for the discrepancy became clear.

When the designer demonstrated his calculation method, the builder shook his head. The designer had only included the inside dimensions of the individual spaces, and had omitted crucial elements such as wall thickness, closets, and other "accessory" spaces like halls and bathrooms. Of course, a house cannot be built with pencil-line-thin walls, and closets do cost money to build. As you might imagine, the resulting discrepancy was quite significant, but the disappointed client finally understood the reason for it and accepted the reality of the builder's numbers. The moral to this story is: learn what's required to calculate square footage.

That may be more difficult than you might think because not only does the exact method vary from region to region, it varies from person to person. In addition to builders and designers, square footage figures are calculated and used by appraisers, real estate agents, and developers. To help, here are some widely accepted standards for calculating square footage.

• Square footage, as we saw in the example above, is not a measure of floor area or room area. Walls, halls, and closets are included in square footage figures.

• The base number for most square footage calculations is the area of the finished, insulated space as measured from the outside of the exterior walls. This is typically called "primary" living space.

• Rooms with walls less than full height ($7' 6''$), but higher than 4 feet are typically considered primary living space. If not, they are usually listed separately as "useful" space.

• Below grade space is seldom, if ever, included in square footage figures, even if it's a finished basement.

• Garages (attached or detached), porches, and attics are not included, but listed separately.

HOW MUCH DOES A SQUARE FOOT OF HOUSE COST?

Now that you know what a square foot represents, you need to know how much each square foot of house is going to cost. As I mentioned earlier, at this stage it's virtually impossible to determine a precise dollar amount, but right now we're only interested in an approximation. For instance, residential construction costs in my area of New England typically run between $60/s.f. and $100/s.f. Sometimes they may even be higher, but rarely lower. If we were to use the house mentioned above and do some quick calculations, we'd discover that the house might cost between $135,000 ($60/s.f. × 2,250 s.f. = $135,000) and $225,000 ($100/s.f. × 2,250 s.f. = $225,000). The difference between the two is $90,000. That discrepancy is so large that you might be ready to toss the whole notion of cost-per-square-foot estimates in the trash. But wait, not just yet. There are ways to reduce that discrepancy, and to find a reliable per-square-foot cost that will more accurately reflect costs in your part of the country.

One way to refine that estimate is to utilize your local newspaper's "house of the week" feature that I mentioned in Step 2. Typically, the houses shown reflect styles that are locally preferred, commonly built, and available through plans services. It's not particularly important whether you like or hate the houses. What is important is the information you can glean from them. For instance, the "house of the week" piece in a Sunday paper I read usually contains a written description, a set of "statistics," floor plans, and exterior (and sometimes interior) perspective drawings of the featured house. All of this is valuable, but what's most valuable is the set of statistics. Utilizing those statistics, you'll be able to refine the per-square-foot cost estimate. Here's a sample description given for a "house of the week" designed in what's described as a "farmhouse" style.

> *Design F-15 has a "great room," country kitchen, three bedrooms, and two baths, total-ing about 1,950 square feet of habitable space. There is a lavatory, laundry, utility area, pantry, two-car garage, and covered porch. Doors from the great room lead to another covered porch. The overall dimensions of 65' -8" by 43' -10" include the garage. Con-struction blueprints include slab, crawl space, or full-basement versions. House of the Week F-15 can be built in this area for about $165,900, according to estimates provided by the local Home Builder's Association. Land and development costs are not included in the estimates.*

There's some useful data in that paragraph, and it's yours for the taking. Let's concentrate on three items: the size of the house, the cost of the house, and what's included in the size and cost. The house contains 1,950 square feet of "habitable space." We don't really know what is meant by habitable space, but for our purposes we don't need to know. This house will cost about $165,900 to build. Notice the use of the word *about*, recognizing the approximate nature of this figure. Simple math will tell you that this house would cost about $85 per square foot to build ($165,900 ÷ 1,950 s.f. = $85 per square foot). Now that's more like it: one tangible number, not a wishy-washy range, to crunch through your budget. Now, in addition to the main house, the price includes a garage and a covered porch. In a minute, I'll explain why these "extras" are important.

The price of the land, or building lot, and the development costs (improvements such as the driveway, septic, well, and unusual excavating or grading) have been left out of the estimate, and for very good reasons. While the "normal" expense for excavating and rough-grading a house site is usually included in the square foot cost, there is no way of knowing what the price of the land and the cost to develop that land will be until after the land is purchased. You'll need to take these costs into consideration when using this method. If you already own your lot, you know its cost, and you've probably already accounted for it in your budget figure. If you don't, you'll have to estimate the amount you expect to spend on a piece of land and deduct that amount from your budget. In either case, you'll have to decide whether you want to count on an extra cushion: if so, deduct several thousand dollars to cover unusual site development costs that might arise. But, as I've said, don't be too concerned with accuracy at this point; you're only interested in an approximate figure for now.

To increase the credibility of the estimated cost of construction calculated using this approach, I recommend that you do three things:

1 Look at more than just one house of the week.

2 Make sure that all the houses come from the same source. This way you can assume that the same square footage calculation method was used for each example, and that the "extras" were treated equally.

3 Choose houses that include similar features and extras, and note any differences.

This was my approach. Over a several-month period, I selected ten houses. Nine of the houses were in a style usually built in this locale. Seven of the houses cost between $85 and $89 per square foot, for an average cost of $87. Of the three remaining houses, two cost less than $85 ($78 and $75) and one more than $89 ($115). The houses costing $78 and $75 were simple rectangles with fewer extras; it's clear why these two houses cost less than the average. Can you guess which house came in at $115? That's right, the one that was not typical for the local area. The exterior perspective showed a rambling stucco house, with large roof areas and extensive custom windows. The caption read, "Sunny Mediterranean shores come to mind with this design." At a total estimated cost of $332,500, if you're building in New England there are more appropriate ways to build.

ANOTHER SOURCE OF PER-SQUARE-FOOT COSTS

As I mentioned, designers, builders, and realtors use cost-per-square-foot figures every day, and they will know the current costs in their region. I'm not suggesting that you pick names randomly out of the Yellow Pages and call them; you'd probably be rebuffed. A more effective approach is to go to home shows, open houses, and workshops. Keep an eye out for one of my

HOMEWORK Seminars. (See the Appendices to learn more about them.) These are all places you can ask questions concerning costs. Before you do, however, make sure you've done some homework and learned the terminology.

HOW MUCH HOUSE WILL YOUR MONEY BUY?

Let's take a minute and apply what we've learned about square footage costs to the example budget in Step 3. If you look back at the worksheet you'll find that the calculated budget was $155,440. Using the average per-square-foot costs of the "houses of the week" described above, this budget will build an 1,786-square-foot house ($155,440 ÷ $87/s.f. = 1,786 s.f.). By using your own budget and per-square-foot cost figures, you will discover approximately what you can afford. If that turns out to be much less than you had hoped, don't panic. Remember, this is just a rough guide for you to use in the preliminary stages of the planning process. Do not act as if this figure is cast in concrete, or feel that you need to abandon an apparently sinking ship. As you move through the steps in this book, you will learn many ways to increase your buying power, save money, and maximize what you can afford. We all have eyes bigger than our wallets and dreams bigger than our budgets. At this point in the process, although your dreams may be dampened a little by reality, they are still important; don't let them go.

Addition Alert

As a rule, the per-square-foot costs for additions are more than for new construction. This is true for several reasons. First, there are some up-front costs such as demolition, protection of the existing building, and saving materials for reuse. Second, it takes time to "fit" the new structure to the existing when tying in walls, roofs, and floors. Also, the fixed costs of building, such as overhead and transportation, cost more per square foot because of the relatively small area of the typical addition. A major reason for the higher cost of additions is the fact that additions often include a bathroom or kitchen, or both. These are the two most expensive rooms in a house, but when they're part of an entire house, their high cost is offset by the many lower-cost spaces. Not so in an addition, where they can dramatically affect the per-square-foot price. To get a general idea of the cost of your addition, first determine the per-square-foot cost of new housing in your area. Then, taking into account the complexity of your addition, add between 10 and 30 percent of the cost—or more if you're adding a fancy kitchen. Because of the idiosyncrasies of additions, professional advice is really helpful here.

SURVEYING THE SCENE

Now that you've got a handle on the cost of construction, it's time for the more pleasant activities I mentioned earlier. It's time to go house-touring and discover the results of others' dreams turned into reality. The world around you is filled with built examples of what you're planning to do, some more successful than others. You should tap this valuable resource, not only for ideas and information about what to build, but also for the wisdom to be gained from other people's experience. Here's how you can go about it.

The most obvious way is to tour your local neighborhoods looking for examples of houses and additions that appeal to you. Whether you're walking or driving, there are a few things you should do. First, keep a record of the areas you explore, and when you come upon something you like, make a note of what it is and the address of the house. If you want to take a second look later, it will be easy to find. Second, bring a camera along and photograph what you think is important, particularly those things that might be difficult to describe or remember. In the first workshop I ever led, one of the participants corroborated the importance of looking at existing buildings by relating her experience. She and her husband, early in their planning process, took many long drives looking at houses in the surrounding area. Among all the houses they saw, there were three that really turned their heads. With some luck and a little investigation, they were able to talk to the owners of those three houses, and they learned some surprising things. First, all of the homeowners simply loved their houses and had few, if any, complaints. Second, all three houses were designed by the same person. And third, all three houses were built by the same builder. This would not be unusual if the houses were built in the same development, but it would be if the houses were built relatively far from each other, on different types of lots, and for different people with varying needs and situations. The couple was very excited; by finding houses, a designer, and a builder they liked all with one stroke, they felt ahead of the game. Of course their work was only partially completed, and during the course of the next few weeks the couple planned to interview several designers and builders.

Another way to experience houses first-hand is to go to developers', builders', or real estate companies' open houses. One big advantage to seeking out open houses is that it's easy to get inside, and you know you're welcome. Check the real estate or home section of your local newspapers for advertisements announcing open houses. Although there won't be any owners on hand to tell you about their experiences with the house, there will probably be some professionals to show you through the house and answer your questions. In addition to the developer, the builder, real estate agent, designer, banker, or some of the subcontractors might also be there. Take this opportunity, as you did when you cruised the home shows, to interact with the professionals present, pick up their business cards and any information or literature they provide, and make notes about your impressions. If you are told the cost and size of the house, you can calculate the per-square-foot cost the way you did for the house of the week. Remember, be sure to find out what's included in the total price you are given.

A final way to view houses is to visit construction sites. One big word of caution here, though; I do not recommend going onto construction sites without first getting the permission of the person in charge. Not only is it potentially dangerous, but, if you go during working hours, your presence will most likely be a nuisance and interrupt the flow of the work. Needless to say, this is not a way to make friends. Most builders put up signs, complete with their phone number, at job sites. If so, copy the number, call the builder, and ask if you can set up a time to tour the site. If there's not a sign, come back to the job site around quitting time and try to get the appropriate phone number as the workers leave, and then make your phone call. If you do this well, and at more than one construction site, you'll get a lot of good information and also learn about the people who are building the house. In addition, by watching a house progress through the various stages of construction, you will begin to learn about building materials and the construction process. If you're planning an addition, you'll want to pay particular attention to the construction conditions around the house. Is the site kept relatively neat and safe, with the appropriate trash containers available and precautions taken?

I touched on something earlier that I'd like to return to, and that's the notion of learning from others' experiences. Nothing teaches like experience, and while yours will be different from everyone else's, there's a lot to learn from those who have gone before you. You should seek out people who have done building projects similar to yours and ask them to share what they have learned. Some of the questions you might ask are: *What went as you expected? What surprises did you encounter? What would you do differently if you could do it over? What is the one most important piece of advice you would pass along?* And don't forget the $164,000 question: *How much did it cost?* Most people are happy to share their experiences with you, and unlike a lot of the advice you'll be getting during this process, it's free.

TOOLS OF THE TRADE

Earlier in this step, you learned about per-square-foot costs and how to calculate the area of a house. That was an exercise in theory. As you make the rounds of houses, you should try to get of sense of what that area means in the real world. For instance, it's not unusual for a client, when asked about the size of his or her proposed bedroom, to respond with, "I want a really big bedroom." To which I answer, "How big is big?" The client's reply, more often than not, is a shrug of the shoulders, and then we're off, scurrying about, measuring the rooms around us to determine what "really big" means to that person. The point here is that size is relative; what is big to one person may be small to another. You should begin to learn the dimensions of your dreams. A more effective answer to the size question would be, "About 14 feet by 18 feet, or 250 square feet." You can learn to think and talk in those terms, it's not hard.

To begin, carry a tape measure everywhere you go. Get in the habit of measuring everything that you find pleasing or want to learn about. Measure the sizes of rooms, windows, and trim; the widths of porches, stairways, and doors; and the heights of ceilings, counters, and window sills. As you do, you will compile a growing vocabulary of the built world, and before you know it you'll be conversing in a whole new language. Get in the habit of recording these measurements, along with a few descriptive comments, and adding them to your files.

 Insider's Tip

When you forget your tape measure or you can't reach the thing you want to measure, here are a few tips to get you by. Use your body as a measuring device and learn the length of your stride, your walking shoes, or the spread between your outstretched thumb and little finger. Use elements in the building, such as floor tiles or siding, to estimate dimensions. For example, if you like the proportions of a window, but can't use your tape to measure its height, first measure the exposed width of a piece of siding (assuming it's horizontal siding) and then multiply it by the total number of siding courses that occur from the bottom to the top of the window. This will give you a fairly accurate figure.

With all this language and knowledge you've been acquiring, you're beginning to take on the air of a building professional. But there is something most professionals have that you don't: a tool kit. We've already mentioned a few items that should be included in your tool kit; let's take a closer look at those and add some others as well.

- **TAPE MEASURE**   This may be the most important tool in your kit. I suggest that you buy a 25-foot or 30-foot, metal-bladed, spring-loaded tape measure. They're rugged, they will measure most rooms with one pass, and their blades can be extended up to 8 feet before bending. This is a feature that you'll appreciate more and more as you use the tape. You might also consider buying a small auxiliary tape, 6 to 8 feet long, that you keep in your pocket or purse—or even the key chain variety—for times when you want to be more discreet.

- **CAMERA**   The pictures you take are very important. Not only are they a record of what you like, but they will also help you communicate your wishes to others. Almost any camera will do, but a 35mm camera equipped with several lenses will give you useful flexibility. (I suggest a wide-angle lens for whole-building shots, and a telephoto lens for long-distance shots. A "bridge" camera with a built-in zoom lens is a less expensive alternative.) Polaroid pictures don't usually show enough detail, and they cost a lot per shot, but they're better than nothing.

- **ARCHITECT'S SCALE**   An architect's scale, also called a scale ruler or just a scale, will come in handy as you begin to look at building plans more frequently and perhaps work on some of your own. The multipul scale with a triangular cross-section may be a bit confusing to use, but is the most versatile. Although there are 10 different scales plus a 12-inch ruler on this scale, you will use the ¼″ = 1′-0″ scale the most. Clearly mark that scale and practice using or "reading" it so that when it comes time to use it, you'll be ready.

- **MECHANICAL PENCIL**   I like mechanical pencils because they're always ready to use, their points are always sharp, and the lead can be retracted when not in use. They're available in various lead thickness, from .3mm to .9mm, and lead hardness, from 7H to HB. While it's mostly a matter of personal preference, a .5mm or .7mm with an F or HB lead is a good choice.

- **GRAPH PAPER**   In Step 2, I told you to put away your graph paper. Well, you can take it out now. If you don't have any yet, the most useful type is divided into 4 squares per inch (essentially ¼″ scale) and comes in a 8½″ x 11″ pad. At this point in the process, graph paper is very useful if you want to make a quick, scale drawing of something you're measuring in the field or in your existing home. However, it's still too early for you to use graph paper as a design tool to create floor plans. Graph paper is just too limiting, so try to be patient.

- **TISSUE TRACING PAPER**   If you haven't yet bought a 12-inch foot roll of white tissue tracing paper, buy one now; if you already have one, add it to your tool kit. See the "Insider's Tip" in Step 2 (page 26) for a description of its uses.

- **MICRO-CASSETTE RECORDER**   This is the small, hand-held type of tape recorder, often used by news reporters. They can be used to take oral notes at those times, such as driving in your car, when you just can't write, or to record an interview (with the person's permission, of course) or conversation when taking notes would be a distraction. Reasonably priced recorders are available; I use one all the time and find it indispensable.

- **DIRECTIONAL COMPASS**   Learning how to read a compass and locate the compass points (north, south, east, and west) can be a useful skill when planning a construction project. Knowing climatic data such as the direction of the sun at noon and the direction of the prevailing winds, will be valuable whether you're assessing a piece of property to buy or beginning the design process.

- **TOOL BOX**   I recommend that you get a carrying case for your tools, perhaps a plastic tool or fishing tackle box or a brief case. Check your local art supply store or the catalogues listed in the Appendices for both the tools and the carrying case.

OTHER CONSIDERATIONS

At this time, it's important for you to consider three issues that may not have occurred to you yet: energy efficiency, "green building," and "healthy houses." These often are not addressed until later in the process, if at all, but, if you follow The Principle of Sooner, Not Later, they deserve your attention now. Although an in-depth discussion of these issues is beyond the scope of this book, but by beginning to learn about them now, you will have more time to understand and assess the wide range of options. When, with the help of your designer or builder, you do make your final choices, your decisions will be informed ones.

ENERGY EFFICIENCY

Energy efficiency primarily means keeping the heat in during winter and out during summer. To some, energy efficiency means building thicker walls with extra insulation; to others it means sealing and insulating a house so well that it could be heated with a candle. The approaches to efficiency are seemingly endless, and the "right" solutions sometimes appear blurred. One issue, however, is very clear: there is a world-wide need to save energy. Your job here is to recognize that you play a part in energy consumption, acknowledge that you have energy-conservation responsibilities, and decide how and to what extent you are going to meet them. To do this effectively you must be informed. There are a number of good books on the subject (see the Appendices) that make worthwhile reading. Magazines and local newspapers often have articles on the subject of energy efficiency. In addition, numerous energy conservation programs have been developed by both public and private agencies (again, see the Appendices for a listing). These programs offer a wide range of services that include informational workshops, educational literature, plans evaluation, builder training, and on-site inspections. These services are typically offered either free or for a minimal cost.

GREEN BUILDING

Ever since the first Earth Day in 1970, a lot of attention has been focused on the need to conserve the world's natural resources and reduce environmental pollution. "Green" designers, builders, and manufacturers are addressing these concerns in construction by using environmentally friendly and sustainable design and building techniques. The possibilities of including green building techniques in your project are many. The options run the gamut from designing a building that uses less material, to constructing one that is almost completely made of recycled materials. As with energy conservation, the key is to understand that your project, no matter how small it may appear in comparison with the larger world, will have an impact and is a piece of the environmental puzzle. Again, it is your responsibility to become informed (see the Appendices for reference and reading material), decide where you stand on the issue, and then, with the help of the appropriate people, determine how your project will fill its place in the environmental landscape.

HEALTHY HOUSE

Closely related to the issue of environmental pollution is indoor pollution. Most indoor pollution concerns are centered around contaminated, unhealthy air. These contaminants, emitted into the indoor air by household chemicals, building materials, and mechanical equipment, can cause severe problems during times, such as winter, when a house is closed up for extended periods. "Healthy House" design, construction, heating, and ventilating techniques address this problem by minimizing the amount of contaminants released into the air and eliminating the ones that do escape. As with energy efficiency and green building, the range of options is great, but this time the choice is a more personal one. If you have specific allergies to things like pollen or dust, or know that you're chemically sensitive, it probably goes without saying that you'll be careful about indoor air quality. If a member of your family has asthma, it may be important to install a mechanical device called a Heat Recovery Ventilator (HRV), which reliably changes the air in your house. There is one indoor pollutant that you should consider no matter what, and that's radon gas. Even if there's no evidence of radon gas in your area, it makes sense to take the relatively inexpensive steps during construction to eliminate radon gas from your house. Again, do some reading so that, in consultation with the appropriate professionals, you can make educated decisions.

THE HOUSE AS A SYSTEM

Of the energy conservation programs that I alluded to above, the one that I'm most familiar with is called The Energy Crafted Home Program. This program, sponsored by a consortium of New England utility companies, calls their approach to residential energy conservation "the house as a system." Instead of the traditional way of building, in which a house is seen as a loose collection of individual parts, the "house as a system" approach views the house as a dynamic system, composed of integrated components working together to form a whole. Construction methods, insulating and sealing techniques, and mechanical systems all help to save energy, control pollution, and clean the air. This is a refreshing and long-overdue approach to the centuries-old activity of house building. I urge you to do some investigation and try to find a similar program in your area.

CONSOLIDATING YOUR THOUGHTS

As with Step 1, the process of identifying what's realistic could take a long time, but this is an important part of the process, and time spent here is not wasted. On the other hand, while it is important to take your time with this step, remember that your goal here is to describe and define your building ideas and objectives *more fully*, not exactly or precisely, so that in the next step you'll be able to communicate them to the building professionals you'll be interviewing. After that, there will still be the opportunity to work out many of the details. So, when the broad scope and nature of your project becomes clear to you, it's time to move on and consolidate your thoughts. To do this, you should commit your thoughts to paper by completing the Preliminary Project Description Sheet on pages 65-71. This sheet, which you should give to the designers you interview, will accomplish several things.

First, it sets a precedent for implementing The Principle of the Written Word, which you should strive to follow throughout the rest of the planning process. Second, the act of writing helps you focus your attention, and encourages you to be concise and efficient. Third, you demonstrate to the designers you interview that you are serious, well organized, and prepared —all qualities they will greatly appreciate. Finally, because each candidate you interview will receive and respond to exactly the same set of data, you are assured that when you do your evaluation, you will be comparing apples to apples.

CLEAR COMMUNICATION

Before you begin, I'd like to comment on two of the pieces of information you are asked to provide in the Preliminary Project Description Sheet. The first is "Owner's desired amount and/or type of involvement." As I have said, a construction project is as much about construction people as it is about construction materials, and successfully planning and building a residential project is largely about establishing and maintaining good working relationships. Therefore, it makes sense to hire people that *you* work well with, that *you* think are best, that are right for *you.* One of the most important things you can do to ensure this is to be clear about how you want to be involved before you hire somebody.

There is another piece of information that you're asked to note on the Preliminary Project Description Sheet—your budget for the design and construction of the project. Most people are uncomfortable discussing their building budget, let alone disclosing it to designers. There is no hard and fast rule that governs budget disclosure but let's set up a benchmark against which you can measure your situation and make your decision. First, let's assume that the processes of designing and building your project are separate activities, done by different people—a designer and a builder. (If this is not the case, I'll tell you in Step 7 how you can effectively create the same scenario.) Unless you have an endless supply of money, the designer must know what your budget is in order to design something that meets your budget. Later, utilizing the plans and specifications prepared by the designer, the cost of your project will be determined during a bidding or estimating process. This is where the builder enters the picture. To bid on the job, the builder really shouldn't care what your budget is, only what it is going to cost to build your project. Once a builder is hired, you may need to revise the scope of the project to fit the budget. At this time, the builder should be informed of the budget as you work to bring costs into line. The bottom line is if your project is going to fit your budget, you have to reveal your budget to the appropriate people (such as designers).

Now, it's time now to get down to the nitty gritty, complete the Preliminary Project Description Sheet, and begin to identify what's realistic.

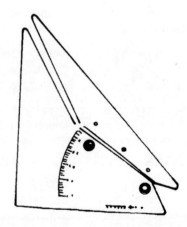

Preliminary Project Description Sheet

Owners' names, address, and phone number:

_____

_____

_____

_____

Type of project:

_____

_____

_____

_____

_____

_____

Reasons for undertaking the project:

_____

_____

_____

_____

_____

_____

Generally describe what you want, including the problems you want to solve, a list of spaces/rooms you want, and the activities that will take place in them (see Step 6 for help):

_____

_____

_____

_____

_____

_____

_____

_____

_____

_____

_____

_____

_____

_____

_____

_____

_____

Describe the styles that appeal to you and those you dislike:

_____

_____

_____

_____

_____

_____

_____

_____

_____

The number, ages, and special needs of the people that are to be accommodated:

_____

_____

_____

_____

_____

_____

_____

_____

_____

Size, in square feet:

_____

_____

_____

Owners' desired amount and/or type of involvement:

_____

_____

_____

_____

_____

_____

_____

Your budget for design and construction of the project:

_____

_____

_____

_____

Items, such as site work (driveway, well, power, etc.), that have already been completed, and materials the homeowner will provide:

_____

_____

_____

_____

_____

_____

_____

_____

_____

Critical dates of construction:

Design

Start: _____

Completion: _____

Construction

    Start: _____

    Completion: _____

Owner's Time Constraints

    Must vacate current residence: _____

    Vacation: _____

    Other: _____

    Other:

Prioritize items and features you would like to include. (Your descriptions do not have to be extremely detailed):

Can't live without:

_____

_____

_____

_____

_____

_____

_____

_____

_____

Would be nice, if possible:

_____

_____

_____

_____

_____

_____

_____

Probably in our next life, but we still want to consider it:

_____

_____

_____

_____

_____

_____

_____

_____

SUPPLEMENTARY MATERIALS

In addition to the Preliminary Project Description Sheet, you might want to include other materials from your files to give to the people you interview. These might include photographs, sketches, floor plans, samples of materials, or anything that you think might be helpful in communicating the nature and scope of your project.

YOUR OWN DESIGN

Now you can use your graph paper to create some hard-line floor plans. Perhaps you've found a floor plan that you like, but you want to change a few things. Or maybe you have an idea for a window arrangement. Graph paper makes it easy to draw elevations as well as plans. Or perhaps you'd like to play around with some of your own ideas and create a totally new plan. Don't worry about the design details (how do the closets fit in, where should the windows be placed, and what about those stairs anyway?). All these details and many more will be put into their proper place as you continue to work through the process.

Be sure to make copies of the Preliminary Project Description Sheet and all the supplementary materials to give to every person you'll be interviewing. Now that you've consolidated all the information and determined what's realistic, it's time to move on to Step 5 and hire the appropriate professionals.

STEP 5 **Hire the Professionals**

I f you've been doing your homework up to this point, you've probably met and had some casual conversations with a number of building professionals. Now it's time to get more serious.

THE GOAL FOR STEP 5   To identify and hire the most competent and appropriate professionals possible—the people you will work with to help turn your dreams into reality.

Step 5 represents a significant juncture in the planning process—a juncture that you probably will encounter more than once. If you accept the premise that the planning and building processes are largely about relationships, then you can see how the choices you make during this step will have a huge impact on the tone and success of your project. Keep in mind that you will not only be hiring people, such as designers and builders, but also companies and businesses. If you buy materials, you are "hiring" that material supplier; if you decide to build a panelized home, you are "hiring" that manufacturer; and when you take out a loan, you are "hiring" the lending agency. You are about to become a major employer in the marketplace, and you should take your responsibilities seriously.

When you think about hiring professionals, three questions should come to mind:

- *When* should I hire someone?

- *What* type of professional should I hire?

- *Which* individual among all the choices in a profession should I hire?

Before the *which* question can be addressed, we must find answers to the *when* and *what*. Basically, there are two reasons for hiring professionals: the first is that you are required to, and the second is that you choose to. In the first case, the choice of when to hire and what type of professional to hire is typically decided by the state in which you live or some other jurisdictional body. In the second case, after assessing your situation, skills, and resources, you decide whether or not to seek the services of a professional. Let's look at some of the reasons why you might be told to hire professionals.

WHEN YOU'RE REQUIRED TO HIRE

In general, we humans don't like being told what to do, and we take particular exception when we are told to do something by a governmental agency. However, you should know the facts of building life; sometimes you are told when and who to hire, and if you want to get your project built, you must do what you're told. The mandate to hire is usually declared in the state or local building codes, zoning ordinances, or other jurisdictional regulations. For instance, in many states anyone is permitted to design a house, and in others building codes require that houses be designed by architects or engineers who are licensed to practice in that state. When it comes to building a house, the states vary tremendously in their requirements for builders; in some states builders must be licensed, in others insured or perhaps bonded. Some states may require one, both, all, or none. Homeowners are also told what they can and cannot do on their own houses. Some building codes allow homeowners to do certain types of work on their own house—electrical work, for instance—but not others, typically plumbing. And just to keep things interesting, building codes are often written to permit flexible enforcement by local officials. As a result, one local building inspector may require something —perhaps that a specific beam be designed and certified by a professional structural engineer —while another inspector may not.

As you can see, exact requirements vary widely from jurisdiction to jurisdiction, and at times appear to be a maze of interconnected and overlapping offices and enforcement bodies. To do your homework properly, you should check with your local building department and learn the local requirements *before* you get too far into the hiring process. By learning your local requirements early, you will not only avoid hiring inappropriate or unnecessary professionals, but you can also transform your reluctant capitulation to what you might have regarded as odious regulations, into a valuable opportunity to save time, money, and aggravation.

WHEN THE HIRING CHOICE IS YOURS

When my children were younger, their school days were filled with many activities. Some of them they were required to do; these were called "have to's." When it comes to hiring, you just learned about your "have to's." During what was called "choice time" at school, my children could select from among a number of options. It's now your "choice time"—time to decide how involved you want to be in your project. I truly believe that your involvement in your project is crucial to its success—after all, that's why I wrote this book, and that's why I so enjoy presenting preconstruction workshops. But as a companion to that encouragement, I want to offer a few words of advice. There are many ways to be involved in your project, from running errands, cleaning up the job site, or doing some work such as painting, all the way up to attempting to be your own general contractor. There are also a lot of good reasons for wanting to take on these tasks, including capitalizing on a skill you have, learning new skills, achieving a sense of satisfaction and accomplishment, and saving money. But here's where I need to raise a big red flag of caution: *do not*, I repeat, *do not* let your desire to save money be the major motivation for doing a task yourself. You might have other motivations, such as wanting the satisfaction that comes with doing it yourself, or not trusting anybody to do anything, but it most often seems to be the glare of the dollar signs reflecting in our eyes that causes even the most clear-headed of us to squint, look past, and ignore reality. When this happens, the visions of savings can sometimes turn out to be a mirage. Let's look at a some of the reasons why this happens.

MISTAKES

When was the last time you did anything perfectly, without making any mistakes? Let's be realistic; mistakes happen, even in construction projects—or should I say, especially in construction projects—and you can rest assured that you will make your share. That's okay; after all, you're only human and you'll learn from your mistakes. But that's the catch. Mistakes in planning and building a home can be quite costly, and learning from mistakes is a costly approach. While building professionals have to "eat" their mistakes, they also have the opportunity to apply what they've learned to many other jobs. But if you make a mistake, its cost must be deducted directly from any savings you had hoped to realize. If you're unfortunate, you might end up spending more than you would if you had a professional do it.

INFERIOR RESULTS

Many of the tasks performed during the course of planning and building require a high degree of skill and experience, as well as special tools. Consequently, most professionals have spent years perfecting their craft and investing in their business. If you're going to attempt a job that is new to you, you will have to acquire some new skills, tools, and experience. But keep in mind that most of your training will be "on the job." Your rookie status will probably display itself in substandard work that can't compare in quality to a professional job. That might be okay for now, but as your eye for quality matures with time, what you once admired as a fine piece of work might transform into such an eyesore that one day you will hire a professional to come in and "do it right." So much for savings. Even if you're happy with your work, others might not be and, as I've learned from experience, that could cost you money. For example, I'm sometimes asked by friends to walk with them through a house that they're considering buying, and share my professional opinions. On one such occasion the real estate agent said with a sweep of her hand, "the owners did a lot of the work themselves." I nodded in agreement, and whispered to my friends, "Yes, and it shows." I discouraged them from buying the house, pointing out that they could find a better value elsewhere. In this case, the inferior quality of the work snuffed out the sale, but it could just as well have been the firm basis for negotiating a lower price. I am *not* trying to discourage you from doing work yourself, but I *am* trying to encourage you to carefully choose the work you attempt and to do the best job you possibly can.

TIME IS MONEY

As you learned at the beginning of this book, no matter how you approach it, a building project will take a lot of your time; this fact just comes with the territory. If you invest your time by taking on a task that might otherwise be done by a professional, you need to account for that time. If, for example, you take this time at the expense of lost work or earning power, you should calculate how much money you would have made and include this as part of the cost of the job. This will reflect the *true cost* of the jobs that you do, and give a more accurate accounting of the money you actually saved.

THE GENERAL CONTRACTING TRAP

Doing your own general contracting is frequently held out as one way an owner can save large sums of money. Figures of 10% to 20% savings on the cost of building a house are typically quoted, and I know of one book that touts the unrealistic figure of 25% to 35% savings. Even if these figures were attainable—and in most cases I seriously doubt that they are—you need to look beneath the surface of these numbers. Problems can arise that will minimize any potential savings.

Time is, once again, a major consideration. To make sure your project is done right, as a general contractor you should spend a good portion of every day—and most nights too—either at the job site or on the phone, overseeing, scheduling, and coordinating everything. Acting as your own general contractor can be a full-time job. If you have this kind of time on your hands, great; but if you're sacrificing earning power to be a general contractor, as I said above, you should include that lost income as part of the cost of your project.

And speaking of time, how long do you want your project to drag on? One book promoting the owner as general contractor suggests that an addition might take between six and twelve months to complete. I don't know about you, but that's just too long for me to be living in a house while it's essentially a noisy, dusty, smelly factory. In contrast, a 2,600-square-foot addition that I designed was recently constructed by an excellent builder and his two-person crew in four months.

Frankly, if you have enough time to do your own general contracting, you will probably save more money by starting early, doing in-depth research, and shopping for the best deals on materials, the people you hire, and the mortgage you obtain.

Even if you find the time to be your own general contractor, it may be difficult to find qualified subcontractors to work for you. Most subs prefer to work for experienced general contractors for whom they have worked in the past. Subs might worry that your inexperience will cause unnecessary delays and subsequent disruptions in their schedules, not to mention concerns about getting paid. If you do find reliable subs to work for you, it is likely that they will protect themselves against your inexperience by quoting you a higher price than they would for a professional general contractor. Where are the big savings? And what happens when the sub's work is completed—or if they don't complete the work at all? Will you be qualified to judge
a job well done or have the leverage to make them finish the job properly? If not, you should hire someone—perhaps a Construction Manager—to do the job. Of course, if you do, you can kiss another large portion of your potential savings goodbye.

What about borrowing money? If you act as your own general contractor, you will find it more difficult to obtain financing. Many lending institutions will not lend to homeowners acting as their own general contractor. This will reduce the number of borrowing options, and you may not be able to get the best financing deal. As I mentioned above, this could prove very costly.
In Step 8, you will learn how the right deal on the right loan can save you tens of thousands of dollars—much more than you could save by acting as your own general contractor.

One final thought: how much is your peace of mind worth? If you think that merely being involved as the owner of a building project is stressful, just try general contracting. Weather delays, scheduling snafus, no-show subs, and misordered materials are just a few of the headaches that are a part of everyday general contracting life. If you value your sanity, you should put a price tag on it—or at least total up your therapy bills—and deduct this from what is turning out to be an ever dwindling amount of "do-it-yourself" savings.

My intention is not to suggest that homeowners can't successfully do some of the actual construction work on their project, or even their own general contracting. Many homeowners have done so in the past, and will do so in the future. My point is that, before you make a decision to do something yourself, you should be aware of what you're getting into; don't open a can of worms you aren't prepared to eat.

THE CHOICES

In Step 1, I gave an indication of the different types of professionals associated with residential construction. Let's take a closer look now at what separates one professional from another. To help you make your decisions about which person to hire for what job I've provided you with the following breakdown, which enumerates most of the necessary tasks and suggests types of professionals that might be qualified to execute them. Some of your choices will probably be made with the help of a professional that you've already hired, and certainly they will be affected by local practices, customs, availability, and regulations.

THE ARCHITECT

An architect is a designer who has met strict standards and is licensed to practice architecture. The first requirement is an architectural degree from an accredited school of architecture. Next, the graduate must receive an Intern Development Program Certificate issued by the National Council of Architecture Registration Boards. The requirements of this certificate are fulfilled by serving a three-year apprenticeship in a licensed architect's office. After receiving this certificate, the architectural candidate can take the state licensing exam, and, upon passing, become an Architect. It is illegal for someone to call themselves an architect unless they have completed all three requirements. A person who has done the first two, but not the third, can be thought of as a building designer. Architects may or may not be members of professional organizations such as the American Institute of Architects (AIA). Architects are qualified to design commercial buildings as well as residences.

THE BUILDING DESIGNER

The building designer is a designer who may or may not have any amount of formal training or experience in residential design. The ambiguity surrounding the qualifications of building designers is a fact of life, unless clarified by the requirements of local jurisdictions or professional organizations. For instance, the American Institute of Building Design (AIBD) sets the following qualifications for professional membership and status:

- **PROFESSIONAL BUILDING DESIGNER**   At least six years of professional experience, in which 50% or more of the designer's working time is devoted to building design.

  Up to three years of related education may be substituted for an equal amount of experience.

- **BUILDING DESIGNER**   At least four years of professional experience, for which up to two years of related education can be substituted.

- **INTERN**   Building designers who have had less than four years of professional experience.

- **CERTIFIED PROFESSIONAL BUILDING DESIGNER**   A Professional Building Designer who has completed the AIBD certification program.

While it is uncommon for someone to be called a building designer without at least some qualifications, it does happen. Checking professional affiliations is one way to verify qualifications; you will learn others later in this step.

THE DRAFTSPERSON

A draftsperson typically has a year or two of technical education and is trained to draw—or "draft"—construction drawings. Draftspeople do not necessarily have any design training or experience, and often work under the direction of other professionals such as architects, building designers, or builders.

THE PROFESSIONAL ENGINEER

A professional engineer (PE) is an engineer who is certified by the state, has passed an examination, and is licensed to practice in a particular field—structural, civil, or mechanical engineering.

THE MECHANICAL ENGINEER

A mechanical engineer is trained to design heating, ventilating, or air-conditioning systems.

THE STRUCTURAL ENGINEER

A structural engineer is educated and trained to design the structural systems and members of a building. In a residence these usually include floor, roof and wall systems, beams, posts, and foundations.

THE CIVIL ENGINEER

A civil engineer has been trained in a wide variety of disciplines, usually associated with the "infrastructure" of our built environment—structures such as roads, bridges, water and drainage systems, foundations and retaining walls, and structural systems. A civil engineer generally has one or two areas of specialization, and will often work in consultation with other professional engineers. In residential construction, a civil engineer might calculate the size of a beam, design a septic system, or do a topographical survey for a site plan. A civil engineer cannot establish property boundaries; that must be done by a surveyor.

THE REGISTERED SANITARIAN

A registered sanitarian is permitted by the state to design sewage disposal systems. In residential construction where the house cannot be connected to a municipal sewer system, this usually means designing a septic system, which includes a septic tank, distribution box, and leaching field. Sewage disposal systems that require training beyond the qualifications of a registered sanitarian are typically designed by a sanitary engineer.

THE SURVEYOR

A licensed surveyor is the only professional who can establish new property line boundaries on a piece of land, or verify existing ones. Before a piece of property is sold, the boundaries generally have to be set or confirmed by a survey. If you have *any* questions about the location of your boundaries (even if you're planning an addition), you should have them clearly marked by a licensed surveyor.

THE BUILDER

A builder is a building contractor who also performs the "general contracting" jobs required of the project manager's role, including estimating the job, hiring the subcontractors, and overseeing the construction of the project from start to finish. For a more complete discussion of the builder and project manager, refer to Step 1.

THE GENERAL CONTRACTOR (GC)

The general contractor is one of the three types of project managers. The other two are the builder (mentioned above) and the construction manager. The general contractor is responsible for compiling the individual prices from subcontractors and submitting a bid or estimate for the entire job, hiring and paying all the subcontractors, scheduling and coordinating the work of all the subcontractors, and overseeing the subcontractors' work to assure the quality and timely completion of the job. The major difference between a builder and someone who is strictly a general contractor is that the GC is usually a manager only, while the builder also does physical work on the building. General contracting, whether it's done by a builder or GC, is the most common type of project management.

THE CONSTRUCTION MANAGER (CM)

The two major differences between a construction manager and a general contractor are the relationships each has with the homeowner and subcontractors. The GC is employed by the homeowner to provide a product—a finished home. The CM works for the homeowner and provides a service—construction advisement. The relationship between a homeowner and GC can sometimes be adversarial, as the GC attempts to balance his own best interests with those of the homeowner. The CM's job is to watch out for the homeowner.

Under a general contracting arrangement, the subs work directly for the GC, whereas with a CM the subs typically work for the homeowner. While a CM will help you develop a line-item budget, gather and evaluate subcontractor estimates, schedule the project, inspect subcontractors' work to assure compliance with the construction documents, and *approve* payments, the CM does not pay the subs—the homeowner does. Some CMs offer preconstruction services such as land selection, design, and construction document preparation. The construction management approach may make sense for someone who would like to be more involved in their project, but realizes they don't have the skill or desire to act as a GC. The GC typically acts as project manager, while with a CM that role is shared with the homeowner.

DESIGN/BUILD COMPANIES

Design/build companies employ designers and builders under one roof. Typically the "builder" portion of the company came first, and the designers were added to the staff later. A major advantage that design/build firms offer is early builder involvement in the design process. As a result, the design can be developed rapidly, practically, and with a close eye on costs. The working relationship between the designer and builder, traditionally viewed as a strained one, should be smoother when working with a design/build firm. The trade-off is that the checks and balances of the traditional separation between designer and builder is compromised, because the person who prepares the construction documents is essentially the same one who bids on them and then builds the project. If a design/build firm takes a project straight through from conception to construction, you have no assurances that the price you were charged was fair. I recommend that, if you decide to work with a design/build firm, that you contract with them separately for the design work, put the project out to bid, and then decide who will build it. Or employ a construction manager to review the construction documents and cost estimates, or build using the cost-plus method outlined in Step 6. These approaches can restore the checks and balances.

THE CHICKEN OR THE EGG

Over the years, as I have presented my home planning workshops, two questions related to hiring get asked most frequently: "What comes first, hiring a builder or getting my project designed?" and "Who should I hire to design my project: an architect, building designer, or builder?" The answer to the first question is straightforward, the second is not.

Can you build anything if you don't know what it's going to look like? Of course not. That means that before you hire someone to build your project, you must hire someone to design it. And when I say "design," I mean much more than just producing a rough floor plan and a few exterior elevations. The design of your project must include sufficient construction documents—construction drawings *and* specifications—to, among other things, obtain written price quotes and permit the orderly construction of your project. We'll talk more about construction documents and their importance in Step 7, but for now understand that they're a must. Some of you might be saying, "Yeah, that might work for the typical custom home, but my situation is different." Yes, your situation may be different, but the basic premise holds true. Let's look at some examples.

STOCK PLANS

There are about 20 companies offering hundreds, if not thousands, of ready-made plans that you can buy, complete with construction drawings and specifications. It is the rare stock house plan, however, that does not need some adjustment. Perhaps the floor plan needs to be changed, the window placement needs altering, or the specifications must be revised. Sometimes the changes are significant enough to require a designer's services, but more often a builder is asked to make the changes. In this case, would you have to hire the builder before the design is finished? I say yes and no. Yes, you should hire the builder, but only to do the design work necessary to complete the construction documents. Don't hire the builder at this time to build the house. When the builder, acting as a designer, finishes the construction documents, you can distribute them to *several* builders—including the one who made the revisions—and proceed to get the best price from the best builder.

SYSTEMS-BUILT OR FACTORY-BUILT HOMES

If you decide to build a systems-built home, you might think that all the design work is done, or at least mandated by the houses in their catalogues, and that all you have to do is hire a builder. This is not true. As a result of the time-saving advantages of Computer-Aided Design (CAD), most manufacturers of systems-built homes offer hundreds of options with their standard plans. You should work with the manufacturer's designer to develop the plan you want and a complete set of construction documents *before* you hire a builder who is experienced with their system. Most manufacturers can offer builder and dealer referrals, and you should interview and obtain bids from several before hiring your builder.

What About Additions?

The order of hiring for an addition is no different than any other project: first you should get the addition designed, then hire someone to build it. However, additions *are* different in another way that's worth mentioning. From my 12-plus years of design experience, I've learned two things about additions: (1) Additions are often more difficult and more challenging to design than a new house, because they typically have more constraints—such as zoning restrictions, the existing floor plan, and existing structural considerations—to address. (2) There is usually at least one good design solution that isn't immediately obvious and takes some searching to find. I believe that this search demands someone with considerable creativity and design experience to develop the best design alternatives. As a result, when someone says to me that their addition is simple and straightforward, and that they are going to have a builder design it, I say, "That's fine, as long as you check the builder's design experience and skill in designing projects like yours."

WHAT KIND OF DESIGNER TO HIRE?

Now that we've answered the first question—"Who should I hire first, the builder or the designer?"—let's tackle the second: "Which designer (architect, building designer, or builder) should I hire?" If you've chosen to build a systems-built house, the answer is easy: you use the manufacturer's designer. But for those of you revising stock plans, planning a custom home, or planning an addition, it's not as simple. There are opinions on this subject that range from one extreme to another. There are factions that maintain that all "good," thoughtful housing must be designed by architects, factions that believe that architects are over-qualified and aloof, and factions that believe that houses should be designed by either architects or builders and that building designers are just superfluous.

My belief is quite simple, and can be applied to all the professionals that you will interview and hire during the course of your project: *If the person meets all the necessary legal requirements, has a proven ability to do the kind of work you need done, and is someone you believe you can work with successfully, then this person is right for the job, and this is who you should hire.* So if you want to decide whether an architect, building designer, or builder should design your project, interview one or more of each, see how they measure up, and make your choice accordingly.

HOW MUCH WILL IT COST ME?

Close on the heels of the "Who should I hire?" question are usually three more:

- "How will I be charged for design work?"

- "Is a building designer cheaper than an architect?"

- "How much is this design going to cost me?"

This time I cannot offer you any universal or pat answers because every situation is different and each question must be addressed on a case-by-case basis. I *can* give you guidance in finding the right answers for your situation.

HOW IS THE DESIGN FEE CALCULATED?

There are three ways that design fees are typically charged: on a hourly basis, as a percentage of the construction cost, or on a flat- or fixed-fee basis. A fee could also be calculated using a combination of two or more of these methods. Each has its pluses and minuses, and most designers have their preferred method.

HOURLY RATE

Billing on an hourly basis is the most straightforward approach to calculating a design fee. Most designers offer hourly rates, typically for short-term consultations or in cases when fees are difficult to determine using other methods. The advantage to the client is that you only pay for design time actually spent; if you are good at making decisions, and the process moves quickly, you could save money in comparison with one of the other methods. Of course, you have to trust the designer to account for the hours accurately. The designer is also assured of getting paid for all the work done, and not being penalized for miscalculating how long the job would take. On the negative side, some people feel that the designer has no financial motive for being efficient and completing the job as quickly as possible. Furthermore, the client has no guarantee of what the total design fee will be. One way to address both of these problems is to establish a "not-to-exceed" figure, above which the fee will not go without the client's approval. This gives the client a figure to rely on, and the designer some incentive for efficiency.

PERCENTAGE BASIS

Fees that are calculated using this method are figured by multiplying the actual cost of construction—typically the amount of the fixed price or bid, adjusted by any change orders—by a fixed percentage. If your project cost $100,000 to build, and the percentage was 10%, the fee would be $10,000. Because the final fee cannot be fixed until the bids for construction are received, the fee is initially based on an estimate of construction costs as determined by the designer. The fee is then adjusted up or down to reflect the bid price. On the plus side, once a bid has been accepted, the client knows exactly how much the design fee will be. However, many clients do not like the percentage method because the fee can be so easily affected by construction costs. The client may believe that this does not encourage the designer to produce efficient, cost-effective designs, essentially rewarding the designer for including more expensive materials, and not necessarily for doing more work. This problem can be overcome by the third method: flat fee.

THE FLAT FEE

There are two ways to calculate a flat fee: as a percentage of a fixed cost, or by the square foot. The percentage-of-a-fixed-cost method is a close cousin to the percent-of-the-cost-of-construction method, with one major difference: the fixed-cost fee is based on the *estimated* cost of construction, and will not change even if the bids come in higher or lower. The one exception would be if there is a substantial change in the scope of the job, requiring more or less work of the designer and therefore a revision in the fee. With the flat-fee method, if the estimated cost of construction is $75,000 and the fee percentage is 10%, the design fee would be $7,500 even if the bids come in at $100,000.

When a designer uses a by-the-square-foot method, the design fee is set by first determining the size of the project in square feet, and then multiplying that by a fee per square foot. You'll remember the cost-per-square-foot concept from Step 1 and the importance of understanding what is and is not included in the square footage figure. This is crucial here because if you're paying by the square foot, you want to know what you're getting for your money.

In the preliminary stages of a project, the cost and size are usually not known with any degree of accuracy. For this reason, designers using the flat-fee methods often work on an hourly basis until the scope of the project becomes clear, and then, with the client's approval, they switch to their preferred method.

Although all the billing methods mentioned above employ different means, their goal is the same: to secure what the designer believes to be fair compensation for work performed. Therefore, the choice of one option over another is really a matter of the designer's preference, not a financial matter. If the same designer were to set fees for a job using all of the above methods, the totals should be reasonably close to each other. However, as we shall see, this does *not* necessarily mean that the fees charged by different designers for the same job will be comparable.

AGAIN, WHAT'S THIS DESIGN GOING TO COST ME?

When I'm asked this question in a workshop, my response is, "How much work needs to be done?" In addition to the factors mentioned above, the total cost of design work is related to the amount of work a designer has to do. Most designers offer a range of service levels, from brief consultations lasting a few hours to a "full-service" package. The vast majority of clients choose an option that falls somewhere between the two extremes. Once you understand the services offered, and the cost of those services, you should choose the type of service that best fits you and your situation.

A designer providing full services to a client will be involved in a project from the very beginning, guiding you all the way until the last nail is set, the last wall is painted, and the last light bulb is installed. The full-service designer will design the project and prepare the construction documents, helping the client choose everything—flooring, siding, roofing, windows, trim, cabinets, light fixtures, wall color, and so on—that will become part of the building. When the construction documents are completed, the designer will recommend and help the client interview builders, procure and evaluate bids, and help to negotiate a building contract. During construction, the designer will monitor the progress to ensure that the building is constructed according to the construction documents, approve and sometimes even disburse the payments to the builder, and compile a "punch list" of tasks that must be completed before the project is declared finished.

That's a lot of work, but it's all part of a building project, and it must be done by somebody—if not solely by a designer, then by some combination of the homeowner, designer, builder, and construction manager. If you do choose to hire a designer on a full-service basis, how much will it cost? Ordinarily I don't like to name standard prices for anything; my experience says that we tend to hold on to the first or the lowest price we hear, even if it is accompanied by all manner of disclaimers. But this time I'll take a chance, and follow it with a disclaimer I hope you'll take seriously. Typically, the full-service design fee ranges between 10% and 15% of the cost of the project. The disclaimer is this: I say "typically," because there are designers who charge less, and designers who charge more, but 10% to 15% is very common. Not only is it fairly typical, it's also a broad range. The design fee for a $200,000 house could be $20,000 to $30,000 under a typical full-service contract. Obviously, you need to shop around and, if all their other qualifications are equal, hire the designer who will do the work for $10,000 less.

Not many houses are designed under a truly full-service fee. It's much more common for a designer to perform some of the services, but not all. Of course this means less work for the designer, which should be reflected in a reduction in the fee. For instance, in my practice I set my fees using the flat-rate, fixed-fee method, and I've charged anywhere from 2% to 15%.

That brings us back to the beginning. The size of the design fee is a function of two things: who you hire to do the work, and how much work the designer does. There are no instant answers; you'll have to keep reading and doing your homework.

I cannot stress enough how valuable good design is and the positive impact a good designer can have on your project. However, it's been my experience that many people balk at the notion of working with a designer and blanch at the fees they charge. Perhaps they've only heard others' tales of disastrous experiences with designers. Unfortunately, this happens, but the opposite is true too. There are many competent designers who will provide you with excellent service at a fair price. Your job is to search carefully for those people and realize that the money you spend on good design can truly be considered a wise investment in your future.

THE MAJOR PLAYERS

Although it is likely that many professionals will work on your project, I would like to focus our discussion of the hiring process on the two most important construction professionals and tasks. This hiring process can easily be modified and used to hire other professionals as your situation requires. The two professionals we'll concentrate on are the *designer* and the *builder*. It's important to keep in mind the broader definitions of designer and builder used in this book (for more detailed definitions, see pages 6–7), so that you won't limit your choices unnecessarily. The first order of business is to find good candidates to interview.

THROUGH THE GRAPEVINE

In spite of the fact that we are living in a time of electronic communication, it's an age-old method of finding designer and builder candidates that's most widely used, effective, and trusted: word-of-mouth. Word-of-mouth is how most of the people attending my workshops find candidates, it's how the majority of the builders I know get most of their jobs, and it's how I get all of my work. Even if a designer or builder uses some form of advertising, it's typically bolstered by word-of-mouth. Word-of-mouth is a major reason why designers and builders work hard to maintain solid professional reputations.

The place to start your search for good prospects is with your friends and co-workers—people you know and trust. Perhaps they've worked with someone they can endorse, or know someone who has. These people aren't going to intentionally recommend an incompetent or dishonest professional. Another excellent source of qualified candidates is the professionals themselves. Designers typically have experience working with a number of builders, and know their work intimately. The same is true of builders. If your first point of contact is with a designer, ask for some builder referrals; if you know some builders, ask them to recommend designers. One advantage of having a designer recommend a builder, and vice versa, is that the two have probably worked well together. As I have said, a good working relationship between a designer and builder is extremely important.

Other word-of-mouth sources include real estate agents, lending agencies, building inspectors, and building supply houses. If you are searching for a builder, one good test of their reputation is their standing in the local business community. If you ask a locally owned lumber yard for builder referrals, it is unlikely that you will be given the name of a builder who is irreputable. After all, the lumber yard's good name is on the line, and they want to keep it intact.

When you ask for references from sources other than your friends, remember The Principle of Threes; ask your sources to give you at least three names. Although it is unlikely that a professional or business would try to steer you to one person, you want to make sure that you avoid the "favorites" game.

There are, of course, other ways to learn about designers and builders: advertisements, yellow pages, home shows, and professional organizations. For instance, the National Association of the Remodeling Industry (NARI) will send you a pamphlet briefly outlining the remodeling process and a list of NARI members in your area. (See the Appendices for NARI's toll-free telephone number.) You might use these sources to cross-reference or supplement the names you've gathered by word-of-mouth, but you should not limit your choices to candidates gathered in this way. That would be contrary to another age-old practice of not putting all your eggs in one basket.

WHO'S THE ONE FOR YOU?

You should not hire a designer, builder, or anybody merely on the advice of someone else, even if a candidate comes with the highest recommendation and has an impeccable reputation. I don't care if the candidate was recommended by your dearest friend, that candidate is essentially a stranger *to you*, and you shouldn't be hiring strangers. The fact that one person had a good relationship with a particular designer or builder is no guarantee that this will be true in your case. To learn if a candidate is "right" for you, you have to get to know each candidate and decide for yourself.

THE THOROUGH INTERVIEW

Given the fact that you are going to be working with the person you choose for anywhere from a few months to a year, you should make every effort to hire a compatible designer or builder. To do this, you need to get to know the candidates extremely well, almost intimately, by following a four-part interviewing process to carefully evaluate each one. I emphasize four parts because, all too often, only the first of the four essential parts is actually carried out. Those four parts are: (1) a face-to-face interview; (2) an investigation of the candidate's references; (3) a visual, on-site inspection of the candidate's work; and (4) a verification of the candidate's professional credentials and reputation.

1. FACE-TO-FACE INTERVIEW

The process of getting to know a candidate begins with a face-to-face meeting. This meeting may be held at the candidate's office or at your current residence or building site. While there are some good reasons for meeting at the candidate's office (the candidate may have designed or built it, giving you an opportunity to view their work first hand, and reference materials are nearby), I recommend that you hold the first meeting on your turf. During the interview, you want to think straight, communicate clearly, and avoid feeling intimidated by either the process or the person. Meeting at your home will help accomplish this, for several reasons.

First of all, you will be in familiar surroundings, which will help you to relax and stay focused. Second, the candidate is removed from the many distractions of the office, almost guaranteeing his or her undivided attention. Finally, when you are in your own home, you will have at least some of the topics of conversation close at hand: a particular room arrangement you like or a piece of furniture that you want to accommodate in your future home. This is particularly applicable if you're planning an addition. Personally, I would insist on meeting a client in their home if they're interviewing me to design an addition. Even if you don't hold the initial meeting at your residence, at least find out if the candidate would be willing to do so. Their willingness or reluctance may give you a measure of their interest in your project.

After making initial contact with a candidate and setting up a meeting, you should do three things: send each candidate a description of your project (a completed Preliminary Project Description Sheet for a designer, or the construction documents for a builder), ask them to bring a portfolio of their work to the meeting, and request that they provide you with a list of references. Let me be more specific about references. The names of one or two *random* people that the candidate has done *some* type of work for, *sometime* in the past does not constitute a proper list, and won't be of much use to you. A good reference list should include the following:

- A minimum of six references, including the first and last names of the owners (the names of both people if the owner is a couple) and their current telephone numbers, the type of project (addition, new construction, renovation), and the start and completion dates of the project. If the candidate wants to include more names, that's fine, but be sure the information you've requested is clearly indicated.

- The names of the candidate's three most recently completed projects, regardless of the type.

- The names of the candidate's three best projects, again regardless of the type.

- The names of at least two different people who hired the candidate for projects that are similar in style or type to yours, if these are not included in the above six references (this is one reason why the Preliminary Project Description Sheet is so important).

- The times when it is acceptable to phone the references. (This is not only a courtesy to the reference, but also in the candidate's best interest; someone who's called at an inappropriate time is not likely to give the most glowing recommendation.)

TAKE CHARGE

By making these specific requests you accomplish two things. First, it puts you in the driver's seat and demonstrates to the candidates that you take the hiring process seriously and are not going to settle for less than the best. This attitude will not only earn the respect of those you interview, but may bring out the best in a candidate. And second, you will get the most accurate picture of the candidates' past performance. Although past performance is no guarantee, it's your best indicator of the future.

Begin your interview with a review of the Preliminary Project Description Sheet or construction documents, and be prepared to answer any questions the candidate might have about them. Inform the candidate that you will be interviewing others for the job and that you have given the same information to each candidate. Then, let the meeting flow, and as it unfolds be aware of its tenor:

- Is the candidate listening attentively to you?

- Does the candidate seem to understand you and your situation?

- Is the candidate responding favorably to your ideas and your project?

- Are you connecting with this candidate on a personal level, perhaps making comfortable eye contact?

- Does the candidate offer opinions without monopolizing the conversation?

As the conversation winds down, perhaps after touring your building site or existing home, take some time to complete the interview by making sure you have gotten answers to all the questions on the worksheet on pages 91-103. Some of these questions may have been answered during the course of the meeting, but the interview is not complete until they have *all* been answered. So don't be shy or embarrassed, pull out the interview sheet and ask away.

2. INTERVIEW THE CANDIDATE'S REFERENCES

After the face-to-face interview, you will probably begin to form an opinion about the candidates. But you've only spent a couple of hours, at the most, with each one, and it's difficult to form a sound opinion about someone in such a short time. You need to listen to the seasoned opinions of the candidates' references—people who have spent weeks, months, perhaps even a year working with that person. Keeping in mind The Principle of Threes, you should speak to at least three references, and more is better. Better advice would be to encourage you to talk with as many references as you must to get a good picture of a candidate. It's important, of course, to talk with the owners of the projects that are most similar to yours.

How you handle this phone call or meeting is crucial to the success of a reference interview. I hate to bother people, and consequently, when I want information, I tend to rush things, asking hurried or incomplete questions. You cannot afford to do this here, and if you plan ahead you won't. So, before you call be sure you have enough time (typically 15 minutes to half an hour) to conduct a proper interview. Listen carefully to the answers to your questions. Keep in mind that the reference may be reluctant to criticize the candidate. Listen to what's being said, and what's not being said, using the following guidelines:

- Are your questions about a candidate answered enthusiastically, without hesitation, or does the reference respond slowly, as if searching for the right words?

- Does the reference go beyond mere "yes and no" answers, perhaps elaborating by relating personal experiences to make a point?

- Do the reference's responses seem unequivocal and convey a feeling of confidence in the candidate?

Make notes to yourself on the interview sheet as you move through the questions. It is important for you to ask the hard questions, especially those about time, money, and responsibility, so be sure to ask all the appropriate questions included in the worksheet at the end of this step.

3. EXAMINING THE CANDIDATE'S WORK

The next move is to take a first-hand look at the candidate's work. Once again, it's good to look at three examples. Sometimes the site visit is arranged by the candidate, who will accompany you on the visit, and sometimes you can set up the meeting and go without the candidate. As long as you've already interviewed the reference, either option is fine. I'm often asked, "I don't know anything about construction, how can I tell good quality work when I see it?" The answer is: "Bring help with you." What kind of help? If the candidate is a designer, you could consider just bringing along an interested, knowledgeable friend. With all the work you've done in the previous steps, you have a good idea of what you do and don't like in the way of house design, and you and your friend can "talk your way" through the project and see how it measures up. If you have more technical concerns—perhaps about how the designer organized the space or addressed energy conservation—you could turn to an appropriate professional, such as a construction consultant, home inspector, builder, or even another (impartial) designer for help. If the candidate is a builder, your designer can come with you on the site inspection and help you evaluate the work. If you haven't hired a designer, seek out the help of one, or another professional.

When you call a professional seeking help to evaluate a designer or builder's work, explain your situation and give the name of the person whose work you would like help evaluating. Don't expect *free* help, you should *hire* and pay this professional on a consulting basis. Make this clear from the start. Remember The Principle of Pay Now and Save Later: any money you spend to get qualified, professional opinions will be well worth it.

As you view the work you might want to take written or tape-recorded notes of your impressions, and complete the questionnaire titled "Viewing the Candidate's Completed Projects" (page 113) when you return home. But be sure to have the questionnaire with you to refer to, and cover all the issues that are raised by the questions.

4. CHECK THE CANDIDATE'S PROFESSIONAL STANDING

By now, you have developed a fairly accurate, comprehensive assessment of each candidate, but there is a final piece of research you should do: you should check the candidate's reputation and credentials. Contact the local offices of professional associations (see the Appendices for a listing for the national offices), the Better Business Bureau, the Chamber of Commerce, or the Bureau of Consumer Affairs. You want to learn about the candidate's history, and any financial, legal, or customer-relations problems they might have had.

Here are some warning signs that might indicate trouble ahead. Keep them in mind during the interviewing process and make sure any problems are resolved *before* you sign a contract.

- You are unable to verify professional information about a candidate—name, address, phone number, license, insurance, or professional credentials.

- The candidate does not comply with your request for references, or you cannot contact the references.

- The candidate does not return your phone calls promptly, is late, or misses meetings.

- The candidate tries to high pressure you into signing a contract by using scare tactics or intimidation.

- The candidate says that a "special price" is available only if you sign the contract today.

- You are asked to pay for the entire job in advance.

- You are asked to pay for the job in cash.

Before you conduct your interviews, read over the following questionnaire, and add any other questions that are important to you.

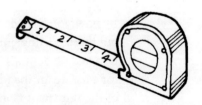

Interview the Professionals

Complete a copy of the following questionnaire for each candidate you're considering hiring.

Candidate's Name: _____

Company Name: _____

Address: _____

Phone No.: _____ Fax: _____

Secretary/Administrative Assistant:

_____

_____

Some of the following questions can be asked of both a designer and builder (indicated as D/B), some asked only of the designer (D), and some only of the builder (B).

(D/B) When would you be available to do the work?

_____

_____

(D/B) Have you done work similar to the project I'm contemplating?

yes _____ no _____

Number that are similar and names of people for whom the projects were completed:

_____

_____

_____

_____

(D/B) Do you meet all the legal requirements (professional certification, state licensing, etc.) to do the job?

yes _____   no _____

License numbers:

_____

_____

(D/B) Are you familiar with the local building codes, zoning regulations, and other regulations?

yes _____   no _____

Summarize:

_____

_____

_____

(D/B) Summarize your relationship with the local building inspector?

_____

_____

_____

_____

(D/B) What is your fee structure and payment schedule?

_____

_____

_____

_____

(D/B) How would you describe your style of working with clients?

_____

_____

_____

_____

_____

(D) How do you expect to involve me in the design process?

_____

_____

_____

_____

_____

(B) How can I be involved in the actual construction of my project?

_____

_____

_____

_____

_____

(D/B) How would you describe your past working relationships with builders or designers?

_____

_____

_____

_____

(D/B) Will you provide a list of references?

(Remember to ask for at least their last three and their best three and, if possible, at least one or two projects similar to your own.)

yes _____   no _____

(D) How long will it take you to design my project?

_____

_____

_____

_____

_____

(D) What do you feel will be the approximate per-square-foot cost of my project?

_____

_____

(D) Do you work with any particular consultants (engineers, other designers, etc.)?

yes _____   no _____

Names:

_____

_____

_____

_____

_____

(D/B) How large is your company? (Is it large enough to do the job, but not so large that I run the risk of being ignored?)

Summarize:

_____

_____

(B) Who will be supervising my project?

Name:

_____

_____

(D/B) How do you handle disputes or disagreements?

_____

_____

_____

_____

_____

_____

(B) Are you insured?

yes _____   no_____

(B) Can you supply me with a copy of your insurance certificate?

yes _____   no_____

(B) Are you bonded?

yes _____ no _____

(B) Can you supply your bond certificate?

yes _____ no _____

(B) Can you give me a bank reference?

yes _____ no _____

Name: _____

Address: _____

Contact person: _____

Phone No.: _____

(B) Can you give me a building-materials supplier reference?

yes _____ no _____

Name: _____

Address: _____

Contact person: _____

Phone No.: _____

Interview the Professionals for Additions

As I've said, additions are special. They have all the requirements of new construction, and then some. As a result, someone designing or building an addition should be experienced, and should possess certain skills not always required by new construction. A builder must be prepared to take special precautions to effectively deal with any foul weather that might arise during construction, and be able to balance the necessities of construction with needs of the homeowners, demonstrating sensitivity to the activities of day-to-day life. There are builders who specialize in additions and remodeling, so if you're planning one, you would be wise to include at least one such specialist among your candidates. To supplement the previous questions, you should also ask the following:

(D/B) Have you had much experience designing/building additions?

     yes _____   no _____

     Summarize:

_____

_____

_____

_____

_____

How many per year for the last five years?

     Summarize:

_____

_____

_____

_____

_____

(D/B) What are some of the "problem areas" that might need particular attention?

_____

_____

_____

_____

_____

_____

(D/B) What building codes or regulations might impact my addition?

_____

_____

_____

_____

(B) What types of precautions do you take to minimize the problems of bad weather, noise, dust, and dirt?

_____

_____

_____

_____

_____

_____

(B) What steps do you take to ensure the peaceful co-existence of construction life and home life?

_____

_____

_____

_____

_____

_____

(B) Are there certain aspects of the design that make construction difficult? In your opinion, can they be (easily) changed?

_____

_____

_____

_____

_____

_____

Interview the Professionals for Stock Plans and Systems-Built Houses

Stock plans and systems-built houses also present special design and construction circumstances. Remember, if you're planning to use a stock plan or systems-built design, you are in effect hiring the company's designers. In the case of a stock plan, you'll probably never actually meet the designer, and if you do, you need to approach the "interviewing" process somewhat differently. Much of the information you'll glean about the company's designer or designs will come from a third party, such as past customers or builders that have built houses designed by the company in question. Here are some questions to help you interview a stock-plan (SP) or systems-built (SB) company:

(SP/SB) Have your plans/houses been built in my geographic location?

yes _____ no_____

How many, and where are they located?

Summarize:

_____

_____

_____

_____

_____

(SP/SB) Do your plans meet all the building codes for my geographic location?

yes _____ no_____

Summarize:

_____

_____

_____

_____

(SP/SB) If your plans don't meet all the building codes for my geographic location, will you change them at no charge?

yes _____   no _____

Summarize:

_____

_____

_____

_____

(SP/SB) Have you experienced any special circumstances that affect the use of your plans in my geographic location?

yes _____   no _____

Summarize:

_____

_____

_____

_____

_____

(SP/SB) What is your company policy on changes before purchase or revisions afterward?

Summarize:

_____

_____

_____

_____

_____

(SP/SB) Could you give me a list of homeowners and builders who have purchased? (Note: When requesting references from a systems-built company, be sure to ask for some that are about five years old so that you can check on the long-term quality of their product. If the company isn't that old, you should check them out very carefully).

yes _____   no_____

Summarize:

_____

_____

_____

_____

When you get the company's references, be sure to follow up on them by asking the relevant questions on the first questionnaire ("Interview the Professionals," page 91)above and including the few I've added here. If a company has had a plan or house constructed in your area, you might also call up the local building inspector, explain what you're doing, and ask what their experience was with the company's house. A local inspector that I know once told me that systems-built manufacturers sometimes miss the finer points of the building code. For instance, in Massachusetts the area over an unheated basement must be insulated. Obviously this means the floor, but an area that often gets overlooked is the basement stairs. The interior walls of the basement stairs and the door at the top of the stairs must both meet code mandated insulation requirements. Checking for problems such as these and remedying them *before* you buy can save you a lot of aggravation, and money. Ask the following questions of both homeowners (H) and builders (B) that were given as references:

(H/B) Was the company open to changes and revisions of their plans?

yes _____   no_____

Summarize:

_____

_____

_____

_____

_____

(H/B) Were the construction documents (plans and specifications) complete, professional, and in compliance with all the local and state building codes?

yes _____   no _____

If not, was the company helpful in revising the plans as required?

yes _____   no _____

Summarize:

_____

_____

_____

_____

(H/B) Were you satisfied with the quality of the product?

yes _____   no _____

Summarize:

_____

_____

_____

_____

(H/B) Did you experience any severe or unusual problems with the company, their plans, or house?

yes _____   no _____

Summarize:

_____

_____

_____

_____

One final caution: if you're considering buying plans or a systems-built house, but are unable to talk to builders who have actually used that company's services, I recommend that you hire a designer or builder to do a thorough review.

DOUBLE-CHECK YOUR HOMEWORK

Just to verify that you have asked the most important questions, see if you can say yes to the following items:

❏ The candidate has given, or will send me, a list of references.

❏ I thoroughly understand how the candidate charges for their services.

❏ I thoroughly understand how much service the candidate will provide for that fee.

❏ I have received, or will receive written verification that the candidate is insured and/or bonded.

As I said earlier, all too often the interviewing process stops here, but there is much work yet to be done, so don't quit here. You will be well rewarded.

Interview the Candidate's References

(D/B) Did the candidate return your phone calls?

always _____ usually _____ not often _____

Comments:

_____

_____

_____

(D/B) Did the candidate keep scheduled meetings, arriving punctually?

always _____ usually _____ not often _____

Comments:

_____

_____

_____

(D/B) Did the candidate meet the agreed-upon deadlines?

always _____ usually _____ not often _____

Comments:

_____

_____

_____

(D/B) Did the candidate meet fee, price, or cost estimates?

always _____ usually _____ not often _____

Comments:

_____

_____

_____

_____

(D/B) Was the candidate a good listener?

always _____ usually _____ not often _____

Comments:

_____

_____

_____

_____

(D) Did the candidate effectively grasp and translate your thoughts and wishes into reality?

always _____ usually _____ not often _____

Comments:

_____

_____

_____

(D/B) Was the candidate open-minded and easy to communicate with?

always _____ usually _____ not often _____

Comments:

_____

_____

_____

_____

(D/B) Was the candidate accessible throughout the course of the project?

always _____ usually _____ not often _____

Comments:

_____

_____

_____

_____

(D/B) Was the candidate practical?

always _____ usually _____ not often _____

Comments:

_____

_____

_____

_____

(D/B) Was the candidate creative and imaginative?

always _____ usually _____ not often _____

Comments:

_____

_____

_____

_____

(D/B) Was the candidate's work professional, complete, and accurate?

always _____ usually _____ not often _____

Comments:

_____

_____

_____

_____

(D/B) Did the candidate honor warranties and fix mistakes?

always _____ usually _____ not often _____

Comments:

_____

_____

_____

(D/B) Did the candidate effectively handle problems or disputes?

always _____ usually _____ not often _____

Summarize:

_____

_____

_____

_____

(D/B) Was the candidate honest?

yes _____ no _____

Comments:

_____

_____

_____

_____

(D) Did the candidate work well with the builder?

always _____ usually _____ not often _____

Comments:

_____

_____

_____

_____

(B) Did the candidate work well with the designer?

    always _____ usually _____ not often _____

    Comments:

    _____

    _____

    _____

    _____

(B) Did the candidate work well with the subcontractors?

    always _____ usually _____ not often _____

    Comments:

    _____

    _____

    _____

    _____

(B) Was the job site kept neat and safe?

    always _____ usually _____ not often _____

    Comments:

    _____

    _____

    _____

    _____

(D/B) What was the candidate's greatest strength?

Summarize:

_____

_____

_____

_____

(D/B) What was the candidate's biggest weakness?

Summarize:

_____

_____

_____

_____

(D/B) Are you happy with your home or addition?

yes _____   no _____

Comments:

_____

_____

_____

_____

(D/B) Would you hire this person again?

      yes _____   no _____

      Comments:

_____

_____

_____

_____

(D/B) Is there anything I didn't ask that you think I should know?

      yes _____   no _____

      Comments:

_____

_____

_____

_____

(D/B) Rate the candidate overall on a scale of 1 to 5, 1 being the least favorable and 5 the most.

      1   2   3   4   5

      Comments:

_____

_____

_____

At the conclusion of your conversation, be sure to thank the person for his or her time. It's a good idea to ask the reference if you may call back if you think of another question. And when you hire somebody, implement The Principle of Acknowledgment by making a call or sending a card to the references of the person you hired. They will appreciate the thought, and can take satisfaction in knowing they helped someone out.

Viewing the Candidate's Completed Projects

Rate the following questions: 1 is the least favorable, 5 the most favorable.

Overall, does the building make a favorable impression?

    1   2   3   4   5

Comments:

_____

_____

_____

Does the building fit the site?

    1   2   3   4   5

Comments:

_____

_____

_____

Do I like the style?

    1   2   3   4   5

Comments:

_____

_____

_____

Do I like the detailing?

    1   2   3   4   5

    Comments:

_____

_____

_____

Is the plan well thought out and functional?

    1   2   3   4   5

    Comments:

_____

_____

_____

Is it easy to see how guests or visitors enter the building?

    1   2   3   4   5

    Comments:

_____

_____

_____

Is the work—cabinetry, flooring, trim, and painting—high-quality construction?

    1   2   3   4   5

    Comments:

_____

_____

_____

Are there any particular features that catch my eye?

      Comments:

_____

_____

_____

Are there things that I don't like?

      Comments:

_____

_____

_____

Would I like to live here?

      yes _____ maybe _____ not on your life _____

      Comments:

_____

_____

_____

Check with Local Professional and/or Business Organizations

How long has the candidate been in business?

Number of years: _____

Has the candidate had any financial troubles, bankruptcy, or non-payment of bills?

yes _____ no _____

Comments:

_____

_____

_____

Has the candidate had a history of customer complaints?

yes _____ no _____

Comments:

_____

_____

_____

Has the candidate been a party to any lawsuits?

yes _____ no _____

Comments:

_____

_____

Has the candidate won any professional awards or had other formal recognition?

yes _____ no _____

Comments:

_____

_____

_____

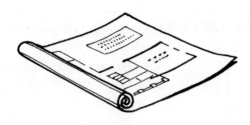

You've gathered a tremendous amount of information about your candidates. Now you need to evaluate the data and make an informed decision about whom to hire. To help with this task, you can use the following evaluation sheet. As you weigh the candidates' qualities and qualifications, keep three things in mind: make fair comparisons, be aware of the factors that are most important to you, and understand the true meaning of "the best deal."

APPLES TO APPLES

Information obtained from different sources and answers given in response to different questions are difficult to evaluate. That's why asking them the same interview questions is so important. These responses will allow an "apples to apples" comparison, and your decision can be made with the knowledge that your evaluation will be fair.

WHAT'S IMPORTANT TO YOU?

Are you searching for someone very creative, extremely practical, or both? Do you place more importance on the initial cost, or are you searching for someone who's noted for standing behind their work? There is no one right answer to these questions. Your job during the evaluation process is to identify all of the factors that you want to consider, determine those that *you* believe are most important, and then choose the candidate who is right for *you*.

THE BEST DEAL

Is the best deal always indicated by the lowest price? Most of the people attending my home planning workshops say "No." At every workshop, I ask the participants to rate the importance of three or four criteria including cost, and cost always loses. Most people understand that there are many issues that are as important as cost, if not more so, and that value is not measured by price alone. So beware of the "good deal" that is based solely on price; in the long run it might not turn out to be the best deal.

After you've chosen your designer and builder, be sure to notify the candidates you didn't hire, and thank them for their time (The Principle of Acknowledgment). If any ask why they didn't get the job, be honest with your answers. It will help their professional development.

Mark the column which most closely describes how each candidate measured up to the criterion. Number 1 represents the lowest, and 5 the highest, level of approval.

EVALUATION CRITERIA	1	2	3	4	5
Personal connection					
Open-mindedness					
Practicality					
Creativity					
Professional demeanor/competency					
Problem-solving abilities					
Accountability					
Typical fee					
Level of knowledge					
Amount of experience					
Reputation					
Other					
Other					

Comments:

_____

_____

_____

_____

_____

_____

MAKING A COMMITMENT

After you've completed your thorough evaluation of all the candidates and chosen the designer or builder you want to work with, it's time to make a commitment and hire them. If you have any doubts about whether you are ready for this step, now is a good time to do some soul searching to reaffirm your resolve, because the next move calls for implementation of The Principle of the Written Word: entering into a formal contract.

Did the word "contract" make you panic? This is a common reaction. In my experience, people will often try to avoid construction-related contracts. Do people associate contracts with terms that are difficult to understand? Perhaps there is a fear that any contract will be skewed in favor of the other party. Whatever your excuses, set aside your fears and understand that good contracts are in the best interest of both parties. Both you and your designer or builder have everything to gain by entering into a contract, and everything to lose if you don't. By clearly stating who will do what for whom and how, a contract forms the cornerstone of a good working relationship and can eliminate many problems before they occur.

WHAT'S IN A CONTRACT?

In this case, a contract is a written agreement between you and a designer or builder for the design or construction of your project.

Design and construction contracts are fairly common, and while it's possible to have a lawyer draft one specifically for you, it's generally not necessary. Designers and builders typically use standard contract forms and modify them to fit the requirements of each job. While a good and fair contract does not have to be lengthy or written in "legalese," it should be comprehensive and protect the interests of both parties. A contract should include:

- All relevant statistics: the names, addresses, and phone numbers of both parties; the location of the project; the date the contract is entered into; and the builder's license number or other legal requirements mandated by state and/or local authorities.

- An accurate description of the services and/or work that is to be performed. In the case of a designer, the services are usually specified in terms of one or more "design phases" (the design phases will be explained in Step 6). If you've hired a designer to prepare full construction documents, you might include a clause stating that such documents will be of sufficient scope and detail to obtain a building permit and delineate the requirements of construction. The scope of the builder's work is described in the project's construction documents (the plans and specifications). Also be sure to account for anything that is specifically not going to be done—any *exclusions* to the work.

- The total fee or price for the services or work to be performed. In the case of a designer, be sure to state what services are and are not included as part of the designer's fee. For example, is the cost of consultants such as engineers, interior designers, and landscape architects included in the design fee? In a contract with a builder, is the price stated as a fixed bid, an estimate with a not-to-exceed amount, or a "cost plus" amount? (In Step

7, we'll look at these methods of pricing a construction project.) Typically the cost of permits, fees, and licenses are paid for by the builder. Be sure this is accounted for in the contract.

• A fee-disbursement schedule. The designer's fee payment schedule is usually keyed to the design phases, and disbursements to the builder usually coincide with actual construction phases. One common approach is to link payments to the builder to the release of loan money from your bank. Make sure the amount of any fee advance or down payments are clearly stated. If you're contracting for an addition or remodeling, you should not pay more than one-third of the total cost of the job up front. Some states regulate the exact amount of any down payments. Except for down payments, you should not pay for any work until it has been completed.

• The amount of retainage and the point at which the final payment will be made. Retainage is a portion of a fee or cost that is held by the homeowner as an incentive and a guarantee until the job has been completed. A retainage of 10 percent of the cost of the project is recommended by consumer affairs professionals. The retainage should not be released until the job is completed according to the construction documents, the terms of the contract have been honored, you have received a certificate of occupancy (C.O.) from the building inspector, and you have obtained the signed "waivers of mechanics liens" from the builder and *all* of the subcontractors. Many lending institutions will not release their final payment until a C.O. has been issued and the lien waivers secured. A "mechanic's lien" is a legal right assigned by a court to general contractors, subcontractors, laborers, and material suppliers to secure payment for work performed or material supplied. If a bill has not been paid, a mechanic's lien allows the plaintiff to "attach" your property as a way of securing payment.

• A clause invalidating the contract in case you are unable to obtain financing. Be sure to state the type and rate of financing that you wish to secure.

• The approximate dates for the beginning and completion of the services or work. Approximate dates are typical in residential construction projects. Penalty clauses, which penalize a contractor financially for finishing after the stated completion date, are rarely used in residential construction. If one is used, it should be tied to an "incentive clause" which rewards the builder equally for completing construction ahead of schedule.

• A description of unforeseen construction conditions. This should include not only a definition what constitutes unforeseen conditions, but also how they will be paid for and by whom. Such conditions are more likely to happen with additions or remodeling, but can also occur during new construction. For example, in new construction, underground rock ledge (bedrock) might be uncovered during excavation and have to be removed before the foundation can be poured. During the demolition phase of an addition, rotten sill beams might be discovered and have to be replaced.

• A list of delays that might occur. Include a description of the types of delays (weather, material shipments, equipment breakdowns) and how they will be handled.

• A provision for handling changes. All changes and revisions, no matter how minor, should be executed through the use of written and signed change orders. A change order should include a description of the proposed change, the amount of any additional cost or credit due, and any adjustment in the completion date made necessary by the change.

• A definition of reasonable "wear and tear." A certain amount of "wear and tear" can be expected to an existing structure during the construction of an addition or renovation, but if an unusual amount of damage occurs, the contract should describe how it will be handled and who will pay for repairs.

• A description and the terms of any warranties that are offered by the builder. A warranty covering materials and quality of work for a minimum of one year should be part of the contract. The warranty should be identified as either "full" or "limited." Under a "full warranty," all faulty products must be repaired or replaced, or your money refunded. A "limited warranty" indicates that the replacements and refunds of damaged products are limited in some way. Make sure that the length of the warranty and the name and address of the party who will honor the warranty is clearly specified. In addition to a warranty provided by the builder, there may be other warranties provided by manufacturers or suppliers. You should ask to see, and read, copies of all warranties.

• A statement indicating the acceptable quality standards for the work. As a bare minimum, the contract should require that all work be done in accordance with local and state building codes and zoning regulations. A more thorough approach would be to refer to specific construction standards or to a detailed description of guidelines that are to be satisfied.

• The types and amount of insurance or bonding to be carried by the builder. You should not hire a builder who is not properly insured. In fact, many states require that builders carry certain types of insurance in order to do business. Workers' compensation and liability insurance are the two main types of insurance. You should ask to see your builder's insurance certificate, and check with an insurance agent or lawyer to make sure that the types and amounts are sufficient to adequately protect you. In some states, "bonding" is required of builders (see Step 10). All subcontractors should also be licensed, insured, and bonded as recommended by an insurance agent or lawyer and in accordance with all regulations. See Step 10 for a description of the different types of insurance.

• A clause assigning subcontractor liability and responsibility. If you are hiring someone to do general contracting work, the contract should clearly state that any subcontractors are the sole responsibility of the party doing the general contracting work.

• Miscellaneous items. Issues such as saving particular items (plantings and building materials) and safety precautions (covering holes and fencing off areas) are often addressed in the specifications, but can also be added to the contract if desired.

• A termination clause. A statement that describes how the contract can be terminated in the event that either party fails to abide by the terms of the contract.

• A failure-to-complete clause. A statement that describes what will happen in the event that work is suspended by either party, or the builder fails to complete the project.

- An arbitration clause. If you are unable to resolve a dispute, your contract should contain a clause that provides for the parties involved to seek arbitration. State arbitration laws vary widely, and some allow either party to refuse arbitration even though one might have agreed to it in a contract. In any case, arbitration is less costly than litigation and is worth pursuing.

- Places for signatures of both parties. The signatures of all the property owners and the designer or builder should be included and dated. Check with a lawyer about the need for witnesses and/or notarized signatures.

- Blank lines or spaces. Do not leave any blank or incomplete lines or spaces on the contract.

Before you sign a contract with a designer or builder, it is important to have your lawyer review the contract to verify that it doesn't contain any omissions, oversights, or ambiguities, that it protects your interests, and that it constitutes a legal document. Even after you've signed a contract with a builder, if you have second thoughts or change your mind, you may have some recourse. If the contract was solicited somewhere other than at a builder's place of business or trade premises (your home for instance), federal law gives you the right to cancel the contract without penalty by written notice within three business days.

Before we move on, I'd like to share something else from my workshops. I often ask my workshop participants if they think it's important to have contracts when they hire a family member or friend. Many aren't sure it's a good idea in the first place, and for the rest the resounding answer is, "Are you serious? Absolutely." I cannot stress enough the importance of contracts. Before you begin *any* work, with *anyone*, on *any* project, you should have a written contract. There is no job too small or too simple, and no situation that doesn't call for a written contract!

Step 5 covers a lot of ground and has been hard work, but now you should have surrounded yourself with competent and dedicated professionals who will help make the rest of your work easier and enjoyable. So it's on to Step 6 for some things that are more fun.

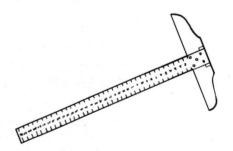

STEP 6 **Begin the Design Process**

The design process actually began back in Step 2 (Explore the Possibilities) and has continued right up through the present, but hiring your designer formally marks the beginning of this stage.

THE GOAL FOR STEP 6 To develop a design for your project that fits the building site, meets all governmental requirements, and satisfies your needs and wishes.

WHAT IS THE DESIGN PROCESS?

The design process is essential to every building project and is basically the same whether you are planning a dog house or a $500,000 home. If you're buying a design from a plans service, or planning a systems-built home, you may not be aware of or involved in every part of this process but it happens nonetheless. The design process has been divided into five phases, beginning with initial planning and ending with the completion of construction. The five traditional design phases are: (1) Schematic Design (also known as Preliminary Design), (2) Design Development, (3) Construction Document, (4) Bidding/Estimating, and (5) Construction.

The Schematic Design phase is a time for gathering information and considering preliminary design schemes. Before beginning actual design work, the designer's job is to help you develop and become thoroughly familiar with your program—your lifestyle, your budget, your goals, the building site, and all applicable codes and regulations. The designer then uses this program to develop some preliminary designs—typically two to three—and present them to you. Your job here, and throughout the design process, is to provide input in the form of comments, criticisms, and suggestions. After all, it's your project, and if you're working with a designer who thinks otherwise, perhaps it's time to change horses before you get too far into the stream. Over the course of several meetings, the preliminary designs coalesce into one design which is then developed further.

During the Design Development phase, your preliminary design is refined and details are developed. Exact room dimensions, window placement, and building materials are among the issues that are settled. There are many decisions to make during this phase and, depending on the scope and complexity of your project, it may require many meetings and take weeks or months to complete. At the end of this phase, the design of the project is ready to be translated into construction documents.

During the Construction Documents phase, the designer prepares a set of construction drawings and written specifications (see Steps 1 and 7 for an explanation of plans and specifications) called construction documents. The construction documents must be sufficiently detailed to communicate the requirements of construction, solicit bids and/or estimates from builders, and demonstrate compliance with applicable codes. Again, the scope and complexity of the job determines the amount of work and time required to produce the construction documents.

The Bidding/Estimating phase encompasses the builder-interviewing process described in Step 5, and is the phase in which the cost of your project is determined. To accomplish this, the construction documents are given to several builders (remember The Principle of Threes) who use them to calculate the price for which they will do the job. When all the bids have been gathered and evaluated—typically with the help of the designer (or perhaps a construction manager)—and the other information has been gathered through the interview process, you should be ready to hire your builder. Any revisions to the construction documents should be completed now, before construction begins, and reflected in the price.

During the Construction phase, the Project Manager (perhaps your designer or construction manager) monitors progress, verifying that the construction documents are being accurately followed. The designer should be available to answer specific questions concerning the construction documents and to make any additional revisions that may be necessary. At the end of construction, the Project Manager will certify the project's completion.

Although this traditional five-phase process plays a part in every design, it is subject to so many variations and modifications that you might not always recognize it. These modifications are a result of two major factors: (1) the type or scope of the project and (2) the working style of the designer. The type or scope of the project can affect the amount of emphasis that's placed on each phase. For instance, if you were planning a small entry addition that could only logically be built in *one* spot, less of the total design time would be spent on the Schematic Design phase, and more on the Construction Document phase. If you were to choose a systems-built house and decide to build one of the company's stock plans, the Schematic Design and Design Development phases would already be done; your experience with the design process would be limited to perhaps some minor revisions to the construction documents, and the Bidding/Estimating and Construction phases.

As you probably found out during the interviewing process, each designer has an individual style of working with clients, and you no doubt made your choice accordingly. Designers' styles also affect the way they approach the five design phases. One common difference is the level of autonomy the designer desires. Some designers prefer to limit the sources of input, retaining more control over the entire design process. But many designers, recognizing the limitations of the traditional five-phase process, strive to be more inclusive, welcoming input from many sources. For instance, I place great value on the knowledge and expertise of competent builders, and search for ways to involve them in the design process as early as possible.

WHERE DO YOU BEGIN?

The Schematic Design phase begins with the creation of your design *program*. You'll remember from the definitions in Step 1 that a program is a collection of data, jointly prepared by you and your designer, that delineates all the requirements of the building project. A good program acts as a solid framework for the planning process, upon which the plans of your project are assembled. It is key to ensuring the success of those plans. Creating a good program requires that you think carefully about what you really want and need. A good program is essential even for a small or simple project—it's just a smaller, simpler program. In fact, when planning a small living space, much more precise programming may be required. And don't think that you can avoid writing a program if you're building a systems-built home or buying stock plans. If you're going to choose such a "ready-made" match to your lifestyle, you really should understand your lifestyle. The more thoughtfully you prepare your program, the more likely you are to achieve that goal.

You may have thought that you created your program when you filled out the Preliminary Project Description Sheet in Step 4, but much more in the way of specifics is required now. However, that worksheet is a good place to start, so review it with your designer. Then, using the questions, worksheets, and checklists below, as well as other questions or techniques suggested by your designer, begin to develop your program. Remember, be as specific as possible, and think carefully about how you live and how you want to live your life, what you want to include and exclude, what makes you unhappy, and what brings you joy. Avoid trying to make your project exactly like "the one you saw in the magazine." Search your memories—perhaps those from your childhood or travels—for the buildings, the spaces, and the experiences that are special to you. By doing this, you increase the likelihood that the building you create will be uniquely yours.

Let's begin with some questions that are designed to get you thinking about the broader issues at hand. These questions are formulated to help you think about your project from the inside out, which I believe is an effective approach to design.

Program Questions

What do I want my site to be like? Do I want distant views? Visual privacy? A southern exposure? Lots of space for outdoor activities? (Look ahead to the section on land purchasing for more specific information.)

_____

_____

_____

_____

_____

How can I best utilize my site both aesthetically and functionally? Can I orient the house to capture particular views, emphasize a special feature, or create privacy?

_____

_____

_____

_____

_____

What types of activities will I be doing at home? Eating, sleeping, playing, working (home office), hobbies, relaxing (TV, video games), entertaining?

_____

_____

_____

_____

_____

What are the daily tasks (dishes, laundry, cleaning, etc.) that I will have to do, and where and how do I want to do them?

_____

_____

_____

_____

_____

How many and what type of spaces do I need to accommodate my activities? Can one space handle more than one activity?

_____

_____

_____

_____

How will my needs change over the years? Should I make the house easily accessible in the event of injury or disability? Consider the possibility that, at one time or another, a member of your family may have a broken bone or serious illness that could make getting around the house difficult.

_____

_____

_____

_____

How do I want the different spaces to relate to each other? Which spaces should be close to each other and which ones far apart? Do I want some spaces separated by walls or open to each other?

_____

_____

_____

_____

How do I want the spaces to feel? Light or dark, open or closed, grand or cozy, private or exposed, noisy or quiet?

_____

_____

_____

_____

Which architectural styles are the most appealing to me?

_____

_____

_____

_____

_____

What special features or elements, such as a window seat, loft, or attic hideaway, do I want to include?

_____

_____

_____

_____

_____

How do I want the spaces to relate to the outdoors? Do I want some spaces to be at ground level, others high above, and still others underground?

_____

_____

_____

_____

_____

Do I want any transitional spaces such as a covered entry, porches, or decks?

_____

_____

_____

_____

_____

What do I want to do with the car(s)? Park them in an attached garage, in a detached garage, in a carport, or under the open sky?

_____

_____

_____

_____

_____

When I come in from my car, into what space do I want to enter?

_____

_____

_____

_____

_____

How will I accommodate things (people, pets, food, trash, dirt, recyclables, clothes, guests, adults, children, and paper, paper, paper) as they move through the different spaces I'm creating?

_____

_____

_____

_____

_____

How do I want to address energy efficiency and environmental concerns? Do I want a super-insulated or sun-tempered structure? Do I want to choose environmentally responsible building materials whenever possible?

_____

_____

_____

_____

_____

How can I make my house safe? Should I include special child-safety features? What about general safety concerns—slippery surfaces, security systems, smoke alarms, sprinklers, and other safety measures?

_____

_____

_____

_____

_____

How can I be sure the indoor spaces provide a healthy environment? Do I want to take special precautions to build with nontoxic materials? Do I have asthma? Do I want to consider installing a whole-house ventilating system?

_____

_____

_____

_____

_____

How can I make sure that maintenance doesn't become a major issue over the years? Do I want to choose materials that may cost more initially, but are also more durable? Do I want to have to repaint my house frequently?

_____

_____

_____

_____

_____

As you answer these questions, you can make lists, write short descriptions, or draw simple sketches, but be sure to recognize the importance of each question and give each one plenty of time. Use additional sheets of paper if necessary.

Exterior Program Checklist

Now that you've addressed some of the larger issues, it's time to focus on the details. You can use this checklist and the following worksheets to guide you, and as you do I'd like you to keep one important thing in mind. You are trying to record *all* your needs, desires, and wishes, even the somewhat impractical ones. For this reason do not leave anything out simply because you think you can't afford it. After all, as The Principle of Asking for What You Want states, if you don't ask for it, you can't get it. At this point in the process, you don't have to choose one thing over another, so don't leave something off your program because you believe it may conflict with something else. Your designer will help you determine which items may have to go and which will stay, or may be able to find a way for you to have both a wide-open southern exposure and the visual privacy you desire. It might be helpful to support this checklist with photos where appropriate.

Check all those that interest you and elaborate or clarify if you wish.

CHARACTER OF HOUSE

❑ Traditional, historic _____

❑ Modern, contemporary _____

❑ Formal, elegant _____

❑ Informal, casual _____

❑ Open, airy, welcoming _____

❑ Private, secluded _____

❑ Other _____

SHAPE OF STRUCTURE

❑ Regular, symmetrical _____

❑ Irregular, asymmetrical _____

❑ One story _____

❏ One-and-a-half story, Cape Cod or salt box style _____

❏ Two story _____

❏ Split entry, living areas one-half level up and down from the entry _____

❏ Other _____

ROOF TYPE

❏ Gable _____

❏ Hip _____

❏ Gambrel _____

❏ Salt box _____

❏ Shed _____

❏ Mansard _____

❏ Flat _____

❏ Dormers _____

shed

gable

❏ Other _____

EXTERIOR FINISH

Wood Siding:

❏ Horizontal clapboards or bevel siding _____

❏ Shingles _____

❏ Shakes _____

❏ Horizontal "shiplap" or "drop" siding _____

❏ Vertical tongue and groove, shiplap, or board-and-batten _____

❏ Composite material _____

Finish:

❏ Painted _____

❏ Stained _____

❏ Clear finish _____

❏ Other _____

Other Materials:

❏ Vinyl siding _____

❏ Aluminum siding _____

❏ Brick veneer _____

❏ Stone veneer _____

❏ Stucco _____

❏ Other _____

ROOFING

❏ Asphalt shingles _____

❏ Asphalt/fiberglass composite shingles _____

❏ Wood shingles _____

❏ Wood shakes _____

❏ Metal—steel, copper, aluminum _____

❏ Clay tile _____

❏ Single membrane _____

❏ Other _____

WINDOWS

❏ Casement _____

❏ Double-hung _____

❏ Sliding _____

❏ Awning _____

❏ Fixed _____

❏ Special shape _____

DOORS

❏ Entry—standard 3 feet wide _____

❏ Entry—door with side lights _____

❏ Entry—double door _____

❏ Sliding glass doors _____

❏ Swinging French doors _____

❏ Interior—panel door, solid wood _____

❏ Interior—flush door, solid core _____

❏ Interior—flush door, hollow core _____

❏ Interior—bi-fold _____

❏ Interior—by-passing _____

❏ Fire door—between garage and house _____

❏ Other _____

LANDSCAPING

❏ Plantings—near house or around _____

❏ Lawn or ground cover _____

❏ Stone walls, walks, or patios _____

❏ Trellis, arbor, gazebo, or secluded area _____

❏ Flower or vegetable garden _____

❏ Sculpture _____

❏ Pond or fountain _____

❏ Play equipment or swingset for children _____

Interior Program Worksheet

From the outside, we move back into the inside to take a close look at some of the issues and possibilities to be considered.

FOOD PREPARATION AND EATING

Do you want the food preparation area and the eating area separate from each other, or combined in one larger space?

_____

_____

_____

If they're separated, do you want them connected with a pass-through, single door, or double French door?

_____

_____

_____

_____

Do you want more than one place to eat—dining room, counter in kitchen, breakfast nook, outdoors on a deck or porch?

_____

_____

_____

_____

What is important to see from the kitchen—children's play areas, front yard, driveway?

_____

_____

_____

How many people typically prepare food at the same time? Do you need more than one sink?

_____

_____

_____

_____

Do you have a preferred countertop layout—"U,""L," galley, center work island, peninsula?

_____

_____

_____

_____

How many and what types of appliances do you want?

_____

_____

_____

_____

What style and type of cabinets do you want—custom or factory made? Solid wood or plastic laminate? Modern or traditional?

_____

_____

_____

_____

Do you have any need for counters and cabinets built to unusual dimensions? Are you short or tall? Do you have a physical disability? Do you do a lot of baking, grilling, or other specialized cooking?

_____

_____

_____

Do you want built-in trash and recycling bins?

_____

_____

_____

_____

Do you want a walk-in pantry, broom-and-mop closet, ironing board, or other built-in features?

_____

_____

_____

_____

What type of floors do you want? (Hard floors—ceramic tile, quarry tile, and slate—are durable but hard on your feet and dropped items. Wood floors are beautiful, but more difficult to maintain. Resilient floors—vinyl, rubber, and linoleum—come in a wide variety of colors, patterns, and price ranges.)

_____

_____

_____

_____

_____

If you wish, sketch the area—or portions of it—below:

ADULT SLEEPING AREAS

Do you want to be close to or far from the children's sleeping areas?

_____

_____

_____

_____

Do you want enough space to do other activities—exercise (space to leave equipment set up between use), sewing, watching television?

_____

_____

_____

_____

Do you want a "master suite" with sleeping, dressing, and reading areas plus private access to a master bath?

_____

_____

_____

_____

What type of closets do you want? One long, two-foot-deep closet, separate side-by-side closets, or a large walk-in with a window?

_____

_____

_____

_____

Do you want any special amenities—fireplace, balcony, or refrigerator for midnight snacks?

_____

_____

_____

_____

Do you need bookshelves or wall space to display collections or artwork?

_____

_____

_____

_____

If you wish, sketch the area—or portions of it—below:

CHILDREN'S SLEEPING AREA

Will the children have separate or shared bedrooms?

_____

_____

_____

_____

Do you want a common play area adjacent to the bedrooms?

_____

_____

_____

_____

Where will the children do schoolwork—at a desk in their room, in the shared common space, or in a family room?

_____

_____

_____

_____

Where will the children watch television?

_____

_____

_____

_____

Will the children have a computer? Where?

_____

_____

_____

What kind of toy storage do you want—shelves, closed cabinets, toy chests, closets?

_____

_____

_____

_____

_____

If you wish, sketch the area—or portions of it—below:

FAMILY AREAS

When you are not cooking, eating, or sleeping, where will you spend most of your time, and doing what?

_____

_____

_____

_____

Where will the family be together to play games, watch television, listen to the stereo, or just hang out?

_____

_____

_____

_____

Where will you entertain and how often?

_____

_____

_____

_____

Do you need spaces for music, hobbies, crafts, or other leisure activities?

_____

_____

_____

_____

Would you like an out-of-the-way place where members of the family can go to for "quiet time"?

_____

_____

_____

_____

Do you have any collections, art, or special pieces of furniture that you want to accommodate?

_____

_____

_____

_____

Do you want to include or plan for some special amenities—a swimming pool, deck, hot tub, sauna?

_____

_____

_____

_____

If you wish, sketch the areas—or portions of them—below:

BATHROOMS

How many do you want and where?

_____

_____

_____

How many and what type of fixtures do you want in each one—sinks, tub, shower, whirlpool tub, toilet (perhaps separated for privacy), bidet?

_____

_____

_____

Do you want a free-standing sink or one installed in a vanity cabinet? (If you're tall, the standard bathroom sink is too low and a real pain. Test it out.)

_____

_____

_____

Do you want a make-up area?

_____

_____

_____

Where will you store medicines and toiletries—wall-hung cabinet, shelves, vanity? Be sure to make provisions to keep medicines out of the reach of children.

_____

_____

_____

Would you like a large wall-sized mirror?

_____

_____

How will you light the bathroom? Good, bright lighting around the sink areas for shaving and make-up is a must. Do you want a heat lamp near the tub or shower?

_____

_____

_____

Where will you store towels—in the bathrooms or in linen closets just outside the bathrooms?

_____

_____

_____

How will you make your bathrooms safe—non-skid floors, soft floors, grab bars?

_____

_____

_____

Do you want natural light and ventilation from windows or skylights? Frosted glass can provide privacy and admit light.

_____

_____

_____

If you wish, sketch the areas—or portions of them—below:

HOUSE KEEPING AND "SERVICE"

Do you need a "service" entrance that incorporates a mudroom, closets, utility sink, or half-bath?

_____

_____

_____

_____

Where do you want the washer and drier? There are better places than the basement— near the bedrooms where the dirty clothes accumulate or near the areas where you spend a good portion of the day, perhaps the kitchen, utility room, or mudroom?

_____

_____

_____

_____

Where will you keep cleaning supplies and equipment—vacuum cleaner, mops, brooms, buckets? In a utility room, hall closet, kitchen pantry?

_____

_____

_____

_____

Would you like a central vacuum system?

_____

_____

_____

_____

If you're planning a two-story house, where will the second-floor cleaning supplies be stored?

_____

_____

_____

_____

How about the windows? If you install double-hung units, will they tilt in for easy cleaning?

_____

_____

_____

_____

If you wish, sketch the areas—or portions of them—below:

What type of flooring materials will you choose? It's a good idea to match the flooring material to the use of the space—perhaps ceramic tile for the entry, wood flooring in a elegant living room, and carpet in the bedrooms. So go through your house space by space.

_____

_____

_____

_____

What about the walls? Again, consider them on a case-by-case basis—ceramic tile in the wet areas, plaster or gypsum board with 4-foot-high wainscoting in the dining area, and solid wood paneling in the study?

_____

_____

_____

_____

Would you like to enhance your painted walls with wallpaper or stenciling?

_____

_____

_____

_____

What type of trim—baseboard, door and window casing, chair rail—would you like? The right trim can really dress up a house, so you might consider installing an unusual or custom pattern. Also, special touches such as molding at the wall-and-ceiling juncture can bring an air of distinction to an otherwise plain room.

_____

_____

_____

_____

How will you finish the trim—paint, stain, or clear finish? If you paint, you can generally use a lower grade of wood trim.

_____

_____

_____

What about hanging things on the walls? If you have any heavy objects, you can plan for them by installing solid wood nailers when the walls are being framed.

_____

_____

_____

_____

MISCELLANEOUS

Do you want pre-wiring for stereo, phone extensions (perhaps for computer modems or "networking"), intercom, and other electronic equipment?

_____

_____

_____

_____

Do you want a security system?

_____

_____

_____

_____

Where do you want outdoor electrical outlets, lighting, and phone jacks?

_____

_____

_____

_____

Do you want roughed-in plumbing or wiring to an unfinished attic or other spaces to facilitate easy expansions or additions?

_____

_____

_____

_____

Do you want an underground watering system for your garden or lawn?

_____

_____

_____

_____

Do you want a fire sprinkler system?

_____

_____

_____

_____

Will you need to install pet doors or plan for a place where a wet dog can dry off?

_____

_____

_____

_____

There is another major element that must be considered in your program: the piece of land upon which your house will be built. Isn't it a little late to explore the subject of land? No, it's not. In fact, I think this is the perfect time to discuss the topic. If I could create a construction utopia, I would decree that everyone planning a new house must wait until just this moment before they could buy the land. Now, I know that in the real world many people buy their property long before they begin the rest of the planning process, but there are some very good reasons for waiting until now. If you're planning an addition or renovation, you still need to take your present house site into consideration, but you can skip ahead to the section on mapping your land (page 163) if you like. If you already own your land, read on anyway; you may discover some things that you still need to do.

One reason for waiting until now to buy your property is that you've already calculated and established your budget, and therefore know about how much you will be able to spend on your project. If you're building a new house and you don't own the land yet, then a portion of your budget must go toward buying the land, and the balance will be available for the construction of the house. The effect on your budget is a simple equation: more money spent on land equals less money spent on house, and vice versa. By waiting until now, when you know your budget and understand how much that money will buy, you can decide how you want the equation to read, and decide on whether your want more land or more house.

Second, you've hired a designer and perhaps a builder, and can employ their skills, knowledge, and experience to potentially save you thousands of dollars in site development and building costs by incorporating their advice in choosing property. Improving land—clearing, excavating, filling—generally requires the use of expensive heavy equipment. If a piece of land is difficult to develop, your property could become very costly, very fast. Such features a professional might point out include excessively long or steep driveways, rock ledge (bedrock), unstable soil, poorly drained areas or wetlands, or other difficult building conditions. Even if you don't spend extra money directly on a difficult site, you might be forced to spend additional, unbudgeted dollars on your house for an expensive foundation or complicated design.

Lastly, you've completed the personal data portion of your program, and should have a good understanding of want you want in a house. This means that you can search for property that is a good match for you and your requirements, rather than having to make major compromises to fit yourself to the requirements of the land. For example, what if you had bought a steeply sloping piece of property with a small buildable area suitable only for a two-story house, but then, while creating your program, you discovered that you'd really like to build a one-story house that's easily accessible to your in-laws? You would have problems because not only is land expensive to "remodel," it's not easy to return or exchange.

SEARCHING FOR A BUILDING LOT

Actually, when I say "buying a piece of land," what I'm really talking about is buying a building lot. A building lot is a piece of "real property" that has been approved under the local regulations or codes—typically the zoning by-laws or the building codes—for use as a building site for a house. A building lot can be a 50-foot-wide by 200-foot-long city lot, or a 300-acre parcel in the country, as long as it meets the jurisdictional requirements. So, unless you're in the market for your own private park or a place to hold family picnics, make sure that the piece of land you buy qualifies as a building lot.

The search for your building lot should be a methodical winnowing process that starts by considering a large geographical area of many square miles, perhaps a county or a greater metropolitan area, and ends with the choice of a relatively small piece to call home. Your first task is to get to know the general area. By this I mean much more than just researching statistical data, although you should do that, too. I mean that you should become intimate with your "regional neighborhood" and develop a sixth sense about the area, moving beyond the sometimes superficial opinions formed as a result of casual contact. If you live or work in the area where you want to build, you've probably done this already, but what if, because of a job transfer or similar reason, you're moving to a completely new location? Should you travel there on weekends to shop for your lot? Move to the area with an unreasonable self-imposed deadline in which to find and buy your lot? I don't think so. You're better served if you slow down, perhaps rent a place to live, and take the time you need to get your bearings. When it starts to feel more like home, it's time to start looking for a place to build one.

WHERE TO LOOK

After you've settled on a region, armed with your programmatic requirements, you can start your search. The most obvious people to turn to are real estate agents who can give you a large number of property listings. Another possible source is through private sale by landowners. These can typically be found in your local newspaper's classified ad section. Don't forget to tap into the word-of-mouth grapevine; that's how I found my property. Remember that lumber yard home-planning center that I mentioned earlier? The staff had compiled a list of building lots available through builders and developers.

Mentioning builders and developers brings me to an interesting situation you should also be aware of. Generally, developers fall into two categories: the land developer and the developer-builder. The land developer typically buys larger parcels of land, subdivides them, makes some improvements—roads, perc tests, clearing—and sells the individual pieces as "bare" lots. The developer-builder will add one additional stipulation: they will only sell you the lot if you contract with them to build your house. With this scenario, your choices usually are restricted to the relatively few designs that a developer-builder typically offers. Also, it's very difficult to compare this deal with another one, first because the land and the house are rolled up into a single "package," and second because you are usually unable to study the construction documents thoroughly. These concerns have been expressed by many workshop participants, who have also pointed out that as development pressures in some suburban areas make land scarce, lots offered by developer-builders are often the only lots available. So, before you get your heart set on a particular region, make sure that you'll have some land options available that appeal to you.

RESEARCH THE REGION

When you've determined that there is acceptable land for sale in a particular area, you should do some general research to learn the region's history, current economic status, and future prospects. The point is to find the most desirable area for you to build your house, live your life, and, in the event that you someday decide to sell, have the opportunity to profit from your investment. The information you seek can be found through Chambers of Commerce, planning boards, building inspection departments, real estate appraisers, local chapters of builders' associations, and real estate agents. You should try to learn:

- The average selling price of the houses in particular sectors. You'd probably like to build in an area where the house you're planning is not the most or the least expensive.

- The location of zoning districts, the possibility of future re-districting, and how that might affect residential property values.

- The existence, or possible imposition of, any building moratoriums due to construction quotas, sewer hook-up limitations, or similar problems.

- The existence of natural environmental problems such as flooding, unstable soil conditions, or water shortages.

- The existence of environmental hazards or annoyances such as toxic waste, air pollution, contaminated or polluted water, traffic or manufacturing noise, and sewage or garbage dump smells.

- Past and future patterns of development. Is the area growing rapidly, at its peak, or in decline?

RESEARCH THE LOCAL NEIGHBORHOOD

Once you have narrowed the choices and found some building lots that interest you (remember The Principle of Threes), it's time to do some conscientious investigation of the local neighborhoods. Your goal is to find out in which neighborhood you would enjoy living. Spend the better part of a day walking through the area, meeting and talking with the residents, observing the daily activities, and getting to know the area on a more personal level. To experience the differences, try to do this both during the week and on the weekend. If the building lots you're researching are part of unbuilt developments, try to find one close by that's similar and spend some time there. Next, check with the local governmental and community agencies to learn more about the local infrastructure. You want to learn about:

- Municipal services, including fire and police protection, trash, garbage, and recycling procedures; water supply and sewage disposal; parks and recreational facilities; road maintenance and snow removal; and legal aid and human services.

- Community services, including schools (student/teacher ratio, strength of the parent/ teacher association, technical school or training, strength of curriculum, transportation, sports programs, and extracurricular activities); medical facilities (modern, state-of-the-art, accredited hospitals or medical centers, the types of physicians and their availability, emergency or ambulance service); social and religious organizations (churches, synagogues, other places of worship, fraternal organizations, senior services, summer youth activities).

- Cost of living: property and other taxes, utility costs, public transportation, variety of shopping facilities, restaurants, and wage scale.

RESEARCH THE LOCAL REGULATIONS

Once you've investigated the surrounding neighborhood, it's time to learn about the local regulations—building codes, zoning regulations, and others—to determine how they will affect the lots you're considering. You don't need to become a regulations expert, you just need to know which ones pertain to your situation. The best place to begin your education is at the local building inspection department. (If you're investigating a lot that's a part of a development or planned community, you should also speak with the developer or governing body.) During the planning and construction process, everything seems to originate in or pass through the building inspector's office, so if the building inspector can't help you, they can tell you who can. Most people seem to avoid building inspectors like the plague, but you really shouldn't. In fact, most of the building inspectors I've talked with are really eager to help, and feel that a large part of their job is to protect the homeowner. Of course, building inspection offices are busy places and, rather than just showing up in person, you should phone ahead, explain your situation, and ask what the appropriate action should be. (See Step 7 for more information about visiting the building inspector.) You should learn the effect on your lot of:

- State building codes and municipal zoning regulations (be sure to ask if there are any impending changes or additions).

- Federal and state regulations: these include wetlands (fresh and salt water) protection acts, historic districts, sewage disposal, and handicapped accessibility.

- Other regulations: any number of restrictions can be placed on a lot, controlling everything from the size of the house to the type of siding that can be used. Make sure you're aware of such restrictions *before* you buy.

ASSESSING PROPERTY

You should also evaluate the lots in terms of your program. There is probably no "perfect" building lot—only the alternative that requires the fewest compromises. With this in mind, try to find the answers to the following questions:.

- Is the lot easy to access, or will the driveway be long?

- If there is no municipal sewer, is the land perc-tested? Does that perc test allow you to build the type of house you want, in a spot that fits your program? Be aware that as more and more marginal land is utilized for building lots, the location and size of private sewage disposal systems can restrict the placement or design of a house. Make sure you have confirmation that the septic system you'll need can be installed on a lot before you consider purchasing it. You could make this a part of your buy/sell agreement. If there are any questions surrounding this issue, implement The Principle of Pay Now, Save Later and seek a professional's advice.

- If there is no municipal water, where will you drill a well, and will its placement conflict with the placement of the house or septic system? The local board of health regulations should provide the distances required between the two. (As a result, don't plan to drill your well until your septic system has been located and designed.) Although it's impossible to know before drilling exactly what to expect in the way of water quantity and quality, the neighbors or the board of health should be able to give you some idea. You could also make the sale of the house contingent on potable water.

- Is there a possibility of any underground hazards, such as contaminated water, a buried oil tank, unstable soil, or other hazards?

- Has the lot been surveyed, and are the boundaries clearly marked on the land?

- Are utilities and services—electricity, gas, water, sewage disposal—readily available?

- Is the lot wooded or open, hilly or flat, wet or dry? Are there features that make building on the lot difficult? If it's sloped, will that cause drainage problems?

- Does the land have views or meet your need for privacy?

- Is the lot's orientation and exposure appropriate for your intentions? Does the lot have solar access?

- What is the microclimate? Where does the sun rise and set, where do the prevailin summer breezes and winter winds come from, and is there protective vegetation? Is the lot in an area that is foggy or subject to temperature inversions that might trap pollutants close to the ground? (Some of this information can be learned by spending time on the lot.)

- Is the lot large enough for your purposes?

- Has the lot been developed sensitively? As land becomes more and more scarce it's important to protect it by appropriate development. A properly developed piece of property is an asset to the world community and will be worth more to you in the long run. (See the Appendices for suggested reading on this topic.)

- Overall, do you feel good about the lot? As an architect friend of mine says, "Does it sing to you?"

One more thing: you can often glean interesting information from the neighbors that would be difficult to discover elsewhere. For example, one workshop participant recalled that, during his search for land, he asked a neighbor about a particular lot. "This looks like a really nice lot," he ventured." "Yes," agreed the neighbor, "it looks a lot nicer now than it did five years ago."

"What do you mean?"

"Five years ago this was part of an old dump."

Use the Lot Selection Worksheet that follows to help you evaluate the information and make your choice.

Lot Selection Worksheet

Fill out a worksheet for each piece of property you consider.

Property Location:

_____

_____

_____

_____

Property Owner

    Name:

_____

_____

    Address:

_____

_____

    Phone no.:

_____

_____

Real Estate Co.

    Agent's name:

_____

_____

    Address:

_____

_____

    Phone no.:

_____

_____

Is the land perc tested? yes_____ no _____

Record the information you gather.

1. Neighborhood research (schools, taxes, etc.):

_____

_____

_____

_____

_____

_____

_____

_____

_____

2. Regulations research (zoning, community regulations, etc.):

_____

_____

_____

_____

_____

_____

_____

_____

_____

3. Program assessment (open vs. wooded, hilly vs. flat, etc.):

_____

_____

_____

_____

_____

_____

_____

_____

_____

_____

_____

4. Legal issues (easements, rights of way, etc.):

_____

_____

_____

_____

_____

_____

_____

_____

_____

Rate the piece of property according to the criteria below, least to most favorable.

CRITERIA	1	2	3	4	5
1. Neighborhood					
2. Regulatory restrictions					
3. Program assessment					
4. Legal issues					
Other					
Cost					
Attractive features					
Unappealing features					

Comments:

_____

_____

_____

_____

_____

_____

_____

_____

_____

_____

_____

_____

_____

DETERMINE THE COST

Asking price .... _____

Your offer .... _____

Purchase price .... _____

Legal fees .... _____

_____

_____

_____

Loan costs .... _____

_____

_____

_____

Total fees and costs .... _____

Total cost of land .... _____

MAKING THE PURCHASE

After you have settled on a piece of property, you must have a lawyer investigate the legal issues before you buy it. First, your lawyer will do a title search to make sure the property is free of any encumbrances such as easements, encroachments, rights-of-way, liens, restrictive covenants, and other deed restrictions. When title is determined to be clear, and after you've negotiated a price with the owner, you are ready to buy the property. This takes place at a "closing." The parties at the closing typically include you, your lawyer, the seller, the seller's lawyer, your loan officer (if you are borrowing money to make the purchase), and the real estate agent. Everyone is there for a particular reason. The lawyers are there for the reasons stated above and to make sure that both the seller and buyer understand the proceedings. The loan officer is there to look out for the lending agency's interests and assure that the borrower (you) follows their procedures. The real estate agent is technically representing the seller, but will usually try to expedite matters by providing pertinent information. If everyone has done their job well and informed you about what to expect, the closing might last an hour. But if both you and the seller have to be educated about all the paperwork and forms you have to sign, the closing could last up to four hours.

MAPPING THE PROPERTY

There is only one more item on the agenda before your designer begins to work on the schematic designs, and that's mapping your lot. I know you're anxious to get started on the design of your house, but the information you gather through mapping is essential to producing an appropriate design, and in some instances it's required by the building inspector or zoning board. You may think that your lot has already been mapped during the survey, but that's not necessarily the case. A survey defines the lot lines, or boundaries, of a piece of property; mapping addresses much more. Mapping your lot is a matter of professionally assessing, locating, and recording all the pertinent physical characteristics, such as existing or planned improvements (buildings, driveways, well, septic system, underground wires or pipes), contours, wet areas, rock outcroppings, proposed house site, potential views, trees and vegetation, and solar access. The resulting "map" is called a site plan.

Addition Alert

If you're planning an addition, it is extremely important for you to map your land, because often making an addition work is a matter of shaping it to meet the needs of the owners and the restrictions of the building regulations. In my practice, I frequently have to work within some fairly close tolerances. Recently, I designed an addition with a roof overhang that came 2 inches from the sideyard setback. I also know of cases in which additions—and even new homes—have actually been constructed on the neighbors' property. For these reasons, if you don't have an accurate boundary survey and know exactly where your boundaries are, you should include them when mapping your lot.

To begin the mapping process, you and your designer will assess the situation and decide what professionals are needed to create your site plan. These professionals might include a surveyor, civil engineer, septic system designer (either a civil engineer or registered sanitarian), landscape architect, or wetlands consultant. At the very least, you must record on the site plan any information required by the building codes, zoning, or other regulations. Typically, this includes the lot lines, well, septic tank, leaching field, and wetlands. These items will have the biggest impact on the location of the house or addition, so their position—existing or proposed—must be determined and delineated before you can choose your house site.

WHERE TO PITCH YOUR TENT

Obviously, choosing your site and locating your house on it is extremely important. Even if your lot is small and the options limited, careful consideration should be given to the exact placement of the building. This is a time when your designer's expertise can be invaluable, because even minor adjustments in orientation, or slight shifts of a few feet, can have a dramatic effect. Whole new views may be revealed or a greater sense of privacy attained as a result of your designer's deft hand. You should, of course, be a major part of the site selection process by taking the time to become intimately aware of the idiosyncrasies of your lot. Spend time observing your building site in the morning, mid-day, and evening until you feel that you know what it's like to live there. This is particularly important if you are trying to select a house site from among several possibilities. Take your time; it will be worth it.

In addition to the esthetic reasons for carefully selecting your house site, there are some financial ones. As we have learned, site development—clearing, stump removal, filling, ledge removal—is a costly proposition. Often, if a house is sensitively sited, many of these expenses can be minimized or avoided altogether. Another issue to be aware of is future construction, both yours and your neighbors. If you have the option, place your house to allow for future expansion. And what will be the impact of future construction around you? Will that gorgeous view from your living room someday be replaced with a view of your neighbors' bath room? Good site planning can address these possibilities.

As a part of selecting a house site, you should include features that are important to it—trees, plants, stone walls, or other natural formations—that you want to preserve. When your house site has been chosen and recorded on your site plan, along with all the other information, it's time for your designer to begin working on the preliminary designs. You can use the forms on the following pages to record the information you gather during the mapping process.

Map Your Lot

DELINEATE WETLANDS

Are there wetlands on your property?   yes _____   no _____

Describe briefly:

_____

_____

_____

_____

_____

Will they impact on your house site?   yes _____   no _____

Describe briefly:

_____

_____

_____

_____

_____

What action will you take to accommodate the wetlands?

Describe briefly:

_____

_____

_____

_____

CHOOSE THE HOUSE SITE

There may be more than one place on your property to site your house. Evaluate the possibilities before making your choice.

Describe alternative #1 briefly:

_____
_____
_____
_____
_____

Pros: Cons:

_____   _____
_____   _____
_____   _____
_____   _____
_____   _____

Describe alternative #2 briefly:

_____
_____
_____
_____
_____

Pros: Cons:

_____   _____
_____   _____
_____   _____
_____   _____
_____   _____

SITE PLAN

	YES	NO
Are the boundaries marked?	_____	_____
Are the wetlands shown?	_____	_____
Is the well located?	_____	_____
Is the septic system located?	_____	_____
Are any problem areas shown?	_____	_____
Are the improvements, if any, shown?	_____	_____
Are the utilities indicated?	_____	_____

Are the noteworthy features (views, solar access, trees, etc.) shown? If so, describe:

_____

_____

_____

_____

_____

_____

Miscellaneous items that could be noted include the health of trees, prevailing winds, soil condition, poor drainage areas, and access for heavy machinery and construction vehicles.

_____

_____

_____

_____

Even though regulatory issues are addressed in depth in Step 7, there may be some (in addition to well and septic location) that could influence the design of the project and could be included as part of your program. If so, note them:

_____

_____

_____

_____

BUDGET REVIEW

When you completed the Preliminary Project Description Sheet, you stated your estimated budget for the design and construction of your project. With all that you've done and learned since then, you should review that figure and revise it if necessary.

Original budget figure .... _____

Reason for and amount of revision:

_____ _____

_____ _____

_____ _____

_____ _____

Revised budget figure .... _____

ADDITIONAL PROFESSIONALS NEEDED

Name/Profession:

_____

Address:

_____

Phone Number:

_____

Name/Profession:

_____

Address:

_____

Phone Number:

_____

Name/Profession:

_____

Address:

_____

Phone Number:

_____

Name/Profession:

_____

Address:

_____

Phone Number:

_____

STEP 7   *Complete the Design Process*

This step is packed with excitement, as the project that you've been dreaming about and working on for so long finally begins to take shape on paper. However, this step can also be long and sometimes difficult, so have patience and perseverance; you *will* reach your goal.

THE GOAL FOR STEP 7   To complete the design of your project and determine its cost so that you're prepared to search for financing.

THE SCHEMATIC DESIGNS

With your program in hand and an accurate understanding of all the requirements in mind, your designer can begin preparing the schematic, or preliminary, designs for your project. As I've noted before, every designer has a different style of working, but the basic progression—from the sketchy to the more detailed—is usually similar. Here's how I work. First, I use "bubble" diagrams (see page 27) to loosely define the possible relationships of the proposed spaces. I try many combinations before settling on several schemes—usually between two and four—that appear worthy of further study. Then I shape the bubbles into freehand squares, rectangles, and other polygons, approximately sized to represent the requirements of the program. When I find an arrangement that's workable, I draft a bare bones plan for each scheme that I'm investigating. This is the point at which the "spaces" begin their transformation into rooms. Next, using the rough plan as a guide, and broad-tip markers on tissue tracing paper as the medium, I further investigate each scheme in both plan and elevation. At this point, I don't pay much attention to details—the exact placement of windows, precise length of the stairway, or the number of lineal feet of closet—because I'm interested in the bigger picture. I find that the broad, loose strokes of the marker free me up to look beyond the trees to see the forest. Later, as each schematic design matures, I will begin to attend to the details.

When I'm satisfied with the schemes, I'll meet with my clients to present and explain each one. At this meeting, I insist that they respond candidly with their comments and reactions. It's the only way I can find out if the design solutions are hitting the mark. If there are questions, I do my best to clarify. If my clients feel I've missed something, I find out where and how. One thing I don't want at this first meeting is a quick decision on their "favorite" scheme. Rather, their job is to take some time and "live" in each scheme until they become familiar with them. When they feel ready, we'll meet again to discuss the various options and determine together how to proceed. One or two schemes are chosen for further study, which typically involves an investigation of numerous possible variations for each basic scheme. When I feel that I've successfully addressed the relevant issues, I'll present the revised design solutions at another meeting. Again, after my clients have had time to digest them, one scheme is chosen for even further refinement. This marks the beginning of the Design Development phase.

This incremental, back-and-forth approach not only allows the design to mature thoughtfully, and at a reasonable pace, but it also permits the client (you) to keep in close touch with the process and sound an alarm if the designer strays too far from the program. Aside from the floor plan and architectural style, there are two other programmatic requirements that should be watched carefully during the Schematic Design phase: your budget and the applicable building codes and regulations.

THE BUDGET WATCH

Obviously, your designer has to design a house or addition that you can afford. Accordingly, the first schematic design solutions should reflect the reality of your budget, but because the schematic designs are rough and preliminary by nature, a precise estimate is not possible. There are, however, two broad indicators of construction costs that you can monitor—size and complexity.

As you learned in Step 4, one method commonly used as a guide by designers to estimate construction costs during the design stage is the "cost-per-square-foot method." If we return to the example given in Step 4, where your hypothetical budget was $155,440, and the cost per square foot for construction was $87, you could afford a 1,786-square-foot house ($155,440 ÷ $87 = 1,786 s.f.). If, during the Schematic Design phase, your designer presents you with preliminary designs of 2,000 square feet, you've got about an $18,500 problem (2,000 s.f. × $87/s.f. = $174,000 − $155,440 = $18,560).

Closely following in the budget-busting footsteps of size is complexity. It stands to reason that the more complicated a building is, the more costly it will be to construct. Not only does a complex structure take more time to build than a simple one—and as we all know, time is money—but a complex structure also consumes more building materials. It is quite possible that your designer could present design solutions that meet the 1,786-square-foot target, but are so complicated that they push the cost per square foot to $97.50. If so, you're staring into the face of that same $18,500-plus problem (1,785 s.f. × $97.50/s.f. = $174,038 − $155,440 = $18,598). Here are some ways to address the potential problems posed by excess size and complexity.

- Be sure that your designer accurately calculates the square footage of each design solution that's presented.

- If the schematic designs are right at the square-foot limit of your budget, beware of the "inflatable plan" that grows almost imperceptibly over time. Study the plans closely to see if anything has been left out—closets, a bathroom, a mudroom—that might need to be added later.

- If the schematic designs are too large, work with your designer to solve the problem now. Review your program and determine whether you really need all the spaces you've asked for; eliminating one could solve the problem. Try reducing the overall size of the plans by combining spaces or utilizing one space for more than one activity. Reducing the size of individual spaces while keeping them intact is also a possibility. However, be careful, as you reduce the size of a plan, not to seriously compromise the function of the separate rooms or integrity of the entire plan.

• The first place to look for complexity is in the corners. A rectangular building with four corners is the simplest structure to build. Each additional corner adds a higher level of complexity, and therefore cost. If your cost estimates are based on a simple Cape-Cod-style rectangle, and the schematic designs show the octagonal towers, walk-out bays, and wrap-around porches of a Victorian, some major re-thinking is in order.

• Level changes can add an air of interest to a house, and may even be necessary because of site topography, but they're not free. Each level change adds to the construction costs. If you're pushing the limits of your budget, you should consider minimizing the number of level changes, or even eliminating them altogether. In addition to cost savings, another benefit to one-level living is that it makes the entire house easily accessible for wheelchairs and walkers.

• Sloped ceilings also add complexity to a structure. Rooms with sloped ceilings are more costly to build, more expensive to heat, and more difficult to maintain than rooms with flat ceilings. While sloped ceilings can add a dramatic effect to a house, too much of a good thing may just be too much. Use them sparingly.

• One source of complexity that might not be as easy to spot is long spans. As a rule, the greater the distance that a structural member has to span, the stronger—thicker, deeper, wider—it must be, and typically an increase in strength means an increase in cost. The length of materials itself is also a factor in cost. The price of standard framing lumber—such as that used for floor joists and rafters—increases significantly at lengths over 16 feet. Cost-conscious designs keep the number of long spans to a minimum.

• A close cousin to complexity is dimensioning. Building materials are manufactured to standardized dimensions. Framing lumber is produced in 2′ increments starting at 8′ long. Plywood, oriented-strand board (OSB), and many other sheet materials are manufactured in 4 by 8-foot standard panels. Gypsum board also comes in standard sizes of $4′ \times 8′$ to $4′ \times 16′$. Other sizes are available, but often at a considerable increase in cost. Buildings that are designed with an awareness of standard dimensions—using multiples of 4′ when possible, or 2 feet when necessary, and avoiding odd overall dimensions ($21′ \times 33′$) —use building materials more efficiently, use less of them, and will consequently cost less to build.

I don't mean to give the impression that complexity is bad, or something to be completely avoided. Quite the contrary, if all of the character and interest that complexity brings to buildings were eliminated, the results would be extremely boring. However, you should avoid the trap of seeking complexity for its own sake, and don't let it get the better of you and your budget.

VISITING THE BUILDING INSPECTOR

A building inspector I know once told me, "For most people, going to see a building inspector is like visiting the dentist—they keep putting it off and putting it off." This is not a bad analogy, and can be taken one step farther. If you put off seeing the dentist, what was once an easily remedied problem can turn into a much larger one, requiring an expensive solution. The same is true with a building inspector; if your plans are not checked early for code compliance, a small problem could become a big, expensive headache. For example, let's say that you're planning an addition that includes two bedrooms and a study, and you decide to take your schematic designs to the building inspector for a preliminary check. The inspector says everything looks fine, with one exception, and suggests that you consult the Board of Health to find out if your present septic system has the capacity to handle the planned addition. When you do, you learn that, although your septic system can handle the addition of two bedrooms, the study must be considered a potential third bedroom, effectively loading your septic system beyond its capacity. You have several options: you can enlarge the septic system, you can eliminate a bedroom from your plans, or you can forget the project altogether. None of these options may be desirable, but, because of the inspector's input, at least you *have* some options. Had the building inspector not seen the plans until you applied for a building permit, you might have been forced into an unwanted decision, or spent money needlessly. Even though your designer will prepare the plans with the building codes and regulations in mind, people make mistakes, oversights occur, and regulations are revised. Enlisting another pair of watchful, well-informed eyes can be helpful. The building inspector will have to enforce the building codes sooner or later; it's wise to remember The Principle of Sooner, Not Later.

Another important reason for meeting with the building inspector early in the design process is to establish a good working relationship. Seeking the inspector's input indicates that you understand and respect the important role he or she plays in the planning process, and demonstrates that you want to work *with* the inspector on your project. In return, the building inspector will probably make every attempt to work with you.

Probably the best time to have the building inspector do this preliminary review is just before the Design Development phase. First, be sure that you read Step 9: The Permitting Process, so that you better understand the workings of the building inspector's office. Then you, your designer, or both of you should contact the building inspector, explain your project, and set up a meeting. Remember, most building inspectors are happy to help at this stage of design, but you should have your questions well prepared and organized. At the meeting, make sure you get, or find out where to get, the answers to the following questions:

- Is there anything about the plans that is in violation of the zoning regulations—setbacks, height restrictions, lot coverage? If so, what is my next step—variance, special permit?

- Are there other regulations that impact my project—wetlands regulations, community ordinances, historic districts?

- Are the plans in violation of any building codes—window egress, insulation levels or placement, fire safety?

- What tasks do I need to complete before applying for a building permit—septic design, source of water, other approvals?

- What other permits will I need—plumbing, electrical, demolition?

- What does your office require in the way of construction drawings and specifications?

- How long does the permit application and approval process typically take?

- What are the common pitfalls that I should watch out for?

Many building inspector's offices have written descriptions of the permitting process that you should take home and study. If you have questions about zoning regulations, you can usually obtain a copy of the zoning regulations to study at home. I can't stress enough, particularly if you're planning an addition, the importance of confirming early in the design process that your plans are on the right track and that you will not be needlessly derailed or delayed by unforeseen problems with codes, regulations, and the building permit process.

DESIGN DEVELOPMENT

After one schematic design has been chosen and checked out with the building inspector, that design is ready to be revised and refined until every detail has been worked out. During the Design Development phase, I shift to mechanically drafted drawings because their precision is necessary to fully investigate the design. I draft floor plans, elevations (exterior and interior if needed), and sections—anything that will help me understand the design and communicate it to my clients. I will often build a model or, if I've constructed one during the Schematic Design phase, modify it to reflect any changes. This revision and refinement, as was the case during the previous phase, takes place over the course of several meetings. Typically, the more complicated or the larger a project is, the longer it takes, but even "simple" additions can require considerable time and attention. I've never had a design spring completed from my mind, straight to the paper, and onto the ground.

COST CONSCIOUSNESS

As the design matures, you will begin to select building materials. You should probably start by making what I call the "primary" decisions first—the types of windows, doors, roofing, siding, and flooring—and leave the "secondary" decisions—the styles, patterns, and colors of materials—until the Construction Document phase. With the help of your designer, review your program and determine which items you want to keep as is, and which you want to change.

During the Schematic Design phase it was size and complexity that needed to be monitored to keep building costs within your budget. In the Design Development phase there is a new trouble-maker on the scene: *level of finish*. Like everything else, building materials come in a range of types, grades, and prices. For example, in my area you can buy fiberglass roofing shingles for $22 a square or $58 a square (a square equals 100 square feet). A house that's 28' × 40', with an 8/12 roof pitch, has about 1,400 square feet of roof area, or 14 squares. The cheapest shingles would cost $308 (14sq × $22/sq), and the most expensive $812 (14sq × $58/sq), for a difference of $504 ($812 −$308 = $504). Sometimes, when spending hundreds of thousands of dollars, the value of a few hundred dollars gets lost. It becomes easy to say, "Yes, let's get the top of the line, it's *only* $500 more." The problem occurs when you utter this phrase a few too many times, and soon you find yourself *only* $5,000, or $10,000, or $15,000 over budget.

At this time, rather than the price of individual items, you should be focusing on the *level of finish* that you can afford as it's represented by the cost per square foot that your designer is using as a guide. If that square-foot figure is on the low end of the scale you should be thinking about the $22 shingles; the high end buys the $58 shingles. I'm not holding this out as a hard-and-fast rule, or suggesting that you can't "splurge" on some things above your "price range," and save on some below it. But to avoid what often happens toward the end of a construction project—when there's not enough money left to buy the kind of finishes and furnishing you really want—I am recommending that you know your "target" level of finish and, with the help of your designer, choose your building materials accordingly.

CONSULTING PROFESSIONALS

During the Design Development phase, and continuing through the Construction Document phase, your designer may seek the services of other professionals to help with specific aspects of the project. As we saw above, a registered sanitarian might be required to verify the capacity of the septic system, to redesign it, or to do both. A beam or structural system might need to be designed by a structural engineer before your designer can proceed with the plans. Your

Remodeling Budget Busters

If you're planning an addition or renovation, there is a special set of budget busters to be on the lookout for: oversights or omissions. The problem with oversights is that they have a way of showing up when you can least afford them. You and your designer should carefully scour your plans, your existing house and surrounding grounds for oversight potential. Some things to look for are:

- Inadequate electric service—The electrical service in many homes, particularly older ones, might not be sufficient to support the electrical needs of a major addition and may need to be upgraded.

- Inadequate septic system—As we saw in a previous example, the construction of an addition might push a septic system beyond its design capacity. Check with the building inspector or board of health.

- Insufficient pipe diameter—Plumbing codes regulate the number of fixtures (sinks, bathtub, showers, toilets) that can be connected to pipe of a given size. An addition that includes many fixtures—perhaps when both a bathroom is added and a kitchen upgraded—might exceed the code. Check this out with the plumbing inspector.

- Hazardous materials—Many older homes contain lead paint, asbestos materials, or underground oil storage tanks which can be extremely costly to remove. Check with your building inspector about the regulations concerning hazardous materials, find out if your house is affected, and learn how to comply with the regulations.

- Unforeseen conditions—Rotted floor joists, inadequate existing footings, rock ledge ("bedrock"), and underground water are all examples of "unforeseen conditions" that generally are not discovered until *after* construction begins. The contract with your builder should state how these situations will be handled, so in that sense they can't be considered true oversights. However, they will become oversights if you don't account for them in your budget.

designer should keep you informed about the need for these consulting professionals, and provisions for hiring them should have been made in your contract with your designer. If the cost of these services is not included in your designer's fee, you should account for them separately in your budget.

CHECK AND DOUBLE CHECK

Once your design is complete and the primary materials are chosen, but before your designer begins to work on the construction drawings, two things should be done: the estimated cost should be double-checked and another brief meeting with the building inspector should be held. To do the double check, you can use the same per-square-foot method as before, but this time with some new input: that of a professional builder. When I get to this stage I will often ask a builder (who is going to have the opportunity to bid on the job) to meet with me, briefly go over the plans and specs, and comment on the cost-per-square-foot figure that I've been using to date. If the builder believes that the figure is inappropriate, I'll report this to my client and together we can decide whether to revise the drawings immediately, or wait until after the bids come in and see where the actual numbers fall. If you decide to use a builder for this purpose, I recommend that you offer to pay for this service.

Asking for the building inspector's input yet again, before applying for a building permit, may seem like overkill, but I don't think it is. First, if the inspector made comments or suggestions at your first meeting, you'll demonstrate common courtesy and respect by indicating how you've implemented the suggestions, or explaining why you didn't. Second, you've probably made some changes in the plans, however slight, since the Schematic Design phase. This second meeting will give the inspector an opportunity to comment on those changes or even catch something that was missed the first time around. I also think it's a good idea to point out any unusual construction materials or methods—ungraded lumber, an innovative foundation, or an unorthodox framing system—and get feedback now, rather than be rejected or delayed later. Third, because the building inspector is familiar with your project, your application might move through the permitting process faster, at a time when speed is usually of the essence.

Addition Alert

Those of you planning an addition have something very important to do at this juncture. You should know by now, either through your visits with the building inspector or your research of the zoning by-laws, whether or not your proposed addition is in violation of any zoning ordinance. If it is, you should apply for a variance now before your designer begins to prepare the construction documents. The reason? Complete construction documents are time-consuming and costly to prepare, and they are generally not required for zoning approval. A dimensioned site plan, floor plans, and elevations will usually suffice, and if your proposed plans have to be altered, the cost of those revisions will be relatively low. If, for some unlikely reason, your plan is totally rejected, you can take solace in the fact that you didn't waste your money on a set of unusable construction documents.

Finalizing the Design

On the following pages record the information you gather as the design process is completed:

1. ADDITIONAL PROFESSIONALS:

Name/Profession:

_____

Address:

_____

_____

Phone Number:

_____

Name/Profession:

_____

Address:

_____

_____

Phone Number:

_____

Name/Profession:

_____

Address:

_____

_____

Phone Number:

_____

2. BUILDING INSPECTOR'S COMMENTS:

_____

_____

_____

_____

_____

_____

_____

_____

_____

_____

_____

Revisions required to meet building codes:

_____

_____

_____

_____

_____

_____

_____

_____

_____

_____

_____

3. PRELIMINARY COST ESTIMATE.

Size of project: _____

Method of estimating: _____

3a. Total preliminary estimate: _____

Costs associated with the construction of projects that are sometimes not accounted for in the estimates or bids:

DESIGN FEES:

Architectural .... _____

Civil Engineer .... _____

Structural Engineer .... _____

Wetlands Consultant .... _____

Interior designer .... _____

Other .... _____

MISCELLANEOUS FEES AND COSTS:

Some of these may or may not be included in your contract with the builder.

Demolition .... _____

Dump/dumpster .... _____

Clean up .... _____

Landscaping .... _____

Furnishings .... _____

Lighting fixtures .... _____

Homeowner's insurance .... _____

Other .... ═══════════

3b. Total associated costs .... _____

Preliminary estimate (from 3a, above) .... + _____
                                                                              ═══════════

3c. Total estimated cost .... _____

As was mentioned in Step 3, no matter how carefully estimates or fixed bids are prepared, building projects usually cost more than anticipated. Some of the causes are ordering additional work, making changes to work already done, and accounting for omissions and/or oversights. For this reason you should add a "cost overrun" amount to your total cost.

Total estimated cost (from 3c, above) .... _____

Cost overrun amount (add between 5% to 20%
depending on the nature and scope of project) .... × _____ %

3d. Total estimated cost and overrun .... _____

4. COMPARE THE ESTIMATED COST WITH YOUR ORIGINAL BUDGET, AND REVISE PLANS, IF NECESSARY, TO REFLECT INPUT OF THE BUILDING INSPECTOR AND/OR BUDGET CONSTRAINTS.

Your budget (from the "Establish Your Budget"
worksheet in Step 3, page 51) .... _____

Total estimated cost (from 3d, above) .... ═══════════

Difference + or – .... _____

List the revisions that are necessary to make the total estimated cost equal to or less than your budget.

Revision   **Estimated Amount of Savings**

_____   _____

_____   _____

_____   _____

_____   _____

_____   _____

_____   _____

_____   _____

Total revisions .... _____

4a. Total cost (from 3, above) .... _____

      Less total revisions .... – _____

4b. Revised estimate .... _____

4c. Your budget .... _____

(Ideally, 4b and 4c should be equal.)

THE CONSTRUCTION DOCUMENT PHASE

As we learned earlier, during the Construction Document phase the designer prepares an interrelated set of working drawings and written specifications. The drawings graphically illustrate how the building should be constructed, and the specifications support and supplement the drawings by describing the precise methods and materials to be used. Construction documents are an essential part of any building project. They must be sufficiently detailed to enable a builder to provide an accurate bid or estimate, allow you to obtain financing from a lending institution, and show how the building is to be properly constructed. But how detailed is "sufficiently detailed"? Unfortunately there is no universally applicable answer. Generally, the size and complexity of a job will determine the scope of the construction documents, but I've seen very large houses built with nothing more than a simple floor plan and four elevations (not something I recommend), and very small additions that involved numerous drawings and many pages of specifications. For most projects, a middle ground probably makes the most sense, but before you attempt to decide what's right for you, let's take a look at who will be using the construction documents and how, and why they're so important.

PUTTING THE PAPERS TO WORK

First and foremost the construction documents are used by you, the homeowner. They should be an *accurate* expression of your needs and wishes—your program—and they are your assurance that you will get what you want. The type of roofing and siding, the style of doors and cabinets—anything that you have an interest in—should be specified in the construction documents. Of course, there may be some things—the grade of framing lumber or the number of plies (thin layers of wood glued together to form a strong sheet) in the plywood for example—that don't interest you at all. These should be specified, too, and your designer will act on your behalf to suggest or make choices for you. The bottom line is that you, or someone working on your behalf, should know exactly what's going into your building.

The next person to utilize the construction drawings is the builder, who will probably use them more intensely than anyone. First, your builder will carefully review the drawings, examine the specifications, and then use the information they contain as the basis for calculating an estimate or bid for doing the job. When a price is agreed on, and the builder is hired, the construction documents become a vital part of the contract documents; the builder agrees, or contracts, to build your project according to the plans and specifications. During the construction of the project, the construction documents become a "construction manual," which the builder will refer to many times a day. Any changes made during the construction process are recorded in the construction documents. The construction documents are subsequently used to clarify any questions, confusions, or disputes that may arise before, during, or after the builder begins work. An accurate, clear, and comprehensive set of construction documents will help to avoid construction and contractual problems, save time and money, and help the builder successfully and efficiently complete the project.

Another party who has more than a passing interest in the construction documents is the lending agency. As part of the loan application process, the lender will hire an appraiser who will use the construction documents, in conjunction with other data, to determine a "value" for your project. The lending agency will, in turn, base the amount of the loan on the appraised value.

The appraiser ascertains the size and style of the project from the construction drawings, and the type and quality of the building materials from the written specifications. Both the drawings and the specifications must be detailed enough for the appraiser to do an accurate appraisal, because the lending agency will use your property to back up or "secure" the loan, and it wants to have confidence that the project is worth the money they are lending.

Next in line is the building inspector and the other enforcement officials, who will use the construction documents to determine whether your project meets all the building code and other jurisdictional requirements. The construction documents may be reviewed not only by the building inspector, but also by an electrical inspector, a plumbing inspector, the zoning board, the board of health, and the fire chief. To assure that all the necessary information is provided on the construction documents, building inspection departments typically have minimum requirements for drawings and specifications. To avoid time-consuming delays in the issuance of your building permit, or perhaps even a rejection, your construction documents must, at the very least, meet all the minimum standards.

HOW MUCH WILL CONSTRUCTION DOCUMENTS COST?

The last item you need to consider before your designer moves forward with the construction documents is their price. If you haven't settled on a price with your designer for preparing the construction drawings, you'll have to do that now; even if you'd previously agreed on a price, it might be appropriate to take a second look at it. If, during the course of the previous design phases, the scope or complexity of the job has changed significantly, and affected the amount of work that needs to be done during the construction document phase, such changes should be reflected in the cost of their preparation.

At my workshops, one of the most frequently asked questions concerning construction documents is, "How much will they cost?" My reply? "That depends on how much work will have to be done." Again, this is a question without a one-size-fits-all answer. In fact, I would be doing you a disservice by quoting even a general dollar figure. If you did your homework during the interviewing process, you most likely learned what an appropriate price would be given your project and your circumstances. I can say with complete assurance that clear, accurate, and appropriately detailed construction documents are worth every penny you spend on them.

WHAT'S IN CONSTRUCTION DOCUMENTS?

Construction drawings are commonly referred to as "the set of plans," which graphically illustrate how a building is to be constructed. By this time, you've probably seen a set of construction drawings and are fairly familiar with what they look like (see the definitions in Step 1). However, this may not be the case with specifications, which include many items you would expect to see and some you may not. If you're interested in really sinking your teeth into it, you could consider obtaining or purchasing a set of specifications (see the Appendices for sources), but the following overview is a good primer.

Specifications are typically organized according to the 16 categories, or "divisions," outlined by the Construction Specifications Institute (CSI), that have become the industry standard.

While the CSI approach works well for large building projects, it is often modified to better suit residential construction, typically by deleting several divisions (10, 12, 13, and 14) and often by restructuring or streamlining some of the others. Additional materials, known as "front end documents," are also considered to be part of the specifications, but we'll look at them a bit later.

Divisions for Residential Construction:
    1—General Requirements
    2—Sitework
    3—Concrete
    4—Masonry
    5—Metals
    6—Wood and Plastics
    7—Thermal and Moisture Protection
    8—Doors and Windows
    9—Finishes
    11—Equipment
    15—Mechanical
    16—Electrical

Each section usually begins by providing general information about the product's use and handling procedures. This is followed by an exact description of the materials and methods of installation. For example, in Division 3—Concrete, if a basement is going to used as living space, my specification for the concrete slab might read:

General: Discharge concrete within 1½ hours of mixing. Slump shall be no more than 4 inches. Protect from freezing.

Basement Slab: Slab to be 4 inches thick, 3,000 lb. poured concrete, reinforced with 6 x 6 wire mesh or fiberglass reinforcing (Fibermesh or equiv.). Slab to be installed over 12 inches of well-compacted gravel, 6 inches of ¾-inch washed stone, 2 inches of extruded polystyrene, 4 mil cross-laminated polyethylene vapor retarder, and 2 inches of clean sand. Provide a ½-inch extruded polystyrene thermal break at foundation walls and thicken slab under carrying walls as indicated on the plans.

This approach leaves little room for error or confusion. The following is a brief description of what's included in all the divisions.

DIVISION 1—GENERAL REQUIREMENTS

The purpose of this division is to establish the overall ground rules that will govern the implementation of the rest of the specifications. While much of the material covered in this division can be viewed as "boiler plate," it provides crucial protection for the homeowner. Much of the information contained in General Requirements is either included or referenced in your contract with your builder.

SCOPE OF THE WORK This section describes the work that is to be done, typically referencing the construction drawings and specifications. This section is particularly important if you're planning an addition, because the line that separates the new work to be done and the existing structure that's to be left alone can easily become blurred. Any exclusions to the work should be clearly stated.

INSURANCE COVERAGE This section states the types and amounts of insurance the builder must have, and a requirement that the builder provide the homeowner with a copy of the insurance certificate. (At one of my workshops, a builder pointed out that a few unscrupulous builders have been known to cancel their insurance policies, but still give photocopies of the invalid certificate to clients. To guard against this he suggested that homeowners obtain the insurance certificates directly from the insurance company.)

QUALITY-OF-WORK STANDARDS Sometimes this is described in a phrase such as "*All work to be done in a workmanlike manner,*" but this is somewhat vague and may be too open to interpretation. A better approach is to reference a specific construction standard such as Architectural Woodwork Institute Quality Standards or Quality Standards for Professional Remodelers (see the Appendices), or to include a more comprehensive description, such as: *Build and install all parts of the work in the correct position—level, plumb, square, and with appropriate tolerances—according to manufacturers' recommendations and sound construction practices.*

CHANGE ORDERS The need for written Change Orders is typically stated in the specifications, while the exact means for their implementation is included in the contract with the builder.

CASH ALLOWANCES Often, even with the most careful planning, it's not possible or desirable to select all the materials before the project goes out to bid. For instance, let's say that you know you'd like wall-to-wall carpeting in the children's bedrooms, but you can't decide on what type or manufacturer. But to get a complete bid, the cost of carpeting must be included. This is accomplished through the use of an "allowance." For example, the flooring specification might call for a carpet allowance of $22 per yard, including installation. It is vital that all allowances include both the cost of the item(s) *and* the cost of the installation.

CLEANING This section defines and assigns responsibility for daily cleaning of the site, providing and paying for trash receptacles, and final cleaning at the end of the job, and gives any special instructions for disposal of trash on the construction site.

MISCELLANEOUS ITEMS These might address such areas as who obtains the building permit, code compliance, warranty coverage, subcontractor responsibility, hidden conditions, cutting and patching existing structures, and hazardous materials.

SUPPLEMENTARY CONDITIONS This section is used to express specific wishes that the owner might have, and is often employed extensively by owners planning additions. Some of the areas that are addressed in the Supplementary Conditions are:

• What items (trees, bushes, etc.) around the site need to be protected?

• When working in a residential area, who will make sure that any regulations concerning work hours are adhered to and that, when appropriate, the neighbors are notified of the impending construction?

• What time of the day is work to begin and end?

• How will the building be secured at the end of the working day if the owners aren't home?

• Can the workers store tools and equipment on site, and whose responsibility are they?

• For additions, what on-site facilities (bathroom, phone, power) can be used by the builder and subcontractors and what areas are off limits?

• For additions, what kinds of precautions will be taken to minimize the impact of construction dust, dirt, and noise on the owners?

• What are the rules, if any, about smoking?

• How will children and pets be protected from the dangers of the construction site?

• Will the builder be allowed to display a sign?

DIVISION 2—SITEWORK

This division specifies the work that is to be done on and around the building site.

DEMOLITION Lists any existing buildings, portion of buildings, or other on-site structures that need to be demolished before new work can be constructed.

CLEARING Describes the clearing of such things as trees, brush, or stumps that must be done before construction begins.

EXCAVATING, BACKFILLING, AND GRADING This section includes foundation excavation and backfilling, utilities (electrical, gas, water, sewer) trench excavation and septic system installation, foundation drainage installation, driveway construction, and landscaping.

DIVISION 3—CONCRETE

This division specifies the structural elements that will be constructed from poured concrete.

FOOTINGS Specifies the concrete footings that will be used to support the foundation walls and lally columns used to support beams.

WALLS Describes the concrete foundation walls.

SLABS Lists the various concrete slabs—garage, basement, walks, patios—that are to be installed.

RETAINING WALLS Specifies the size and type of any necessary retaining walls.

DIVISION 4—MASONRY

CONCRETE MASONRY UNIT (CMU), OR CONCRETE BLOCK Specifies any structures—foundation walls, retaining wall, fire walls—that are to be constructed of concrete block.

BRICK MASONRY Specifies the construction of any brick structures, such as fireplaces and structural walls.

VENEER Specifies any veneer work—brick, stone, simulated stone—that is to be done.

DIVISION 5—METALS

This division deals with the types of metals to be used. In residential work that typically means steel beams, and rarely steel joists and metal floor decking.

DIVISION 6—WOOD AND PLASTICS

This division encompasses many of the areas generally thought of as carpentry.

ROUGH CARPENTRY This section includes framing materials and methods, sheathing materials, subflooring and underlayment, and interior walls, referred to as "partitions."

FINISH CARPENTRY This section includes exterior and interior trim, stairs and handrails, wood paneling, shelving, cabinetry, and countertops.

DIVISION 7—THERMAL AND MOISTURE PROTECTION

This division covers the requirements of protecting a structure from the elements.

FOUNDATION DAMPPROOFING   Describes the method used to prevent water from penetrating the foundation walls. Interestingly, the typical bituminous foundation coating applied to the foundation walls is not "waterproof" and proper above and subsurface water "management"—gutters and downspouts, finish grading, appropriate back fill, footing drains—are the key to a dry basement.

INSULATION   This describes all types of insulation—fiberglass, cellulose, rigid foam, sprayed foam—in all locations—under slab, foundation walls, floor joists, wall cavities, ceiling joists, and rafters.

AIR/VAPOR RETARDERS (A/VR)   Air/vapor retarders are installed to inhibit heat loss due to air infiltration and to prevent the movement of warm, moist air from the inside of a building through the structure—floors, walls, and roofs—where the moisture might condense and cause problems. There are conflicting opinions about their application, but they're generally considered important for good building performance and are required by most building codes. Sealing the building against air infiltration with caulking and gaskets can also be included.

ROOFING   Including all roofing materials—wood, asphalt, fiberglass, metal, tile, single membrane, and roll roofing—and associated materials such as underlayments, ice and water barriers, flashing, drip edge, and gutters.

SIDING   Including all materials and types such as horizontal and vertical wood, vinyl, aluminum siding, and wood shingle siding.

DIVISION 8—DOORS AND WINDOWS

This division lists the type, styles, materials, and manufacturers for the doors and windows, typically organized in the form of a schedule. The required hardware—latches, door knobs, hinges, closers—are also listed in this section.

DIVISION 9—FINISHES

This division specifies the materials that are used to cover or "finish" the major surfaces—floor, walls, and ceilings—of a building.

PLASTER, GYPSUM, AND OTHER WALLBOARDS   This section describes the installation of these materials on the walls and ceilings of the building.

FLOORING   This covers the many types of available flooring materials—wood, quarry tile, ceramic tile, resilient tile (vinyl, rubber, linoleum), and carpeting.

PAINTING   This section specifies how the various surfaces—walls, ceilings, trim, doors—are to be finished and what is to be used—paint, stain, oil, or other.

DIVISION 11—EQUIPMENT

This section, infrequently used in residential construction, lists the appliances and similar equipment to be installed in the building.

DIVISION 15—MECHANICAL

This division describes the mechanical equipment and systems that will be installed in the building.

PLUMBING   Both the water supply and the sewage disposal systems.

HEATING   Including warm air, hot water, and radiant systems fueled by oil, gas, and solar.

AIR-CONDITIONING   Generally only used for whole-house air-conditioning.

VENTILATING   Specifies the type of equipment and accessories to be used to ventilate the building. With the advent of tighter houses, more attention is being paid to whole-house ventilating—regulating the exchange of stale indoor air with fresh outdoor air through mechanical means. In recent years, state-of-the-art construction and installation techniques treat heating, air-conditioning, and ventilating as interrelated systems.

DIVISION 16—ELECTRICAL

This division encompasses most things electrical.

ELECTRIC SERVICE AND WIRING   As was noted earlier, the electric service and/or wiring sometimes has to be upgraded when planning an addition or remodeling.

LIGHTING   Including the switches, dimmers, and lighting fixtures.

OTHER ELECTRICAL DEVICES   These might include fans, telephones, cable television, and wiring for appliances, stereo, computer, and smoke detectors.

ELECTRIC RESISTANCE HEAT   Electric resistance is a type of heat source that is inexpensive to install, but very expensive to operate and consequently is no longer in common use. Another source of electric heat—heat pumps—are more energy efficient and cost competitive with fossil fuel systems.

EQUIVALENTS, ALTERNATES, AND ADDENDA

Often, more than one material can be used to meet the requirements of the project. The designer provides the flexibility to use one of these substitutes either by allowing the use of "equivalent" materials—"the paint shall be the best quality brand name or equivalent"—or by supplying a list of "alternate" materials that can be used as substitutes. This allows the builder to use materials that are more readily available or on sale without compromising the level of quality.

Sometimes, after the construction documents have been completed and sent out to builders for estimates or bids, they have to be revised. Perhaps the owners have changed their minds about something, the designer has discovered a discrepancy, or the builder has noticed an omission. These corrections are executed through the use of "addenda," typically to the specifications. To ensure the fairness of the bidding process, it is vital that every bidder be sent notification of the addenda and given sufficient time to revise their price accordingly.

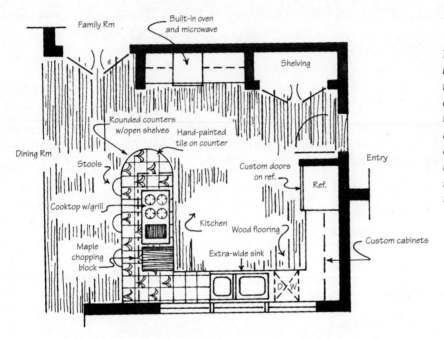

The plan of this kitchen shows some of the items that might be listed in the specifications, but that may not necessarily show on the construction drawings. Some of these items—the rounded counter, hand-painted tile, cooktop with grill, and pantry with custom shelving—indicate a high level of finish and will significantly increase the cost per square foot of this kitchen.

YOUR APPROVAL

When your designer has completed the construction documents he or she will present them to you for your approval. Before you accept them, you should review them very carefully. If there is anything you don't understand, have it clarified. If you discover an error or spot an omission, bring it to your designer's attention and have it corrected. Scrutinizing the construction documents now is yet another way to save money and avoid disappointing results.

THE PRICE TAG

Ideally, when you buy something, you'd like to know exactly how much you're going to pay for it. Can you imagine signing an agreement with a salesperson to buy a car for "around $20,000"? What recourse would you have if the final price turned out to be $24,000? Of course, it's that pesky word "around" that causes the problem—it's just not accurate enough. Granted, pricing a building project is more complex than pricing a car, but it should, and it can, be done with a good deal more accuracy than is implied by the word "around." The estimating/bidding process consists of four parts:

1 Interviewing builders.

2 Soliciting estimates or bids.

3 Reviewing the estimates or bids and revising if necessary.

4 Accepting a price and hiring the builder.

You're already became familiar with items 1 and 4 when you hired your designer in Step 5. As you begin the estimating/bidding process you should return to Step 5 and review the process. If a builder has acted as your designer, you should still follow through with this process. How else will you determine whether you're getting a fair price for constructing your project? So, set up and conduct your interviews according to the procedures in Step 5, and then move on to soliciting estimates or bids.

SOLICITING ESTIMATES OR BIDS

You may be curious about why I separate soliciting estimates and bids from the interview process. This is because interviewing someone doesn't mean you necessarily want to hire them. During the interviews, you may decide that you wouldn't work well with one or more candidates. If so, there's no reason to pursue matters further by asking them to submit a bid. That would be an unfair waste of the builder's time and money. While deciding on who you'd like to have bid on your project, remember The Principle of Threes. In fact, I think that a field of four or five bidders is better, because chances are that one or two may drop out part way through the process; you'd be left with a poor basis for price comparison, and you'd lose valuable time trying to find replacements. When you've selected four or five bidders, give each of them the construction documents.

TO BID OR NOT TO BID

There are two sound approaches to pricing a construction project: the lump-sum or fixed-bid method, and the "cost-plus with a guaranteed maximum price" method, also commonly, and inaccurately referred to as an estimate. Both methods are widely used, and one is usually chosen based on the preferences of the owners, builders, or both. Your designer can help you decide which one is right for you and your situation. Let's start by looking at the fixed-bid method.

As its name suggests, when a project is priced using the fixed-bid method, each builder submits one firm, fixed price for doing the job. There are a number of advantages to the fixed-bid method. First, the exact cost of the project is known before construction begins. Perhaps I'd better qualify "exact" a bit by saying that if nothing were to change during the course of construction, the exact cost would be the original fixed bid. However, change is one of the facts of construction life—changing minds, changing weather, and making mistakes add up to change orders—and it is the rare project that ends up costing the same as the original price. Some of these changes you will have control over, and some you will not, but at least you'll be able to follow the changes and track the cost to its final resting place.

Another advantage to the fixed-bid method is the fact that you'll be able to make a meaningful comparison of all the bids. It is not uncommon for bids to differ so dramatically as to make you wonder if everyone was bidding on the same job. A low bidder may be more efficient, a high bidder less experienced. Another high bidder may be very busy and can only take the job by hiring expensive help, or perhaps the lowest bidder has made a big mistake. No matter what the reason, you'll have the price-spread before you. Keep in mind that there is no magic in the construction world. If one bid is significantly lower than all the rest, there's a reason for it, and not necessarily a "good" reason. The lowest price does not always indicate the best deal and you should weigh the individual bids carefully along with the information you gathered during the interview process.

One distinct advantage of the fixed-bid method is that the owner is less likely to become what I call an "arm-chair supervisor," which is someone who is constantly looking over the builder's shoulder, worrying about the efficiency of the construction crews, and perhaps even under-mining the builder with criticism. This kind of interference is unpleasant and counterproduc-tive for the owner and builder alike. Also, because the owner isn't paying by the hour he or she isn't as concerned about how long the job takes.

When all the advantages of the fixed-bid method are added up, the result is another benefit that I think is truly priceless: peace of mind. As a rule, the fixed-bid method of pricing a job will reduce the homeowners' reasons for concern and level of stress, resulting in a more enjoy-able experience.

THE COST-PLUS METHOD

This method of pricing a job is often used for "fast-track" projects that must begin before the construction documents are complete, for projects that use a lot of new building materials or methods, and for additions that contain a lot of unknown conditions. Builders often like the cost-plus method because it reduces their financial risks by shifting some of the burden for the unexpected construction costs to the owner. This ensures that the builder will recover costs, expenses, and probably some profit. Aside from the advantage of being able to price and start a project when that's not possible with the fixed-bid method, the cost-plus method may have a couple of other benefits for the owner as well.

A major advantage of the cost-plus method is that theoretically the owner is paying only for the cost of the work that's actually being done—materials, expenses, and labor—and not for a large markup that might be a part of a fixed-bid price. As a result, there is the very real pos-sibility that you could save money using this method. But without the stability of the fixed bid, what's to stop the price from escalating out of control? The key to cost control is the guaran-teed maximum price (GMP), and you should not use the cost-plus method with-out one. The

GMP is an amount above which the cost of your project cannot go. The only exceptions would be a GMP increase due to written change orders agreed on during the course of construction.

In addition to potential savings, some people like the level of involvement that the cost-plus method requires. For the cost-plus method to work well, the owner must work more closely with the builder and develop a trusting working relationship. These advantages notwithstanding, the cost-plus method is more complicated and asks more of the homeowner.

One difficulty with using this method is determining exactly what will be included in the cost portion of the cost-plus price. It's obvious that outlays directly related to the job, such as materials, supplies, equipment, labor, fees, and other expenses, should be included; it's some of the indirect costs that can cause confusion. The allocation of these costs—transportation costs, telephone service at the site, long-distance phone calls, time spent preparing invoices and doing other paperwork, and photocopying—are usually resolved through negotiations between the builder and owner, and then written into their contract. I'm sure you can imagine that, even on a small job, the list of costs can be quite lengthy and time-consuming to manage, and this is only the beginning. Periodically throughout construction, when the builder submits a request for payment, the owners (possibly with the help of the designer or CM) will have to scrutinize each and every cost before signing off and paying the invoice. On a large project, this could be quite tedious and time-consuming.

WHAT'S THE "PLUS" PART?

The plus portion of the cost-plus method is the builder's fee, which is compensation for the time and skill it takes to coordinate the project, for time spent negotiating and estimating the project and for the risk of shouldering these responsibilities by providing a fair profit. This fee can either be a fixed amount or a percentage of the cost of construction. One objection to a percentage fee is that it eliminates the builder's incentive to reduce building costs, because as costs rise so does the fee. On the other hand, a fixed fee that doesn't allow for an increase if the scope of the work changes can be unfair to the builder. These issues are, again, usually worked out in discussions between the owner and the builder. After the costs and fee have been determined, the GMP, which is usually the total of the construction costs plus the builder's fee, is established and the cost-plus contract is signed.

Once you've weighed all the factors and decided which method you want to use, you and your designer should complete the "front end-documents"—the Instructions to Bidders, Bid Form, and Itemized Estimate/Bid sheets on the following pages (or use ones that your designer supplies). You might also consider including a cover letter as an introduction, possibly using it to personalize your hopes for the project and communicate the type of working relationship you'd like have. Also, as a point of information, you should make it clear that you're obtaining more than one price for the project.

Request for Estimate or Bid

The owner(s) should fill out the following:

Owner(s)   Bidder # _____

    Name(s):

_____

_____

    Address:

_____

_____

    Phone Number: Fax:

_____   _____

Designer

    Name:

_____

_____

    Address:

_____

_____

    Phone Number: Fax:

_____   _____

Project

The project is described in the accompanying construction documents that were prepared by:

_____

_____

Location:

_____

_____

To set up an on-site visit or ask questions about this request form or the construction documents contact:

_____

_____

Return this form to:

_____

_____

The builder/bidder should furnish all of the following requested information:

Bidder

    Name:

_____

_____

    Address:

_____

_____

    Phone Number: Fax:

_____   _____

The bidder should complete the following:

I/we submit the following estimate or bid for the work described in the construction documents indicated on the previous page.

Indicate one of the following.

Total Fixed Bid: $ _____   Total Estimate*: $ _____

Note:
The bidder should use the Itemized Estimate/Bid Sheet provided (page 198) to itemize the above figures.

This bid/estimate will be valid until:

_____

The owner reserves the right to reject, for any reason, any and all bids.

Signed by:

_____
bidder

_____
(please print names below the signature)

*Describe the exact type (cost plus, estimate with a not-to-exceed amount, etc.) and conditions of the above estimate:

_____
_____
_____
_____
_____
_____

Sample Itemized Estimate/Bid Sheet

Include a copy of the Itemized Estimate/Bid Sheet with your request for estimates or bids. Its purpose is to break down the estimate or bid into some of its parts so that you will be able to easily compare the different bids, make sure the builder included everything, and see where you might be able to cut costs if you have to. In consultation with your designer, go over the specifications and decide what you want to break out. You should list the section numbers (the ones given below are the ones I use, but your designer may use different numbers) and the items you would like broken out. The bidder will fill in the cost. A brief example follows.

SPECIFICATION SECTION NUMBER	ITEM	COST
6.5	Cabinetry	
8.0	Doors	
8.1	Windows	
9.9	Painting	
15.1	Plumbing	
16.0	Electrical	
	All others	

Total Estimate/Bid .... _____

Now move on, fill in the necessary information on the actual itemized sheet and include a copy with the construction documents that you give to each bidder.

Itemized Estimate/Bid Sheet

Owner's Name:

_____

_____

Bidder's Name:

_____

_____

Instructions to the bidder: Itemize your estimate or bid by listing the cost of each item indicated below.

SPECIFICATION SECTION NUMBER	ITEM	COST
_____	_____	_____
_____	_____	_____
_____	_____	_____
_____	_____	_____
_____	_____	_____
_____	_____	_____
_____	_____	_____
_____	_____	_____
_____	_____	_____
_____	_____	_____
_____	_____	_____

Total Estimate/Bid .... _____

Alternates

_____   _____   _____

_____   _____   _____

_____   _____   _____

_____   _____   _____

_____   _____   _____

_____   _____   _____

_____   _____   _____

_____   _____   _____

_____   _____   _____

Alternates Used   Cost

_____   _____

_____   _____

_____   _____

_____   _____

_____   _____

_____   _____

_____   _____

_____   _____

_____   _____

Total Cost of Alternates Used .... _____

Total Estimate/Bid (from above) .... _____

Total Estimate/Bid, Including Alternates .... _____

Addenda   Cost

_____   _____

_____   _____

_____   _____

_____   _____

_____   _____

_____   _____

_____   _____

_____   _____

_____   _____

_____   _____

_____   _____

Total Cost of Addenda .... _____

Total Estimate/Bid, Including Addenda .... _____

Budget/Bid Comparison Sheet

Often items are included in the construction documents, but are intentionally excluded from the estimates or bids. Some of these might include light fixtures, a whirlpool bath, new telephones, or landscaping. To get an accurate picture of your true construction costs, these should be added to the estimates or bids you receive.

1. LIST OF ADDITIONAL EXPENSES

ITEM	COST
_____	_____
_____	_____
_____	_____
_____	_____
_____	_____
_____	_____
_____	_____
_____	_____
_____	_____
_____	_____
_____	_____
_____	_____
_____	_____
_____	_____
_____	_____

1a. Total Additional Expenses .... _____

2. ESTIMATE/BID COMPARISON

Estimate/Bid Amount	#1	#2	#3
	_____	_____	_____
Total Additional Expenses (from 1a, above)	+ _____	_____	_____
Cost	_____	_____	_____
Cost overrun amount	X %	%	%
2a. Total Cost	_____	_____	_____

3. COMPARE THE TOTAL COST TO YOUR BUDGET

Total cost (from 2a, above)	_____	_____	_____
Your budget (from the "Establish Your Budget" worksheet in Step 3, page 51)	_____	_____	_____
3a. Amount Over or Under	_____	_____	_____

If the total cost is under your budget, then you're all set to move ahead. If not, then you must revise your plans or be prepared to come up with more money.

REVIEWING THE ESTIMATES OR BIDS

There's something about seeing a price tag that makes a building project feel real, and gets one's heart pounding with the realization that this project might actually happen. If your project comes in at or below your budget, this is a time for real joy. However, your heart may beat rapidly for another reason. What if, in spite of all your best efforts, your project is unacceptably over budget? What will you do—start over from scratch, wait for the next building downturn and re-submit your project for new prices, or shoot your designer? You needn't resort to measures quite this drastic. There are a number of ways to substantially reduce the cost of your project without seriously compromising its quality or undertaking major revisions. Of course, letting go of some of the things you had your heart set on can be difficult, but often a necessity. The best way to approach this situation is for you and your designer to first assess all the possible ways to reduce the cost, and then pick the ones that have the largest financial and the smallest emotional impact.

- **RECONSIDER THE AMENITIES**   Perhaps the first place to look for cost savings are the "amenities"—the niceties, not the necessities, of life. Steam baths, whirlpools, built-in vacuums, and swimming pools could be considered amenities. Of course, identifying amenities is highly subjective, and one person's luxury might be another's bare minimum, so you'll have to make up your own list.

LEVEL OF FINISH

Earlier in this step, with the example of roofing materials, we saw how the level of finish or quality of materials can affect price. This tactic can be utilized with many other materials. You should be selective in your choices, however. Choose materials that will not be significantly compromised by stepping down a grade or two, that will be easy to replace or upgrade in the future, or that will not negatively affect the overall quality of your home or addition significantly. Less expensive kitchen cabinets, carpeting instead of hardwood, and resilient flooring in place of imported Italian tile, for example, can be effective ways to save, but less expensive windows, doors, and siding may not be.

SIMPLIFY

Again, we touched on this earlier, but it's worth a second look. Changing from sloped to flat ceilings may still be relatively easy to do. If you've included fancy woodwork—stair and hand rails, wainscoting, moldings—consider simplifying or eliminating them. Replacing the garage with a carport or some opening windows with fixed ones are also ways to save money.

PROCRASTINATION

This is one of those rare cases where procrastination can be a good thing. Postponing such items as a garage, deck, finished basement, and landscape plantings can yield substantial short-term savings, although they may cost more in the long run. Again, be careful about what you decide to put off, and don't allow the integrity of what is built to be jeopardized by what isn't. Another little caution: sometimes the things that don't get done right away never get done. Don't let *this* jeopardize your relationship with your partner and family.

SWEAT EQUITY

You may have considered and rejected this approach earlier in the planning process, but if your project is over budget, perhaps it's time for a second look. The type of work you can do and the amount of savings you can realize depend significantly on your level of skill and the builder you hire. The specifics will have to be worked out in negotiations, but here are some suggestions: running errands, painting, demolition, pick-and-shovel work, and job site clean-up.

I'm sure you, your designer, and the builders will also have valuable suggestions about ways to save money. If, after considering all these cost-saving measures, your project is still over budget, your designer may have to revise the design to sufficiently reduce the cost. However, if you retain some of the cost-saving measures you've discovered above, you might be able to minimize the extent of any revisions.

ACCEPTING A PRICE AND HIRING THE BUILDER

When you have a price for your project that you can afford and that price is offered by a builder you have total confidence in, you should accept and hire the builder. In other words, it's time to sign a construction contract with the builder, so return to Step 5 and review the section on contracts. Here are a few additional tips about contracts.

- Make sure that any governmental or jurisdictional requirements—builder's license, insurance coverage—are indicated in the contract.

- Do not enter into a contract with your builder until all the subcontractors have submitted prices for their work.

- Do not begin *any* construction until you have a signed contract with your builder.

- If you're concerned about the amount of money the builder wants up front, you could set up an escrow account from which the builder can draw as each stage of the work is completed.

- If you have to obtain a loan to build your project, your contract with the builder should contain a clause that states that the contract is valid only if you secure the type of financing you want, at the interest rate you specify.

- A payment schedule is usually included as part of your contract with the builder. To ensure that you will have the funds available to pay the builder upon request, you should coordinate the payment schedule with the loan disbursements from your lending institution. Step 8 will discuss these disbursements, and Step 10 will address payment schedules to builders.

A signed contract is not only essential for your protection and peace of mind, it's also a requirement of most lending agencies. Before writing a loan, they will need to see a signed copy of the contract with your builder, complete with cost figures. Now, with the contract, cost estimates, and construction drawings in hand, you are ready to search for and secure financing for your project.

STEP 8 *Secure Your Financing*

You now know what your project is going to look like, who is going to build it, and how much it's going to cost, but there's still one big piece missing: the financing. Now the talk about money gets very serious.

THE GOAL FOR STEP 8   To obtain the money necessary to construct your project.

That sounds simple, but I know from the large number of questions asked by the participants at my home planning workshops, that this part of the process can be confusing, threatening, and even scary. That's not surprising; if you think about it, although your house or addition may appear to be expensive, it's the loan that's the big-ticket item. For example, to borrow— or buy the right to use—$100,000 with a thirty-year, fixed-rate mortgage, written at 10% interest, it would *cost* you $215,925 in interest. That's right, more than twice the amount you originally borrowed. Of course you must also repay the principal, for a total cost of $315,925 for a $100,000 loan. No wonder people get frightened when they hear the word "mortgage."

Mortgages are another fact of construction life, and they actually aren't all bad. Mortgages allow us to trade our future earning power for a place to live today. They allow us to own a home and have money available for life's other necessities and luxuries. And, because they involve such large sums of money, shopping for mortgages offers significant opportunities for savings. Accordingly, this is a crucial time to apply The Principle of Comprehension: make sure that you thoroughly understand mortgages and the loan process so that *you* have some control over the impact that a mortgage will have on your life.

Borrowing money to build a new home actually requires two different kinds of loans: a temporary and a permanent loan. The temporary loan is called a *construction loan*, and the permanent loan is called a *mortgage*. If you are planning an addition or remodeling, you have several options, including refinancing, second mortgage, or home-equity loan, that may not include a temporary loan, but most certainly will require a permanent one. We'll look at all these options in more detail later, but the first order of business is to find out where you might find the money you need.

MONEY—WHERE TO GET IT

Once again, as with so many other pieces of the preconstruction process, securing the funds to transform your plans into reality doesn't happen overnight; it requires careful progression through several steps. Your first task is to investigate all the possible sources of funds and financing. You may recall from Step 3 that if your financial situation is typical, and your building project is of any size, you will have to look beyond your personal savings and the generosity of your family and friends to bankroll your plans. Usually this means looking to one of the many types of lending agencies or institutions. Here's a brief overview:

SAVINGS AND LOAN ASSOCIATIONS

Savings and loan associations (S&Ls) are either state or federally chartered, were originally created as a source of home mortgage financing, and have traditionally been the primary issuer of residential loans. In the 1980s, S&Ls were allowed to enter into many activities unrelated to mortgage lending, and consequently experienced some well-publicized financial troubles. Subsequently, their share of the mortgage market has dropped significantly, but they still remain an important source of residential financing. Although you should care about the financial strength of the S&L you do business with, your concerns as a borrower are considerably less than those of a depositor; if an S&L fails after you've completed your building project, your have their money, they don't have yours. S&Ls offer construction, home improvement, and permanent mortgage loans.

MUTUAL SAVINGS BANKS

Mutual savings banks are state-chartered lending institutions, concentrated mainly in the Northeast, and are also a major source of residential construction funds. They are closely related to S&Ls, and are required by law to invest their savings deposits in safe investments. Therefore, residential mortgages comprise the bulk of their lending activities. Mutual savings banks are "mutually" owned by the depositors. They, too, offer construction, home improvement, and permanent mortgage loans.

COMMERCIAL BANKS

Commercial banks have traditionally concentrated on short-term loans to businesses, and limited their interactions with individuals mostly to credit cards, automobile loans, and personal loans. But recently commercial banks have become more active in the residential loan market. Commercial banks are chartered by the federal government or by the state in which the home office is located, and are owned by stockholders, not the depositors. Commercial banks offer construction, home improvement, and permanent mortgage loans.

CREDIT UNIONS

Employee credit unions typically specialize in consumer and home improvement loans, but if their cash deposits are large enough some may offer construction loans. Credit unions often have rates and terms that are more attractive than other lending institutions, so if you have access to one it's worth looking into.

EMPLOYER ASSISTANCE

Employers sometimes offer loan assistance programs, and may have money available for construction loans. If they don't make loans directly, employers may provide money for loan down payments or might be able to use their influence at a lending agency to help you secure a loan.

CO-OPERATIVE BANKS

Co-op banks are similar to mutual savings banks and are found only in Massachusetts and Rhode Island. They are a good source of residential construction funds, including construction, home improvement, and permanent mortgage loans.

MORTGAGE BANKERS

Unlike other lending agencies, mortgage bankers are specialized companies whose only business activity is mortgage lending. Although most of their loans are permanent mortgage loans —either new or refinanced—they do issue some construction loans. Mortgage bankers do not take deposits from the general public, but get the money they lend from "outside" sources, such as pension funds and large individual investors. They are not as tightly regulated as S&Ls or banks, and they typically sell the loans they issue to other buyers in the secondary mortgage market. Critics claim that mortgage bankers have less incentive to treat you well because they do not offer other banking services, but the opposite case can also be made: without you as mortgage customers, they'd be out of business.

DEVELOPERS

Residential developers, in cooperation with a local lending agency, may offer mortgage loans for the houses they build and sell. Sometimes, in anticipation of making a profit on the house, the developer will "subsidize" the loan and you can get a favorable arrangement. However, it might also be true that, for a commission, the developer would steer you to a particular, perhaps high-priced, financing source. Scrutinize carefully any loan offered through a developer.

STATE ASSISTANCE PROGRAMS

Generally these programs are intended to help low-income home buyers, or home buyers who pledge to rehabilitate substandard housing. While the states usually don't make direct homeowner loans, they encourage private lenders to do so by offering certain types of partial guarantees or subsidies.

MORTGAGE BROKERS

If you are having trouble locating a financing source, you could seek the help of a real estate agent or a mortgage broker. Although neither offers loans directly, they are well connected with lending agencies that do and, for a fee, are in a position to "comparison" shop for the best rates and terms available. However, this close connection can also become too cozy, and the referring agent could be tempted to steer you to the source that provides referral fees, rather than the best deal for you. Accordingly, you should be aware of what is and what is not a good loan deal, and never rely on any one source for your information.

Although each type of lending agency must follow the rules of their chartering or regulating bodies (state and federal governments), there is sufficient flexibility within these guidelines, even among agencies of the same type, to promote healthy competition for your lending business. Differences in these lending practices—qualifying limits, interest rates, points, and fees— are one way lending agencies attract customers. Although it can be confusing at times, part of your job in choosing a lending agency is to weigh these differences. To further complicate matters, not only are there differences in lending practices, but there are also different types of loans.

MONEY—THE PACKAGING

There are many types of mortgage loans to choose from, and while the purpose of all these loans is the same—to provide you with the money for your project—the means are different. Interest rate structures and repayment terms (the length of the loan and the amortization schedule) are the two major characteristics that distinguish one type of loan from another. The following is a brief description of the most common loans available, but because the specifics of each one varies from lender to lender, I recommend that you do a lot of additional reading on the subject (see the Appendices for other sources and information).

THE CONSTRUCTION LOAN

As I've noted, if you are building a new home, the first type of loan you will need to obtain is a construction loan. The construction loan is a temporary, short-term loan that's written to cover the time it takes to build your house, usually for a year or less. During this time the loan money is paid to the borrower in a series of installments, or "draws," until the project is completed and the entire amount of the loan has been disbursed. With the typical construction loan, the borrower pays the lender a specified rate of interest, but only on the amount of money borrowed to date, not on the entire loan amount. When the term of the construction loan expires, it's replaced with a permanent or "mortgage loan." To eliminate the additional time and expense of applying for and obtaining two separate loans, some lending institutions tie the two together with what is called a construction-permanent, or "construction-perm" loan.

Under the prearranged terms of a construction-perm loan, when the construction of your house is completed, your construction loan automatically converts to a permanent mortgage loan. To create a variety of construction-perm loans, lending agencies combine different permanent loans, fixed-rate or adjustable-rate loans for instance, with construction loans. The right construction-perm can result in substantial savings of time and money for you, but because it also means that you are effectively "buying" two loans at one time, you must make sure that you understand the costs and terms of the entire loan package to make an effective comparison of the construction-perm loans offered by different lending agencies.

PERMANENT LOANS

The permanent loan, or mortgage loan, picks up where the construction loan leaves off. A mortgage is a long-term loan, most commonly written for a period of 15 or 30 years (20- and 25-year terms are also available), during which time the borrower makes monthly payments to the lender that include both interest and principal, until the principal has been entirely repaid.

Interest is, in effect, the "rent" you pay the lender for the right to use their money, and the principal is the amount of money that originally was borrowed. If you were to borrow $100,000 at 10% interest for 30 years, you might think that the first year you'd pay $10,000 in interest ($100,000 × 10% = $10,000) plus $3,333 in principal ($100,000 ÷ 30 = $3,333) for a total payment of $13,333. Following this line of thinking, the second year's interest payment would be $9,666.70 ($100,000 - $3,333 = $96,667 × 10% = $9,666.70) plus $3,333 in principal for a total of $12,999.70, and continuing with ever-decreasing payments until the principal is repaid. Sounds sensible? Maybe it does, but it's also wrong.

Mortgages are structured so that, in the early years, the mortgage payment is almost entirely interest, with only a small portion going to reduce the principal. As the years go by, an increasing amount of each payment goes to pay the principal. With the common 30-year fixed-rate mortgage, the payments are divided into 360 equal monthly payments, but in the first year, at 10% interest, the total interest payments for the 12 months would be $9,974.96, and the total payments on the principal would only be $556.00, for a total of $10,530.96, not the figures calculated above. This method of gradually repaying the principal is called "amortization."

Over the years, as you slowly reduce the amount of principal you owe, your "ownership" of your home increases. This ownership, or equity, is the difference between what you owe on your loan (the amount of remaining principal) and the market value of your house. If your house is worth $200,000 and you owe $100,000, your equity is $100,000. As you learned in Step 3, the lender will require that you have some equity in your home before writing you a loan in the first place (and now would be a good time to review the loan application infor-mation in that step).

Here is a brief description of the various available mortgages; some may suit your needs better that others.

FIXED-RATE MORTGAGE

This is the most basic of mortgages, and because of its simplicity and security, it may be the best mortgage for many people. Under a fixed-rate mortgage, the interest rate is established at the time the mortgage is issued and never changes throughout the life of the loan. This means that you'll know exactly how much money to budget per month to meet your loan obligation, because the monthly mortgage payments are always the same. So if you've managed to lock in an interest rate of 10%, and interest rates skyrocket to 17% or 18%, as they did in the 1970s, you won't have a thing to worry about. If, on the other hand, interest rates fall, you can always refinance your loan at a lower rate. Lenders typically charge more for fixed-rate mortgages— higher interest rates, fees, and points—but this may be offset by future hikes in interest rates and the peace of mind a fixed-rate loan provides.

ADJUSTABLE-RATE MORTGAGE

In the wake of the financial losses brought on by the high interest rates of the 1970s and 1980s, lending institutions began offering adjustable rate mortgages (ARMs). With an ARM, the interest rate paid by the borrower is adjusted from time to time to bring it in line with changes in the financial market. This means that when there's a rise in the interest rates, the interest rate on your ARM rates goes up too and your monthly mortgage payment increases. It's obvious why lending agencies like ARMs; they are protected against sharp upswings in interest rates, but ARMs can offer advantages to borrowers too. In the beginning, interest rates are typically lower for ARMs than for fixed-rate mortgages. The resulting lower monthly payments may allow you to qualify for a larger loan, and subsequently to build more house. The downside, of course, is that if interest rates rise significantly, the increase in your monthly payments could jeopardize your ability to repay the loan. Before agreeing to any ARM, read the Federal Reserve Board pamphlet *Consumer Handbook on Adjustable Rate Mortgages*, which outlines what you should know about these basic ARM loan features: the adjustment period, the index, the margin, discounts, interest rate caps, and payment caps (see the Appendices for this and other suggested reading). If you are confident that your income will increase over the years to handle any increase in mortgage payments, and if you'd like to qualify for a larger mortgage, an ARM may be right for you. If not, a fixed-rate might be the better choice.

TWO-STEP MORTGAGE

The two-step mortgage is a new type of ARM that essentially combines an ARM with a fixed-rate mortgage. During the first step, generally a period of from five to seven years, the interest rate is adjusted only once and this new rate remains in effect for the duration of the loan (the second step). The two-step mortgage offers the benefits of lower initial interest, protection against the possibility of numerous hikes in interest rates, and the peace of mind of predictable long-term mortgage payments.

GRADUATED-PAYMENT MORTGAGE

Like a fixed-rate mortgage, a graduated-payment mortgage fixes the amount of your monthly payments in advance, but there is one major difference: the payments increase during the life of the loan. In the beginning, the payment is actually less than the interest that is due, and as a result, the principle increases. The amount of the payment continues to increase for a specified number of years and then remains the same until the loan is repaid. The graduated-payment mortgage is designed for younger, perhaps first-time homeowners who expect their income to rise along with the mortgage payments. This is not very attractive in a climate of job insecurity and layoffs.

BALLOON-PAYMENT MORTGAGE

The balloon-payment mortgage is somewhat unique in that, while it does feature regular, usually equal, monthly payments, the term of the loan is relatively short—typically from two to ten years. This is not sufficient time to repay the loan; in fact the principal is seldom reduced appreciably. The result is that a large "balloon" payment is due when the loan term is up. Balloon mortgages are often used when interest rates are so high that very few people want or can afford to commit to other types of mortgages. They are sometimes used by developers to sell homes that might otherwise remain unsold, or by borrowers who don't want to lock themselves into a long commitment to a high interest rate. Of course, the borrower is betting on the ability to repay the entire balloon amount, or the more likely scenario of refinancing the loan at a more reasonable rate. If this cannot be done, the bet is lost and the balloon bursts.

ENERGY-EFFICIENT MORTGAGES

Energy-efficient homes save their owners money by reducing energy consumption and lowering utility bills, and recently some lending institutions have been giving homeowners the opportunity to capitalize on these savings by writing what are called energy-efficient mortgages (EEM). As you learned in Step 3, lenders regulate the size of the loan a borrower can qualify for by placing a limit on the amount of debt and housing expense they can carry. Because an energy-efficient home will cost less to operate than an ordinary home, EEM lenders will increase the level of allowable housing expense, with the result that the borrower can qualify for a larger loan. To find out more about EEMs, contact your state energy office.

FHA-INSURED AND VA-GUARANTEED LOANS

The preceding mortgages are sometimes referred to as "conventional" loans because they are made according to the regulations and lending practices established by the lender's governing body. Two other types of loans, FHA-insured and VA loans, are not.

The Federal Housing Administration (FHA) and the Veteran's Administration (VA) are government agencies that were created to help people who might not otherwise be able to afford to borrow the money to buy or build a home. The FHA and VA do not lend money directly to the public, but rather insure or guarantee loans that are more affordable—that offer lower interest rates, reduced or no down payments, extended repayment periods, and usually no pre-payment penalty—than conventional loans. FHA and VA loans are only offered through a select number of approved lenders, and houses built under these programs must be constructed according to FHA and VA standards.

LOANS FOR ADDITIONS AND RENOVATIONS

If you are planning to add to or renovate your house, you have three major financing options available to you: refinancing your current mortgage, adding a second mortgage, or securing a home equity loan. While the basis for all of these lending options is the same—the equity you have in your home—there are differences among them. Some of the most important differences are in the interest rates, points, and fees that are charged for different options. Before you decide on any one, you should carefully consider them all, calculate what the total financing costs (not just interest rates) will be for each one, and then determine which one is best for you. You should ask your accountant or financial advisor for assistance in making your decision.

REFINANCING

As we saw in Step 3, refinancing is a viable approach to paying for your addition or renovation, and it works basically the same as taking a first mortgage. The lending agency will have your plans and specifications appraised to determine the value of your addition or renovation. That figure is added to the current appraised value of your house to get a new total appraised value. The loan-to-value ratio (LTV) is then applied to this total value, and if your current equity meets this requirement (and you meet their other loan requirements), the lending agency will be happy to lend you up to the full amount you qualify for. You would use the difference between what you owe on your current mortgage and the amount of refinanced mortgage to pay for your addition. To review the example in Step 3, let's assume the addition you're planning is valued at $30,000 and the appraised value of your house is $160,000. The total value of your property would be $190,000 ($160,000 + $30,000) after the addition was built. This time, let's assume that you were able to find a lender whose LTV was 80%, not the 75% calculated in Step 3. In this case the lending agency would be willing to lend you up to $152,000 ($190,000 × 80% = $152,000). If you had $120,000 left to repay on your original mortgage, you'd have $32,000 available to finance your proposed addition ($152,000 - $120,000 = $32,000), which would be more than enough . Refinancing may not be an attractive option if the current interest rates are higher than your present mortgage, because you will be paying a higher interest rate on the total amount of the loan, not just the portion that will be used to build your addition. On the other hand, if interest rates are lower than your current mortgage, refinancing could make good financial sense. Remember, be sure to check out *all* the costs of refinancing.

SECOND MORTGAGE

The second mortgage has traditionally been a fixed-rate, short-term (5 to 15 years) loan secured by the equity in your home. Generally speaking, interest rates for second mortgages are higher that those for first mortgages, but of course that interest will probably be paid on a much smaller principal. Second mortgages, which still suffer from the bad reputation they got during the Great Depression, are not very common, and in fact have been largely replaced by the home equity loan.

HOME EQUITY LOAN

As its name suggests, a home equity loan is also a loan that's secured by the amount of equity you have in your home. However, a home equity loan differs from a mortgage loan in that, rather than borrowing a set amount of money, the home equity loan establishes a "line of credit." You can draw on this line of credit as you see fit, and borrow up to the established limit, which is generally equal to your equity. Another difference is that there is no set repayment schedule. As long as you keep paying the interest on the outstanding balance, you can borrow, repay a portion, borrow some more, and so on—a practice known as revolving credit. Home equity loans often set a fixed time period during which you can use the line of credit; at the end of that time, you might be able to renew the credit or you might have to repay the full amount. Home equity loans have a number of attractive features: flexibility, tax advantages, low interest rates, and easy access.

One disadvantage to a home equity loan is that you pay the fees, generally in the form of points, up front and based on your total credit line, not just the amount you borrow. However, that may not be much of a concern if you're borrowing for a building project and will borrow up to your limit relatively quickly. The interest rates charged for home equity loans are generally variable rates, although some lenders may allow you to convert to a fixed rate at some time during the equity plan. As with all variable rates, you should be aware of the loan's rate cap. And now a word of caution: the lure of revolving credit can also be a trap. Without the forced repayment plan of the typical mortgage loan, it can be easy to ignore the realities of your financial situation and find yourself over your head in a sea of debt. So borrow wisely and cautiously.

SHOPPING FOR A LOAN

Now that you know something about the types of lending agencies that exist and the loans they offer, it's time to determine which one you want to do business with. Let's face it; lending agencies are businesses, selling the right to use their money. In order to sell their money, lending agencies must have "customers" to buy their loans. When you shop for a loan, understand that you are important to them, you are a potential customer. Maybe it's my imagination, but it does seem like many of us take the opposite view: that the bank is doing us a favor by lending us money. Perhaps that's because we often don't know if we can afford, or "qualify," to buy what the lender is selling. Then uncertain about our financial situation, we rely on the lender to tell us where we stand. Hopefully you took care of that in Step 3, and now you're prepared to choose a lending institution as you have chosen every other professional or business throughout this process.

To choose a lender you must: (1) find a number of lenders with whom you could possibly do business, (2) do some preliminary screening, (3) thoroughly interview the ones who pass the screening, and (4) choose one and secure your loan. But there are a few preliminary issues you need to attend to, if you didn't do them in Step 3. First, you should order a copy of your credit report and resolve any errors or problems *before* you approach the lending agencies and they discover them for you. Failure to do so could result in lengthy delays or an outright rejection of your loan application. Second, if you don't have a credit history, establish one now (see Step 3 to learn how). A lending agency wants to see proof that you are capable of handling the responsibilities of repaying debts. Finally, by now you should have researched the different types of loans sufficiently so that you have narrowed your choices, perhaps down to two or three. This will help keep the interviewing process manageable. The final choice should be made with input from the lender you choose and the help of your financial advisor.

WHERE TO LOOK

Your first task is to generate a list of names—between six and nine—of lending agencies that you will contact and screen over the phone. To make a comparison of the various lending agencies, it is a good idea to include more than one type on your list—three mutual savings banks, three commercial banks, and two mortgage bankers, for example. The first names to put on the list are the institutions, perhaps S&Ls or banks, with which you currently do business.

Word-of-mouth can be a good way to get some other names. Ask your friends about their experiences with lending agencies: was the loan officer helpful, did he or she follow through on promises, was your friend's overall experience a good one, and would your friend choose the same agency again? Next, you should read the financial section of your local newspaper. Not only do many lending agencies advertise there, but papers usually publish a list of local agencies and a comparative chart of their loan rates. This is a quick and easy way to learn the general interest rate and gauge roughly how one lender stacks up against another.

As I mentioned earlier, real estate agents are a good source of leads. In fact, they are often familiar with the lenders in the area, and may know which ones are currently offering the best terms. Lawyers and title companies may also be able to offer suggestions. In this era of electronic communication, you can also utilize computerized databases to seek out mortgage loan information. If you aren't wired you might be able to gain access to a database through a realtor or a mortgage lender. A computer search should either be free or inexpensive. Stay away from service companies that charge a percentage fee based on the amount of the loan you ultimately obtain; you shouldn't have to pay anything for a mere listing of mortgage lenders.

INITIAL SCREENING

Now that you've compiled a list of possible lenders, you should do some preliminary investigation to eliminate all but the strongest possibilities. Comparing lending practices and loan terms can be confusing, so you must be well organized and approach it systematically. The most efficient way to do this is to use the phone. When you call, ask for a loan officer or loan originator. Explain that you are planning to build, are in the market for a loan, and that you are doing some preliminary checking to learn about local lenders' terms and costs. Keep in mind that you will be taking up someone's time, so ask if you've called at a convenient time and mention that you have a list of questions.

When making comparisons, you should probably determine the two or three loan types that you are most likely to obtain—for example, a construction loan, a construction-perm, a 30-year fixed, or a 30-year ARM—and become very familiar with them so that you can obtain pertinent information about each one. Before you begin your phone calling, I recommend you read *Settlement Costs: A HUD Guide*, which is available at most lending agencies. After reading that and the following descriptions, you should take the Questions for Lenders Worksheet that follows and a pencil in hand, and make your calls. Keep in mind that mortgage lenders often apply different names to the same costs, so be sure you understand to what cost each one is referring.

LOAN TERM   The length of time you take to pay back a loan impacts heavily on the amount of total interest you will pay over the life of the loan as well as the size of the monthly payments. Right now, you're just interested in doing a loan comparison, so pick a term that you think you will be comfortable with. Later, when you get closer to actually choosing a loan, you can make your final determination.

INTEREST RATES   Lenders can change their interest rates frequently, sometimes even daily, and the rates can be different for different loans. Over the life of a 30-year loan, a quarter-percent difference in the interest rate represents a lot of money. However, to accurately compare interest rates, you also have to know the number of "points" a lender will charge.

POINTS OR LOAN DISCOUNT   On some loans, lenders will charge a one-time fee known as "points." One point equals 1% of the loan, so if you are charged two points on $100,000, the fee is $2,000. One point equals approximately ⅛ of a percentage point, so a 10% loan with 2 points is roughly equal to a 10¼ percent loan with no points.

LOAN ORIGINATION FEE   This fee is charged by some lenders to cover administrative costs associated with processing a loan, but many banks do not charge this fee. The origination fee is sometimes also referred to as points.

ANNUAL PERCENTAGE RATE   As a result of the 1969 Truth-in-Lending Act, the Federal Reserve Board devised a standard method of computing mortgage charges that must be followed by all mortgage lenders. This single figure, known as the annual percentage rate (APR), is the "effective" interest rate of the loan when all the variables such as points, mortgage insurance fees, and interest-rate calculation methods are taken into account. The APR makes comparison shopping for a fixed-rate mortgage much simpler, but is not as helpful when looking for an adjustable-rate mortgage because of all the variations in terms. The lender is required to express all rate quotes in terms of APR, including the interest rate and points, but does not have to divulge the effects of other charges, such as private mortgage insurance, until three days after receiving your loan application. To assess all the costs, it might be a good idea to try to learn these figures before applying.

QUALIFYING LIMITS   As we saw in Step 3, the amount of the loan you will be able to secure is largely affected by certain qualifying limits, such as the housing expense/income ratio and the total debt/income ratio. Both are expressed as a percentage of your gross monthly income. These percentages vary from lender to lender and from loan to loan, so research them carefully. A higher percentage means that you'll qualify for a larger loan and may be able to build a larger home.

LOAN-TO-VALUE RATIO (LTV)   As we learned in Step 3, the lending agency will not lend you the full appraised value of your property. The amount they will lend you is expressed as a percentage of the property's value, and called the Loan-to-Value Ratio. LTVs vary from loan to loan and lender to lender, and under certain circumstances can be increased above the normal limits.

APPRAISAL FEE   This is the fee the lender will charge you for having your project—the land, any existing structures, and your construction documents—appraised to determine the total current market value.

CREDIT REPORT FEE   This minimal fee, if it's charged at all, covers the cost of ordering a copy of your credit report.

MORTGAGE INSURANCE   This term is used to describe two types of insurance: mortgage life insurance and mortgage default insurance. Mortgage life insurance is a life insurance policy that lists the lender as the beneficiary; however, you may not be required to buy a separate life insurance policy. Since life insurance is cheaper when purchased in larger amounts, you could save some money by purchasing one policy that's sufficient to take care of your family's needs *and* pay off the mortgage. While a lender may require you to prove that you have enough insurance to cover their investment, they cannot tell you where to buy your insurance.

Mortgage default insurance, sometimes referred to as private mortgage insurance (PMI), protects the lender if you fall behind in your payments or default on the loan. Lenders generally don't require default insurance unless you exceed the standard loan-to-value ratio. Also, PMI may be written so that when your equity reaches 20%, bringing the LTV into line, it is no longer required. If you must have PMI, try to negotiate this type of policy.

OTHER FEES   There may be other fees associated with obtaining a loan, such as an application fee, mortgage insurance application fee, attorney's fees, or inspection fee. Be sure you are made aware of all the fees you may be charged. For instance, some banks will charge an application fee that is not refundable if your loan application is denied.

DISBURSEMENT OR "DRAW" FEES   A construction loan is given to the borrower in a series of disbursements or draws. These draws are often contingent on a site visit and subsequent approval by the lending agency's field representative, who verifies the progress of the project. The total amount of these fees and the manner in which they are charged varies with each lender. You might consider obtaining a copy of each lender's disbursement schedule and compare it to your builder's construction schedule.

ESCROW REQUIREMENT   An escrow account is required by many lenders, and is used by the lender to pay your local property taxes and house insurance. At the loan closing, the lender will deduct the escrow amount—typically enough to cover six months to a year's worth of taxes and insurance—from the amount of the loan you get. Over the years, escrow accounts have been a source of controversy, with some lenders being accused of keeping the accounts larger than necessary. Some states now require that lenders pay borrowers interest on escrow accounts.

PREPAYMENT PENALTY   Some lenders charge a prepayment fee if borrowers repay a loan before the full term is up, for instance if you refinance or sell the property. Historically, the majority of mortgages are repaid within seven years, so unless you are certain that you will not repay your loan early you should search for a loan without a prepayment penalty.

RATE LOCK-IN DATE   As I mentioned earlier, interest rates can change frequently, so you'd like to know something about the stability of the loan rates you're being quoted. First, ask how long the lending agency can honor the rates they're quoting you. Second, assuming that you apply for one of the loans you're researching, find out if the lending agency will guarantee or "lock-in," the rate quoted at the time you filed the loan application, and for how long.

PROCESSING TIME   The length of time a lender takes to approve a loan could be crucial in keeping your construction schedule on track. Your builder may have to move on to another job if your financing, and with it the starting date, is delayed. Typically, the approval process takes 30 to 60 days, and sometime even longer; if you're in a hurry, look for a lender that takes the shortest time.

ARM CHECKLIST   To find the ARM that offers you the best protection against the possibility of rapidly rising interest rates, be sure to get answers to the following questions:

• **INITIAL INTEREST RATE**   When will the first adjustment in the interest rate occur? Beware of "introductory discount" or "teaser" rates. At first glance, they may appear to be a bargain, but the low rate may only last for a brief time, perhaps only until the first adjustment period, after which the rate may take a significant jump.

• **ADJUSTMENT INTERVAL**   How often can the interest rate be adjusted? Annually? Every three years? Every five years? The longer the adjustment period, the longer you're protected against rising interest rates.

• **RATE CAP**   Does the ARM have a rate cap and, if so, how much is it? A rate cap limits how much the interest rate can increase. There are two types of caps: periodic caps, which limit the amount the interest rate can increase in each adjustment period, and lifetime caps, which limit the amount the rate can increase over the life of the loan. While a lifetime cap provides the most protection, you should look for an ARM with both types of caps.

• **PAYMENT CAP**   Is a payment cap a good idea? A payment cap limits the amount your monthly payments can increase—a feature that might seem attractive, but that can also get you in hot water. With a payment cap, even if the interest rate rises and you owe the lender more in interest, your monthly mortgage payments do not increase. Does the lender just forget about this unpaid interest? No! It gets added to your loan balance, with the result that the amount you owe increases rather than decreases with each payment, a phenomenon known as "negative amortization." Eventually you might owe the lender more than the original amount you borrowed. Before agreeing to an ARM with a payment cap, be sure you understand the possible consequences.

• **FINANCIAL INDEX**   What financial index is the ARM tied to? Most lenders set their interest rates according to an index, which goes up and down according to the general movement of interest rates. Lenders use a variety of rates, the most common of which is the interest rates on one-, three-, and five-year Treasury securities. These rates are widely published in newspapers and are easy to track. Another common index is the national cost of funds to S&Ls. Whichever index is used, you should find out how often it changes and where it is published.

• **MARGIN**   How much is the margin? The margin is the number of percentage points the lender adds to the index to arrive at the interest that will be charged.

• **CONVERSION**   Is the ARM convertible? Some ARMs can be converted to a fixed-rate mortgage at designated intervals during the life of the loan. A convertible ARM may have a higher initial interest rate, or up-front fees, or may require a fee at the time of conversion. The method for calculating the fixed rate is disclosed to you at the time of the initial closing, and the actual fixed rate is set (according to this formula) at the time of the conversion.

Screening Questions for Lenders

Make photocopies of this worksheet and complete one for every lender you call.

Lending Agency Name: _____

Contact Person: _____

Phone Number: _____

LOAN FACTORS	LOAN #1	LOAN #2	LOAN #3
Type of Loan	_____	_____	_____
Loan Term	_____	_____	_____
Interest Rates	_____	_____	_____
Points or Loan Discount	_____	_____	_____
Loan Origination Fee	_____	_____	_____
Annual Percentage Rate	_____	_____	_____
Income Qualification Limits	_____	_____	_____
Loan-to-Value Ratio (LTV)	_____	_____	_____
Appraisal Fee	_____	_____	_____
Credit Report Fee	_____	_____	_____
Mortgage Insurance	_____	_____	_____
Other fees	_____	_____	_____

LOAN FACTORS	LOAN #1	LOAN #2	LOAN #3
Debt Qualification Limits			
Escrow Requirement			
Prepayment Penalty			
Rate Lock-In Date			
Processing Time			
ARM Checklist:			
Initial Interest Rate			
Adjustment Interval			
Rate Cap			
Payment Cap			
Financial Index			
Conversion			
Margin			

FACE-TO-FACE INTERVIEW

When you've finished your preliminary screening, it's time to carefully assess all the information you've gathered, see how the different mortgage lenders stack up against each other, and narrow the field down to—remember The Principle of Threes—three or four possible candidates that you will interview face-to-face.

Remember, you're going to work with the mortgage lender during the construction of your project and beyond. Therefore, you need to hire a lender who not only offers competitive rates, but who gives you good service and makes you feel comfortable.

Another important thing to remember is that your loan will be very expensive, and the wrong choice could prove costly. In light of this, you should consider seeking professional guidance from your accountant or financial advisor. The size of their fee—The Principle of Pay Now, Save Later—will be miniscule in comparison to the amount of money that sound professional advice can save you.

With this in mind, after you've made your selections, contact the same loan officers that you initially spoke with, and set up your face-to-face interviews. Explain that you've narrowed the field and are meeting with a few mortgage lenders to review the various fees and available options more closely before making a final choice. Make it clear that, although you're not prepared to apply for a loan at this time, you would like to know if there is any preliminary information that you could supply that would be helpful. The loan officer might suggest that you bring in the necessary information to become pre-qualified (see Step 3 and also below); this may save you time if you decide to apply for a loan with them. Bring your telephone interview sheet with you to the meeting and carefully go over the information with the loan officer to make sure that it's all correct and that you understand everything (The Principle of Comprehension). In addition to reviewing this information, there are a few more questions you ought to ask.

FEES

This is a good time to invoke The Principle of Ask for What You Want. Some of the fees that mortgage lenders charge are not etched in stone; they may be subject to negotiation or outright elimination. If, during the course of your initial screening, you find fees that are significantly lower than others or nonexistent, don't be afraid to point this out to the higher-priced lenders and ask if they're open to reducing their fees.

THE SECONDARY MARKET

Many residential mortgages are sold by the original lending agency to what's known as the secondary mortgage market. The secondary market includes three quasi-governmental agencies and one private corporation. They are the Federal National Mortgage Association (FNMA or "Fannie Mae"), the Government National Mortgage Association (GNMA or "Ginnie Mae"), the Federal Home Loan Mortgage Corporation (FHLMC), and "Maggie Mae," the popular name for the buying instrument of the Mortgage Guaranty Insurance Corporation (MGIC). These agencies buy large blocks of mortgages and resell them to large investors such as pension funds, life insurance companies, mutual funds, mortgage brokers, and individual investors. Mortgages may also be sold directly to the other investors.

As a rule, the original lender continues to service the loan—collecting payments, maintaining escrow accounts, paying taxes—and any effect on the borrower is negligible or nonexistent. Problems, such as handling the escrow accounts and resolving repayment difficulties, sometimes do arise when the mortgage is sold and the responsibility for servicing the loan is transferred to a distant location. For this reason you should seek a mortgage lender who will retain the servicing rights even if the loan is sold on the secondary market.

BUYOUTS

It seems that every time you pick up the paper, one lending agency is taking over, or buying out, another. During the last two years, four of the banks sponsoring my workshops have been bought by larger banks. The question arises: what happens to the loans that were written and are currently being serviced by the bank that's bought out? The terms of the loan cannot change, so most of the time the borrower doesn't notice a thing. In some cases, however, the new owner may transfer the servicing responsibilities. As I mentioned above, this might lead to some difficulty during the course of the loan. The loan officer may not be able to tell you the full implications of a possible buyout, but it doesn't hurt to ask if there's one lurking around the corner.

PAYMENT AMOUNT

As you discuss the type and size of the mortgage loan you're interested in with the loan originator, make sure you also go over the likely size of your monthly mortgage payments. Remember, these payments will not only consist of principal and interest, but also money to pay for local property taxes and insurance, and will probably have to be within the lender's preset limits.

THE BLANKET QUESTION

There are times when it just seems impossible to ask all the questions that should be asked. In these situations, I like to ask the catch-all question: "In your experience, what should people in my situation know that they usually don't know?"

Interviewing Lending Agencies

Type of Agency: _____ Date: _____

Name of Agency:

_____

Address of Agency:

_____

_____

Phone Number: _____ Fax: _____

Contact Person's Name and Title:

_____

_____

TYPE OF LOANS AVAILABLE	YES/NO	DATA TO COLLECT ABOUT EACH TYPE OF LOAN			
		EQUITY	RATE	POINTS	ORIGINATION FEE
Construction					
Construction-Perm					
Fixed Rate					
Adjustable Rate					
FHA-Backed					
VA-Backed					
Home Equity					
Home Improvement					
Energy Efficient					
Other					

QUESTIONS ABOUT CONSTRUCTION LOANS:

1. How long does it take for loan approval?

_____

_____

_____

2. What is the loan term or length?

_____

_____

_____

3. Is there an appraisal required and if so what's the cost?

yes _____   no _____   Amount $ _____

4. How many disbursements (draws) are there and what is the cost?

Number of draws _____   Cost per draw $ _____

5. Do you offer construction-perm loans? If so, what are the terms?

yes _____   no _____

Terms:

_____

_____

_____

GENERAL QUESTIONS:

1. What is your 2-year interest rate history?

_____

_____

2. Do you require an escrow account?

_____

_____

3. Which of your fees, if any, are negotiable?

_____

_____

4. Do you sell your loans on the secondary market?

Yes _____   No _____

If you do resell loans, do you retain the servicing rights to them?

Yes _____   No _____

5. Is there a pending buyout of this lending agency, and if so what will be its impact on my loan?

Yes _____   No _____

Comments:

_____

_____

_____

_____

6. What is my total monthly mortgage payment (PITI) likely to be??

_____

7. Is there anything I should know or should ask?

_____

_____

_____

_____

_____

When you ve completed your interviews, assessed the data (perhaps with professional help), and chosen your lending agency, it s time to set up a loan interview. This time the shoe will be on the other foot, and the loan originator will be asking most of the questions. When you set up the loan interview, have a loan application sent to you so that you can familiarize yourself with it before the meeting, and be sure to ask what information and documentation you should bring with you. During the loan interview and application process, the lender must satisfy the requirements of the four Cs of credit that were covered in Step 3. To recap, they are: capacity (can you repay the loan?), credit history (will you repay the loan?), capital (do you have enough up-front money?), and collateral (will the lender be protected if you fail to repay the loan?). Although some of this information may have been gathered if you were pre-qualified, it will probably have to be verified now. Mortgage lenders may vary somewhat in what they want to see, but the following list covers most of what will be required.

EMPLOYMENT INFORMATION   Names, addresses, phone numbers, and dates of employment. If you ve had a number of different employers over the past several years, ask the lender how far back they want to go.

INCOME INFORMATION   W-2 forms, pay stubs, tax returns, or other proof of wages or salary. If you re self-employed, you may need to bring your balance sheets, year-to-date profit-and-loss statement, and several years of tax returns.

DEBT INFORMATION   Names, addresses, and phone numbers of your current creditors, as well as any documentation of your debt repaymen t m ortgage, credit card, or other loan statements, canceled checks, or receipts.

FINANCIAL INFORMATION   Names, addresses, and phone numbers of your bank, S&L, or other depositories in which you have accounts. Your mortgage lender will request from them a verification of the number, type, balance, and activity of your accounts.

PROPERTY INFORMATION   Signed purchase and sales agreement on the land and a copy of the deed.

If you are applying for a construction loan you will need to supply the following:

A COMPLETE SET OF CONSTRUCTION DOCUMENTS   The plans and specifications.

AN APPROVED SEPTIC SYSTEM DESIGN   Indicating verification that all local, state or federal requirements have been satisfied.

A VALID CONTRACT BETWEEN YOURSELF AND YOUR BUILDER   Including cost estimates and construction schedule.

A LIST OF MAJOR SUBCONTRACTORS   Including proof that the builder and subcontractors are licensed and insured.

A note of caution about the loan amount you decide to apply for: don't make it too high or too low. You should be cautious about stretching your financial resources to the limit and removing the safety net you may need in case of a crisis. Consult your financial advisor and determine what type of cash reserves you should maintain. On the other hand, you want to make sure that the loan you obtain is sufficient to cover the entire cost of the project and complete it to the lender's satisfaction. If it's not, and you have the financial resources, you will have to take out another loan or refinance and pay another round of fees and closing costs. Discuss this with your loan originator during the interviewing process.

LOAN PROCESSING AND APPROVAL

When your loan application has been completed, it will be submitted for processing and then, hopefully, will be approved. During the approval process, the mortgage lender will verify the information you've provided, order an appraisal of your project based on the construction documents, order a credit report, and seek other required approvals such as those from a mortgage insurer, the FHA, or the VA.

When your loan is approved, the lender will send you a formal letter of commitment, which is the loan offer. This offer will state the loan amount, the terms of the loan, the points, the origination fee (if any) and other fees, the annual percentage rate (APR), and the monthly payment (including PITI—principle. interest, taxes, and insurance). If the exact amount of the settlement costs and loan fees is not stated in the commitment letter, the settlement agent is required by law to give them to you at least one day prior to closing the loan documents. The loan offer will give you a fixed amount of time in which to either accept or refuse the loan. If you accept the offer, the next step is to "close" on the loan.

CLOSING THE LOAN

With the hard work completed—the loan amount and terms determined and agreed to—the loan closing should really be nothing more than a formality. Sometimes the lending agency will send you a brief letter describing the closing procedures, but if they don't you can ask for a verbal explanation. You, of course, will be present at the closing, along with your lawyer and perhaps the loan officer. Depending on the lending agency or state, some other people may also be involved, such as an escrow agent (which could be a lender, real estate agent, attorney, or an escrow or title company representative) and a settlement agent (typically an attorney). If you are buying your property at the same closing, the seller and seller's attorney will also be present. As I said, all the details should have been taken care of before the closing, but if you have any questions or concerns be sure to get them resolved *before* you sign the loan document, and close the loan.

LOAN REJECTION

If your loan is rejected, you should find out why. Lenders are required to give you a written explanation for their decision, but it might also be a good idea to meet with the loan officer and discuss the reasons in person. Maybe there was an error in transferring some important information, or perhaps something you say can get your loan reconsidered. If not, take advantage of the opportunity to ask for suggestions on ways to improve your ability to get a loan in the future. Also, the fact that you were rejected by one lender is no reason to assume that you won't be approved by another. In Step 3, we covered two issues that might cause a loan rejection: a poor credit rating and excessive debt. Now let's look at a few more.

• **LOW APPRAISAL**   If you're building a new house, it's possible that the estimated cost of construction is significantly higher than the appraised value. The appraiser may determine that the estimated cost doesn't accurately reflect the value of the materials and finished structure. If you're planning a large addition or renovation, the appraiser may feel that the total cost of the new work will not be fully reflected in a corresponding increase in the total value of the property. If you get a low appraisal, you can try another lending agency, or you could re-bid or scale back the project and rework the specifications.

• **INSUFFICIENT DOWN PAYMENT OR EQUITY**   If you don't have enough up-front money to meet the lender's equity requirements, you might have to be patient, begin saving, and wait until you've accumulated more funds before you reapply. Ask your loan officer to help you set up a savings plan. Another option may be to apply for a loan, perhaps one that requires private mortgage insurance, that allows a lower equity amount.

• **INSUFFICIENT INCOME**   If the lender's income qualification limit is the cause of the loan rejection, you might be able to show that there are extenuating circumstances. Perhaps, for example, the rent you are currently paying successfully is equal to the proposed mortgage payment, proving that you will be able to handle the mortgage. Maybe you are due for a raise that will push you over the limit, and you can supply a corroborating letter from your employer. You can also ask the loan officer what other options exist.

HOW TO SAVE BIG MONEY

As I said at the beginning of this step, your mortgage loan will cost you more than your house. I also pointed out that, because mortgage loans are so expensive, they present opportunities for significant savings. Although these approaches are not as simple as they seem on the surface—due to such influences as variable-interest rates, points, loan fees, complex record keeping, the borrower's foregone interest, and lost property tax advantages—they are certainly worth considering.

• **LOWER THE INTEREST RATE**   It almost goes without saying that you should try to get the lowest interest rate you can, but many borrowers don't shop hard enough, perhaps because they don't fully understand the impact a lower interest rate can have. On a $100,000, 30-year fixed-rate mortgage, the amount of interest paid at a 10.5% interest rate is $26,000 more over the loan term than with a 9.5% rate. That seems like plenty of incentive to me.

• **SHORTEN THE LOAN TERM**   This is a simple way to save money, and, although it might not appear very easy, with a little forethought it shouldn't be out of the question. Let's look once more at the $100,000, 10% fixed-rate mortgage. If you were to shorten the loan term to 25 years, you would pay $172,610 in interest, resulting in a $43,315 ($215,925 - $172,610 = $43,315) reduction in interest paid when compared to the 30-year term. Of course, the reductions get bigger and bigger as you make the loan term shorter and shorter. For a 15-year mortgage, the total interest payments would be $93,430, for a six-figure reduction of $122,495 ($215,925 − $93,430 − $122,495). You'll notice that I've called them reductions, not necessarily savings. Because these figures don't take into account the effects of foregone interest (interest that would have been paid on the borrower's additional funds that went toward the mortgage) and lost property tax advantages, the actual savings may be more or less. Either way, for a possible savings of $122,495, a shorter-term loan is definitely worth investigating.

These reductions in interest totals will cost you in the form of higher monthly payments, but perhaps not as much as you think. For instance, the monthly payment (principal and interest only) for the 30-year loan is $877.57, and for the 25-year loan, $908.70—an increase of $373.56 per year. Not a big price to pay for a $43,315 interest reduction. The 15-year loan's monthly mortgage payment is $1,074.61, for an increase of $2,364.48 per year or $45 a week. That's certainly more money, but not astronomically so, particularly when you consider the payoff. If you're trying to find ways to save money on your project, rather than digging trenches or hanging sheet rock, you should find a way to bring home an extra $45 a week and put it all toward a 15-year mortgage. After all, when have you heard of someone being paid $122,495 for digging a few trenches?

• **PREPAYMENT OR MORTGAGE ACCELERATION**   Typically, prepayment money is applied to the loan principal, reducing the number of loan payments, shortening the term of the loan, and lowering the total amount of interest owed. In addition to saving you money, mortgage acceleration is more flexible than some other techniques. You can either choose to make additional payments occasionally, or follow one of two basic regular prepayment approaches: flat-sum acceleration and principal-only acceleration. As an example, looking again at the $100,000, 30-year, 10%, fixed-rate mortgage, if you were to add $100 extra every month to the $877.57 payment, you would save $90,000 in interest payments and reduce the loan term by 10 years. One of the drawbacks to mortgage acceleration is the complexity it may add to the record keeping. Keep in mind that lenders aren't infallible, and they can make bookkeeping errors. But again, these savings are worth a little extra work.

• **REDUCE THE AMOUNT YOU BORROW**   If you have substantial savings, you might want to consider borrowing less money. It may not make sense for you to borrow more than necessary if that borrowed money costs more in interest than your investments are earning. If you do need more financing in the future, there are always the options of refinancing or a home-equity loan to pick up the slack. Of course, you must be sure that you don't deplete your reserves and jeopardize your ability to handle financial emergencies or meet your other financial goals and responsibilities.

Throughout the planning process, I've encouraged you to take all the time you need to be thorough. Given what's at stake here, that advice is especially important now. Take your time, do it right, and reap the benefits.

You've now cleared the last major hurdle between you and the actual groundbreaking for your project. Only two comparatively easy steps remain.

STEP 9 *Obtain Your Permits*

If you want to ride the train, you have to have a ticket. Step 9 is about how to obtain a building permit—your ticket to ride the construction express. Compared to the previous eight steps, this one may seem small and fairly routine; if you've been doing your homework, it should be. If, however, you have not properly planned ahead, you could be delayed or derailed.

THE GOAL FOR STEP 9   To complete all the necessary requirements, and apply for and receive your building permit.

I want to begin by emphasizing two things about the permitting process:

• While the general approach to the permitting process is similar in the various jurisdictions throughout this country—state, county, city, town, and village governments—it is by no means uniform. Each has its differences, some minor, others not. For this reason, it would be futile or misleading for me to give you a single, universally applicable explanation. It is your job (with your designer's or builder's help) to learn and comply with the permitting process that's in place in your local code enforcement jurisdiction. I can only give you the general picture.

• As I said, it is never too early to contact the building inspector and learn about the permitting process. (Be aware that contacting a building official in a small town may take a bit longer than in larger cities because inspectors may only work part time.) I recently asked a building inspector in New York State what the single most common problem faced by people applying for a building permit is. He answered, without hesitation, that they do not start the process soon enough. So, now you must implement two important principles: The Principle of Comprehension and The Principle of Sooner, Not Later.

As I mentioned in Step 7, most local building inspection offices have a written description of the permitting process that they make available to the public. In my area, the city of Northampton building inspection department provides a flow chart diagramming the process, and another chart that shows exactly which city department to contact with your questions. If you lived in Northampton, you would be directed to contact:

• **THE BOARD OF HEALTH**   with questions about the local health code and state sanitary code.

• **THE BUILDING INSPECTOR**   with questions about zoning ordinance interpretation and enforcement, zoning variances and special permits, the building code, flood-plain districts, parking requirements and planning, the watershed protection district, and flood insurance rate maps.

- **THE PLANNING AND DEVELOPMENT BOARD**   with questions about flood-plain districts, parking requirements and planning, the watershed protection district, and flood insurance rate maps (notice the overlap with the building inspector), wetlands identification and protection, open space and recreation planning, traffic and circulation planning, historic buildings, commercial and residential developments, zoning changes, and land-use and development policy.

- **THE DEPARTMENT OF PUBLIC WORKS**   with questions about water and sewer hookups, traffic and road engineering and maintenance, and traffic circulation and planning (again, an overlap).

By providing guidance such as this, your local government makes your journey through the permitting process much easier. Usually, your first stop along the permitting path is to learn about the zoning regulations.

ZONING REGULATIONS

The zoning regulations, typically called zoning "by-laws" in towns and "ordinances" in cities, are the rules established by local governments (following guidelines supplied by the state) to set minimum standards for, and regulate the use of, buildings and land. Zoning regulations serve to augment the building codes; their main purpose is to promote the orderly growth of the community and to protect the health, safety, and welfare of its inhabitants. These regulations define zoning districts—agricultural, residential, commercial, and industrial—and address many issues. The ones you're mainly concerned with are the requirements for such things as the minimum building lot size, minimum road frontage, maximum lot coverage, maximum height of buildings, and the minimum front, rear, and side yard setback requirements (see Step 1 for definitions).

The zoning regulations are administered by the zoning officer, who is, in many communities the building inspector. You or your designer must submit the plans for your proposed project to the zoning administrator, who will determine whether they are in compliance. If your plans conform to the regulations, they will be "approved," and you can then begin the building permit application process. Keep in mind that this review takes time. The city of Northhampton, like many cities, allows up to 30 days for this zoning review. If your plans are found to be in violation of one or more of the by-laws—a circumstance you should not face or should have anticipated if you've been doing your homework—you must seek an appropriate solution.

ZONING BOARD OF APPEALS

This solution—usually in the form of a variance, sometimes a special permit or a finding—must be obtained from the zoning board of appeals (ZBA). After you've submitted an appropriate application, the ZBA will set a time to conduct a public hearing on your appeal, advertise this meeting in the local newspapers, and send notices directly to your abutters (the community members whose land abut yours). After considering your reasons for the appeal, and listening to the comments of the general public and abutters, the board will render its decision. If the board rules in your favor, you can proceed with the building permit process after the abutters' right-to-appeal period has elapsed. If your application is denied, it's not necessarily the end of the road. You still have the option to appeal the zoning board's decision in a court of law. If the court overturns the ZBA's ruling, you can then move on. If not, it's back to the drawing board.

Here's some advice that I have gleaned from years of dealing with the permitting process: when you are dealing with government agencies you must observe The Principle of the Written Word. Any decisions or rulings that are made by the zoning administrator, ZBA, building inspector, or any other public official must be given in writing. Why? Because, as much as I respect the vast majority of the inspectors I've worked with, and in spite of the fact that I encourage you to work cooperatively with building inspectors and value the role they play, I know they are neither infallible—they're very busy and can forget things—nor all saints. Here's a case in point. A couple of years ago, I was retained to design an addition in a local town. The program called for the removal of an existing one-story structure, and its replacement with a two-story addition constructed directly on the existing foundation. After researching the zoning regulations, I discovered that the existing structure was in violation of a zoning ordinance; it was too close to the side lot line. This is known as a pre-existing non-conforming condition. I pointed this out to my clients, but I also noted that work done within the confines of such non-conformity is usually allowed under the zoning regulations. I suggested to my clients that we bring the project through the design development phase, but that, before moving to the construction document phase, we file a zoning application.

We did just that, and when the building inspector reviewed the application and plans, he concurred that the project did not violate the zoning regulations as long as it was built directly on top of the existing foundation. He approved the zoning application. However, for several reasons the project was delayed for a year. When the builder did apply for the building permit, the building inspector—the same one who last year had given his approval—refused to issue the permit. The proposed new structure was two stories high and therefore, he maintained, did not qualify as a pre-existing condition. Although the builder had not included the approved zoning application with the permit filing, he was aware of its existence and mentioned it to the inspector. The building inspector could find no record of the zoning approval, and was going to reject the building permit application. But after a brief, admittedly tense, search of my client's file, I found salvation—an original copy of the approved zoning application, signed in the inspector's own hand. The application clearly showed the approval of a two-story addition, and, after a two-week delay, the inspector grudgingly granted the building permit.

BUILDING PERMIT APPLICATION

After you've cleared the zoning hurdle, you can begin the work necessary to apply for a building permit. Two words are key here: begin and apply. *Begin* indicates that getting a building permit is going to take some time, and *apply* warns you that the building permit is not something that you're automatically given; it has to be earned. There are a number of tasks that must be completed before you can file the application and request a building permit. One of the most important tasks is to show that your proposed project meets all the requirements of the building codes.

In almost every jurisdiction in this country, with the exception of some rural areas, residential construction is regulated through the enforcement of building codes. Building codes typically address every aspect of a building, including structural requirements, plumbing, electrical, heating and other mechanical systems, energy use, and fire safety. Although some major cities write their own codes, most jurisdictions adopt codes written by either one of three major code service organizations: the Building Officials and Code Administration (the BOCA code), the International Conference of Building Officials (the Uniform Building Code), or the Southern Building Code Congress International (the Standard Building Code). The BOCA code has been primarily adopted in the Northeast and northern Midwest, the Uniform Building Code in the Midwest and the West, and the Standard Building Code in the Southeast and most of Texas. While the bulk BOCA, UBC, and SBC regulations address commercial codes, the CABO (Council of American Building Officials) code, the one- and two-family sections of the BOCA code, has been widely adopted in the UBC and SBC jurisdictions.

Contrary to popular opinion, buildings codes were not put in place to harass the homeowner and hog-tie the builder. Although, shouldn't you be able to do exactly what you want with your building and property? At first look that might seem reasonable, but it's not that simple. What you do with your building and property affects others—your neighbors, the community, friends who visit your house, and the people you sell it to—and the building codes safeguard the public and protect their rights. I know I would not appreciate visiting a house that had headroom clearance at the stairway of 5'-11." I'm 6'-1" tall and would probably smack my head going down the stairs. One important issue to keep in mind is that the building codes set and enforce *minimum* standards for construction; it is quite likely that you will want to build to higher standards. Insulation levels, which codes typically set fairly low, is a good example of this.

The building codes are administered and enforced by building inspectors, who review and approve the plans and make periodic inspections of a project during the course of construction. The person we refer to as "the building inspector" (sometimes known as the inspector of buildings or building commissioner) is generally responsible for the structural and safety aspects—foundation, framing, other building materials, and egress—of the building. Other elements of the building, such the plumbing, electrical, and gas installations, must comply with their respective codes and also have to be inspected. Larger cities and towns may have separate inspectors for each one, but in some smaller ones the building inspector wears all of the hats. To ascertain how your project measures up to the building code, the building permit application will request some information. While each jurisdiction is different you will usually be asked to supply the following:

DESCRIPTION OF THE PROJECT   New construction (single-, two-, or multi-family house, garage, deck, swimming pool, etc.), addition, or renovation. The size, in square feet (although some jurisdictions ask for a total cubic footage that includes the ceiling heights), of living space and uninhabitable space. Total height (number of stories and/or height in feet) of the structure, number of occupants, and estimated cost of the project. The cost is used to calculate the building permit fee. Some jurisdictions assign a fixed value to different types of construction and multiply those values by the square footage to determine the permit fee, and others rely on cost estimates supplied by the builder or owner.

BUILDING LOT INFORMATION   The location, zoning district, size (area), street frontage, and lot coverage. Lot coverage is the ratio of building size to lot size, and although generally a zoning issue, it's required information for many building permits. Some jurisdictions require that a house number—which the building department usually assigns—be included in the address. This information helps the tax assessor keep up with new tax-paying arrivals.

OWNER AND BUILDER INFORMATION   Name(s), current mailing address, and phone number of the owner and builder. Each state has different laws and regulations governing the qualifications builders must meet to conduct business. Some states require that builders be licensed, in others they must be insured, in some they must be both licensed and insured, and still others have no requirements. Obviously the builder you hire must, at a minimum, satisfy any state-mandated requirements, and, as you learned in Step 5, you might even set higher standards.

INFORMATION ON ADDITIONAL PROFESSIONALS   Some jurisdictions ask for the name of the designer or architect, especially in states that require construction drawings to be stamped by an architect or engineer. Sometimes the names, addresses, and professional license numbers of the plumber, electrician, or other subcontractors are also required.

CONSTRUCTION DOCUMENTS   While every building inspection department requires something in the way of construction documents, their precise nature varies widely. As a minimum, you will probably have to provide multiple copies of the foundation plan, floor plans, exterior elevations, and building section. It's also not uncommon to need framing plans, a typical wall section, and structural details. In the states that require such, your drawings will have to be stamped by an architect or engineer licensed to practice in that state. Even if it's not required, the building codes usually give the building inspector the right to request that any unusual design or detail be so stamped. If written specifications are not provided by the applicant, individual structural components—joists, rafters, studs, sheathing, etc.—must be included on the application form. A site plan or plot plan showing the location of certain features—such as proposed and existing structures, distances of structures and other improvements to each other and the boundaries, location of well and septic systems, and location and distances of wetlands and streams—may also be required.

SIGNATURES   To be complete, the building permit application must be signed by the owner and/or authorized agent, typically the builder. There appears to be some confusion over who should sign a building permit application. I've known of instances in which owners, to avoid liability, were counseled not to sign their application. But the Massachusetts State Building Code, in section 113.3, states that "application for a permit shall be made by the owner of the building or structure." One reason for this is to show the building inspector that the owner has indeed agreed to the construction that is about to take place. I've heard of other tales where, under the influence of trying to save money, the homeowner has been encouraged to be the sole signatory. This approach opens the homeowner to potential liability problems. The best advice I can give is for both you and your builder to sign the application.

OPEN TO INTERPRETATION

In spite of the fact that building codes are quite lengthy, and often written in very precise language, they are not as rigid as you might think. In fact, the building inspector is allowed some flexibility in how the codes are interpreted and enforced. This can turn out to have both positive and negative repercussions. On the positive side, building inspectors can assess each situation on a case-by-case basis and apply the code accordingly. On the negative side, building inspectors can appear to make arbitrary decisions and are sometimes accused of wielding power inappropriately. In my 20-some years in the construction field, I have experienced this only once or twice. I ve also learned that building inspectors don t always have the last say. Once, when a client and I felt that a building inspector had made an inappropriate ruling, we went before the state building code appeals board, pleaded our case, and got the inspector s ruling overturned. But situations like this are uncommon, and if you have a disagreement with a building inspector, you and your builder and/or designer should meet with the inspector, try to understand the reasoning behind the ruling, and work the problem out together.

APPROVALS, APPROVALS, APPROVALS

In addition to showing compliance with building codes, you will have to provide appropriate information or documentation, and obtain the approval of a number of other jurisdictional bodies. Once again, the regulations vary from place to place, and the enforcing agencies may be known by different names, so you ll have to learn your local requirements. Here s a list of who you might expect to have to contact:

BOARD OF HEALTH   The Board of Health typically oversees the location and installation of private wells and individual sewage disposal systems (septic systems), insuring that the proper distances are maintained between each, and to the buildings on the property. If you are planning an addition, the Board of Health will determine whether your existing septic system has sufficient capacity to handle the potential increase in flow. Examples of other bodies that perform similar functions are County Health Inspectors and State Departments of Environmental Management.

DEPARTMENT OF PUBLIC WORKS   Typically, the Department of Public Works approves connection to the municipal sewer system and water supply. If you will be constructing a new driveway, you may need to obtain a driveway cut permit.

FIRE CHIEF   In some jurisdictions, the fire chief is consulted about fire-related safety measures. An important example is determining the number and location of smoke detectors. Smoke detectors may also be the responsibility of the electrical inspector. The fire department may also control the storage of fuel oil, installation of oil-burning equipment, and sprinklers.

WETLANDS ENFORCEMENT AGENCIES   There are two federal wetlands protection acts that may affect your project: the Coastal Resource Management Act and the Freshwater Wetlands Act. These regulations are enforced by state and local agencies, such as state departments of environmental management and local conservation commissions. Talk to your local building inspector to learn which agencies to contact in your area.

PLANNING BOARD   The planning board may be involved in a number of areas that could affect you—zoning, wetlands, general planning, and historic districts. Some municipalities have "design review boards" that enforce design standards adopted by the town. Again, check with your local building inspector about the existence and potential impact of such planning boards.

DRINKING WATER

If your land does not have access to a municipal water supply, you are going to have to find your own source of water, typically by way of a drilled, deep-water well. Of course, it's not enough to simply have a supply of water, you must be able to safely drink that water; it must be potable. That means that a sample of the water must be taken to a licensed laboratory and certified as being free of contaminants and fit to drink. Some states require that you have a potable water source before applying for a permit. But your state may have different requirements and, again, you can learn more about the procedures you must follow from your local building inspector.

SUBMIT YOUR APPLICATION

Use the following worksheets to record your progress in the approval-gathering process. Remember, your builder can help you with this. When the application is completed and signed, submit it to your building inspector for review and final approval. The issuing of your building permit will not happen overnight, so while you're waiting you should move on to Step 10 and tie up loose ends before those saws begin to sing.

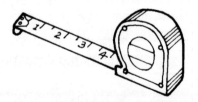

Zoning Application Worksheet

Name of Zoning Administrator: _____

Office Hours: _____

Phone No.: _____

Date Application Filed: _____ Date Approved: _____

Zoning Board of Appeals Members:

_____

_____

_____

_____

_____

_____

Date and Times of Regular Meetings:

_____

_____

Location of Meeting:

_____

Zoning Board Phone No.:

_____

_____

If denied approval, list reasons:

_____

_____

_____

_____

If denied approval, state solution you will seek:

_____

_____

_____

_____

_____

_____

Well Approval and Drilling Worksheet

BOARD OF HEALTH

Date Contacted:_____   Date Well Approved: _____

Board of Health Members:

_____

_____

_____

Board of Health Phone No.: _____

WELL DRILLING:

Name/Address of Well-Drilling Co:

_____

_____

_____

Phone No.: _____

Scheduled Date of Work: _____

Depth of Well/Gallons Per Minute: _____

Cost of Well: _____

WATER TEST

Name and Address of Water-Testing Lab:

_____

_____

Phone No.: _____

Results of Test:

Bacteria:

_____

_____

_____

Chemicals:

_____

_____

_____

Minerals:

_____

_____

_____

Odors:

_____

_____

_____

Taste:

_____

_____

_____

Is a filter needed or desired? _____

If so, type recommended:

_____

_____

_____

Operating Cost Per Year: _____

Approvals-Gathering list

Board of Health

Contact Person/Title:

_____

Phone No.: _____

Type(s) of Approval Required:

_____

_____

_____

Department of Public Works

Contact Person/Title:

_____

Phone No.: _____

Type(s) of Approval Required:

_____

_____

_____

Fire Department/Fire Chief

Contact Person/Title:

_____

_____

Phone No.: _____

Type(s) of Approval Required:

_____

_____

_____

Conservation Commission

Contact Person/Title:

_____

Phone No.: _____

Type(s) of Approval Required:

_____

_____

_____

Other Approvals

Contact Person/Title:

_____

Phone No.: _____

Type(s) of Approval Required:

_____

_____

_____

Contact Person/Title:

_____

Phone No.: _____

Type(s) of Approval Required:

_____

_____

_____

Contact Person/Title:

_____

Phone No.: _____

Type(s) of Approval Required:

_____

_____

_____

STEP 10　**Prepare for Construction**

You must be impatient to break ground, but there are a few more things you should do, and a little more information to be aware of, to truly finish the planning process. Taking care of these last few items may seem like a nuisance, but it's definitely worth it.

THE GOAL FOR STEP 10　To get your affairs in order and prepare for the transition from planning to the actual construction of your project.

INSURING YOUR PROJECT

I've pointed out how important it is to hire builders and other workers who are properly insured. It's also extremely important that *you* are properly protected by the appropriate types and amounts of insurance, both during and after the construction of your project. Buying insurance is a little like buying a car—you are often confronted with complicated, technical-sounding terms and a confusing array of options. In addition to the various types of insurance policies you may need to have, there are also many kinds and levels of coverage you must choose from. To make informed decisions and determine what mix is right for you, I recommend that you read more about insurance (see the Appendices) and consult with your insurance agent. As part of your research, don't forget to shop for the best insurance deal; all policies and prices are not the same. Independent agents represent more than one company and can do some of the shopping for you.

INSURANCE FOR THE HOMEOWNER

• **HOMEOWNER'S POLICY**　An efficient and cost-effective way for you to provide for your insurance needs, from the day you buy your property through to the completion of your home, is with a standard homeowner's insurance policy. These policies provide, among other things, insurance against property damage due to causes such as fire, wind, lightning, and collapse, and provide personal liability coverage in case of owner negligence. Homeowner's insurance is a good choice during construction because most policies cover both your building lot and the house or addition under construction. If you currently own a home, you should check your insurance policy for these provisions, add them if they're not included, or buy a policy from another company that provides them as standard coverage. If you don't own a home, but are currently renting, you should consider buying a "tenant's insurance" policy. This policy provides libility coverage for land and house under construction, but not property damage.

One shortcoming of homeowner's insurance policies is that building materials and supplies that are stored on site are typically *excluded* from coverage until they're actually *installed* as part of the structure. This means that if a pile of 2×4s is stolen from the job site, the loss must be made up by either the owner or the builder. To guard against this, your builder may want you to pay for a "builder's risk" insurance policy (see below), but there is a better, less expensive approach. For between $75 and $150, depending on the company, you can add optional coverage to your homeowner's policy called a "waiver of theft exclusion," which will cover such theft of materials and supplies. This looks like quite a bargain if you've checked the price of 2×4s lately. If your current insurance company doesn't offer such a waiver, it would be worth your time and money to find one that does. This, in combination with a properly written homeowner's policy, should provide most of the insurance coverage you need.

• **COMPREHENSIVE PERSONAL LIABILITY**   This type of policy only covers the personal liability of the insured and is generally purchased to insure a vacant piece of land, for example a building lot. As we saw above, it's probably a better idea to get this type of coverage through a standard homeowner's (if you own a home) or tenant's policy (if you rent).

• **SPECIAL INSURANCE**   Depending on the location of your property, you might want to consider buying one or more "special" insurance policies, such as flood or earthquake insurance, to provide coverage that is not included in your standard homeowner's policy.

If you're planning an addition you should be aware of two important considerations that are often overlooked:

• **INCREASED PROPERTY VALUE**   Your proposed addition or remodeling is going to add to the value of your house; consequently there will be more to insure. You should bring this to the attention of your insurance agent, and determine when, and by how much, to increase coverage to account for this increase in property value.

• **PAYING FOR CODE UPGRADES**   As unlikely as it might seem, there have been a number of instances in which a fire has occurred during the course of building an addition, and damaged both the addition and the existing house. Ordinarily, homeowner's insurance would cover the cost of these repairs, but problems can arise if the building inspector discovers that the work needing repair in the existing part of the home does not meet current code standards. In some cases, building inspectors have required that the substandard work be brought up to current codes, and therein lies the problem. The typical homeowner's policy *does not* cover the increased cost of construction that's necessary to meet the current code. This problem is more likely to arise with an older home. To avoid this potentially costly situation, you might consider adding the optional coverage called "increased cost of construction."

INSURANCE FOR THE BUILDER AND SUBCONTRACTORS

I want to mention the types of insurance that builders and subs must have so that (1) you'll be familiar with them and (2) if you're considering being your own general contractor you'll know what types of additional insurance you'll need to have.

• **WORKERS' COMPENSATION INSURANCE**   This insurance provides cash benefits and medical care for employees of the insured (the builder or subcontractor) who become injured or disabled as a result of an accident or illness related to their work. The general contractor must provide you with proof (in the form of the insurance certificate) of workers' compensation coverage. If you hire workers directly, you should carry this insurance. If *you're* acting as the general contractor, you must be certain that all the subcontractors have workers' compensation coverage.

• **LIABILITY INSURANCE**   General liability, automobile liability, and excess liability insurance protects those on the job site against builder negligence. You have liability coverage through your homeowner's policy, and you must insist that your builder and subs have liability coverage too.

• **PERFORMANCE BOND**   This bond covers you in the event that your contractor doesn't finish the job. If that happens, the bonding company will hire another builder to complete the job, and then attempt to recover their money from the delinquent builder. The process of becoming bonded is arduous and complicated; as a result, only larger builders (usually those specializing in commercial work) are bonded. Requiring a bond for residential construction is not common, although it may be required in some jurisdictions.

• **BUILDER'S RISK INSURANCE**   This insurance provides the same kind of property damage protection that your homeowner's policy does. In addition, however, it covers theft of materials and costs about twice as much as homeowner's insurance. Builders often try to provide this type of insurance at the homeowner's expense, but I recommend against it. First, if you add the "waiver of theft " exclusion mentioned above, you should be adequately protected by your homeowner's policy, but at about half the cost. Second, if you file a claim under your own insurance, you're in control and can negotiate a settlement with the insurance company that's in your best interest. Of course, that's exactly why the builder would like to buy the policy for you. In fact, they may even claim that the insurance will be cheaper this way, but check it out with your insurance agent and learn the truth.

TAKE CARE OF LOOSE ENDS

When construction work actually begins, the pace of life will speed up and at times be quite hectic. Now, while things are calm, take some to time to attend to matters that might get lost in the shuffle. Here are some suggestions:

• You should set up a system—binders, folders, files—that will organize, and provide ready access to, all your important construction papers. You already have some—your contracts, construction documents, and cost estimates—and many more will be generated: Change Orders, additional price quotes for items like furniture, and lien releases. Don't let the papers accumulate in piles on your desk like so much junk mail. Also, consider making "backup" copies and storing these in a secure location such as a safe deposit box.

• While you're shopping for materials, furniture, and appliances, it is a good idea to bring your plans and specifications with you. However, large construction drawings (18″× 24″ or 24″× 36″) can be bulky and awkward to carry. To make transportation easier, you can get your plans reduced, either to 11″× 17″ or 8½″× 11″, and put them in a three-ring binder along with the specifications. Many photocopy shops have oversized copiers capable of doing this photo reduction. These smaller drawings are also more convenient to send through the mail to curious salespeople or family members.

• Keep a daily log of the events and conversations that take place during construction. You should not only keep a written record of your meetings with your builder, but also of your discussions with inspectors and salespeople. This written record can help to resolve misunderstandings and will become a "construction diary."

• If you're planning an addition, you might need to arrange for storage of some of your furnishings or valuables to protect them from damage or theft during construction. Some options include your friends' or family's basements or attics, a self-storage facility, or a storage trailer brought on site.

PRE-CONSTRUCTION CONFERENCE

A pre-construction conference plays a vital role in assuring that your project gets off on the right foot and stays on track all the way through to completion. This conference, which symbolizes the transition between planning and building, should be attended by you, your designer, your builder, and perhaps any significant subcontractors. The topics of conversation should include:

NEIGHBORHOOD ETIQUETTE

If it hasn't been done already, inform your neighbors of your imminent plans and their potential impact. Introduce them to your builder and mention the other workers who are likely to be on the job. Describe the precautions you will take to make the job site as safe as possible, and ask your neighbors to warn their children that construction sites are dangerous places, not playgrounds. Inform them of the starting and quitting times and the expected length of construction. As a courtesy to your builder, ask neighbors to not interrupt the workers with questions during the work day.

GROUND RULES

Many of the ground rules should already have been established through the specifications and your contract with the builder, but it doesn't hurt to review some of the more important ones.

• Who will speak on your behalf and to whom? Designate one person as the official spokesperson for all your communiqués and set up a chain of command so that the spokesperson knows who to speak to. If your designer or construction manager is acting as your representative, most of the communication with the builder may have to be directed through them, but it is rare to have all communication with the builder handled this way. Generally, you will have a lot of direct contact with the builder. Together, you will be responsible for making many mid-construction decisions that were not covered in the specifications, or solving minor problems as they arise. But what if the builder is away from the job and you discover a problem? Can you talk directly to the builder's employee or to the subcontractor to resolve the matter, or must you grit your teeth and wait for the builder's return? Situations like this can cause a lot of tension and wreak havoc with job site moral, so be clear about the chain of command right from the start. If the builder isn't going to be on the job very much, it would be wise to assign communication responsibilities to a member of the crew.

• How will communication between you and the builder be handled? I strongly recommend that you establish specific times for daily and weekly meetings. The short daily meetings, perhaps 10 to 20 minutes in the morning or evening, can be used to talk about the upcoming work day. Longer, one- to three-hour, weekly meetings should be used to review work progress, discuss and make Change Orders, and clarify questions or disputes, among other things. These meetings might include the designer, a subcontractor, or another interested party. You may occasionally have to hold "emergency meetings" to resolve crises.

• What items in and around the building site—trees, bushes, plantings (don't forget those underground bulbs), stone walls, etc.—need to be protected? How will this be done, and by whom? Are there areas that you want to make off limits to vehicles, equipment, and workers?

• How frequently will the job site be cleaned, by whom, and how will the rubbish be disposed of? Are there any materials that can be recycled?

• Do you have any personal "scheduling" arrangements—vacations, nap times for children, sick or disabled family members—that need to be taken into consideration?

• How will you be notified about which subs will be working and when, and be kept informed of scheduling changes? This can become a sticky issue, particularly during the construction of an addition, if you go out of your way to be on the job site to meet or consult with someone and they don't show up.

• What are the rules about providing the crew with refreshments? Some employers frown on the practice; the crew may come to count on it and be disgruntled if you forget, or it could become an annoying burden for you.

• If you're building an addition and you don't arrive home until well after the construction crew has left for the day, who will secure the site? Security may be difficult to provide during certain stages of construction, so you should take steps to safeguard your valuables.

CONSTRUCTION AND PAYMENT SCHEDULING

Another important topic for discussion during the pre-construction conference, if it hasn't been addressed already, is construction and payment scheduling. Up to this point. you've probably paid for the work—designing, engineering, and other consulting—with funds from your personal bank account. This may still be the case if you do not need a loan, or plan to use a home-equity line of credit. But if you'll be drawing from a construction loan, the lending agency will enter the picture, and paying for your project becomes a matter of coordinating the lender's payment schedule with the pace of construction and the builder's need to be paid. Let's look at the construction sequence that your project will move through from start to finish.

FROM THE GROUND UP—A PREVIEW

Whether you're building a 15′ × 20′ cabin or a 10,000-square-foot mansion—whether you're building in the northern woods of Minnesota or on the southern tip of Florida—the construction sequence is basically the same: it's built from the ground up. Of course, the complexity of the project and the type of materials will affect the precise order of events, and not all events occur in every project. In fact, two builders constructing the same house are not likely to follow the same schedule, but, even with all these variables, it's surprising how similar the construction process is from one job to another. I'm going to give you a very brief overview of the process, but it's a good idea for you to read and learn more about it (see the Appendices for recommended reading).

First comes the sitework, which begins with a preliminary "stakeout" of the building. Using the site plan as a guide, you, the builder, and the designer will locate and mark the house, septic system, well, and other improvements on the building site, verifying and maintaining the proper distances from the boundaries and each other. Next, the site is cleared of any unwanted trees and other vegetation, but before this is done you should *clearly* mark anything you want to save. Think this out well in advance, perhaps in consultation with your designer or a landscape architect. I still remember the apple tree on our house site that I wanted to save, but forgot to mark and absentmindedly cut down in a frenzy of tree felling.

With the trees and brush gone, the heavy equipment arrives. At this time a rough driveway to provide access for construction vehicles may be installed, the stumps and large rocks removed, and the building site leveled and graded as necessary. If you don't have access to municipal water, the well is typically drilled now. Remember that the timing of the well installation may be regulated by the building inspection department or your lending agency, so be sure to faithfully follow their requirements. When the building site is prepared, the location of the house is staked out once again, this time more accurately, and all is ready for the excavation of the foundation or cellar.

When our own construction job reached this point, my wife and I were so excited to see what our house was going to look like that we marked the perimeter walls with white lime, entered the front door, and walked from "room" to "room." This was the first of several times during construction when the house looked so small that we were certain a measuring error had been made. We were mistaken; it was just the power of the large "natural" world overwhelming the small built world, playing tricks of scale with our eyes.

Excavation is typically done by a backhoe or excavator. If your project does not include a full basement, only the exterior, supporting walls of the foundation are trenched. Otherwise, the entire area of the basement is excavated and the soil removed. The foundation trenches must be made wide enough to accommodate the footings and to provide room for the workers to construct the foundation (if it's concrete block) or install the formwork (if it's poured concrete). In northern climates, the footings must be installed deep enough to be below the "frost line," a depth typically stated in the building codes. While the excavating equipment is on site, utility trenches for the water line, septic system, municipal sewer hookup, electricity, and phone lines may be dug, the utilities installed, and the trenches backfilled. This can also be done later, when the foundation is backfilled.

The first part of the building to be constructed are the footings that support the foundation walls. Footings, typically made of steel-reinforced poured concrete, are wider than the walls and stabilize the building by distributing the weight of the house to firm, undisturbed, or well-compacted soil. Footings are extremely important to the structural integrity of a building. It's quite common for local building regulations to require the first on-site inspection after the footings have been installed. When the footings have been approved, the foundation walls can be constructed.

Foundations are usually made from concrete block or poured concrete (both reinforced with steel), but pressure-treated wood foundations are becoming more common. As I indicated earlier, foundation walls may be just deep enough to extend below the frost line, perhaps providing room for a crawl space, or tall enough to form the walls of the basement. If your house has a slab foundation instead, the sub-slab material is generally brought level with the top of the foundation wall. As the foundation walls are built, a number of holes are blocked out to provide access for the utilities—water, sewer, gas, and electricity—that will be brought into the house. Wet basements can be a problem, and to keep subsurface water out of basements, a combination of measures generally are used. Exterior footing drains, made from perforated plastic pipe and laid on top of washed stone, are sometimes installed around the building's perimeter. A dampproofing coating or a waterproof membrane are applied to the foundation walls. Polyethylene sheeting is sometimes installed beneath the basement's concrete slab floor—which can also help keep out radon gas—and, in extreme cases, sump pumps may be required. Later, when the foundation is backfilled, care should be taken to make sure the ground slopes away from the building. This encourages the surface water to follow the contour. When the foundation is finished and all the moisture protection measures have been taken, another visit from the building inspector is usually called for.

When I was a carpenter, the next phase—framing the building—was always my favorite, particularly when done in the spring. The numerous bundles of new white wood are unwrapped and rapidly assembled, finally giving form to something which has long existed only on paper and in your mind. The first floor naturally comes first. The main carrying beam (or beams) are put in place, their ends resting on the foundation walls and supported in between by columns. The floor joists are installed next, supported by the foundation walls and the carrying beams, and then covered with the subflooring material. The finished assembly is sometimes referred to as the first floor "deck," and when it's completed the foundation excavation can be filled in or "backfilled." Other excavation jobs that were not done earlier—perhaps the septic or utility trenching—can be completed now.

The exterior walls and interior walls (called partitions) are framed next. The studs are nailed between the top and bottom "plates," with the appropriate openings created for the doors and windows. The sheathing material can either be applied directly to the studs while the wall is lying on the floor deck, then tilted up into place, or applied to the wall frame after it has been put in position. As a carpenter, I preferred the first method and generally found it faster, safer, and more accurate. If the house has two stories, the second floor is constructed now; if not, the ceiling joists and the roof rafters are installed. The ceiling joists, which are attached to the rafters, not only form the ceiling of the rooms below, but also act as horizontal ties, counteracting the spreading forces of the rafters and holding the building together. The rafters meet at the peak, or ridge, and are usually installed from one end of the building to the other in opposing pairs to keep the ridge running straight. This is my favorite point in the framing process; when I was a builder, I always paused to appreciate the angled, rhythmic shadows before moving to the next task. There just seems to be something magical about the combination of the solid, enclosing walls and the open, skeletal framework of the roof. When break time is over, the rafters are sheathed and the building's profile is complete.

Next the building is roofed. While the roofing materials—drip edge, flashing, underlayment, and roofing shingles—are being applied, the carpenters, who up until now have pretty much had the run of the construction site, make room for the other building trades who will do the "rough-in" for their work. Drilling holes in the studs and joists, the plumbers install the water supply and sewage disposal piping, electricians thread wires throughout the walls and hang electrical boxes for the light switches and outlets, and the mechanical contractors install the ductwork for the heating, ventilating, and air-conditioning systems. If you want a built-in vacuum system, it's roughed-in now. When all the "rough-ins" have been completed, it's time for another inspection. This time the plumbing and wiring inspectors get the call, but the building inspector waits for a few more things to be done.

If the house is going to have a chimney or fireplace, it is generally built at this time. Also, depending on the design of the home and the local building codes, fire-stops might have to be installed in the walls or floors. While the walls are open, it is also a good idea to install blocking or "nail backing" to attach things like cabinets, shelves, and towel bars to after the walls are finished. The building is now ready to be insulated, but this will hide much of the structure, so before this happens the building inspector must be called in for a final framing inspection.

While this interior work is going on, the carpenters often move outdoors and begin the exterior finish. The windows and doors must be installed before exterior wall finish and trim (corner boards, soffits, and frieze boards) can be applied. Then the siding is installed. The construction of any decks and porches is often coordinated with this exterior finish work.

When the building has been insulated, and after the doors and windows have been installed, work on the inside can continue. Most codes call for the installation of an interior vapor retarder (usually some type of polyethylene sheeting is used), over which the interior wall and ceiling finish is applied. In most houses, gypsum board—also known as sheetrock or drywall—is used, but a close cousin called "skim coat" or "veneer" plaster is becoming more popular. In both cases, the joints and screw-heads in the wallboard are concealed—the gypsum board with paper tape and joint compound, and the skim veneer base with a thin coat of special plaster.

While the interior finish work is being done, the outside "finish" work can be attended to. The finish grade (the level of the ground surrounding the building) is established and any steps, walks, and patios are constructed. If the siding and trim require painting or staining, it, too, is done. Other landscaping elements such as plantings and stone walls are completed now, and often the finish driveway is constructed.

Meanwhile, back inside, after the walls and ceilings are completed, wood floors are installed, but not sanded and sealed yet. Next, the interior trim—casing, baseboard, wainscoting, and molding—is applied to the windows, doors, walls, and ceilings, and the walls, ceilings, and trim are then either painted, wallpapered, or stained. Other finish work—stairs, handrails, and railings—is also done. Then any wall-to-wall carpet, resilient flooring, tile, or other finish flooring is installed. Plumbing fixtures, electrical trim and fixtures, heating elements and trim, cabinets, and shelving come next. The last major task is to sand and finish the wood floors. Finally, the odds and ends are taken care of and the house is given a thorough cleaning. The building inspector is called for a final inspection and, if all is in order, issues the certificate of occupancy (C.O.). The house is ready to be transformed into a home.

Although the length of time it takes to build a house varies widely depending on many factors—the size and complexity of the house, the size of the construction crew, and the weather, for example—a typical 2,000- to 2,500-square-foot house should require four to six months to complete. As you can see by the graph on pages 254-257, although the number of "working weeks" totals more than this, many of the jobs are done concurrently so the actually construction time is less.

THE DRAW SCHEDULE

You may have noticed that one important element was missing from the preceding construction sequence: the money to pay for it all. Usually, funds are disbursed in large chunks rather than smaller, perhaps weekly, installments. The lender probably has a standard "draw schedule", and your builder will bill you based on the need to pay workers, subs, and material suppliers. To regulate the flow of cash, it's good to synchronize these two schedules as much as possible.

The lender's draw schedule will most likely make the release of funds contingent on the completion of a specified amount of work. Most lenders have a field inspector who makes a visual verification before money is released. This ensures that the required work has been done and protects their interests. When your builder submits a bill to you for payment, you, too, should have a way to protect your interests and ascertain that the work has been done in compliance with the plans and specifications. Approval by the lender's inspector and the building inspector are not sufficient; you need something more. This type of construction supervision can be done by your designer or a construction manager. If you're not working with either a designer or a construction manager, and you don't have the technical knowledge to do the job yourself, it's probably wise—and cost effective in the long run—to hire a professional who can.

Construction Schedule

No. & Amt of Loan Draw	No. & Amt of Payment to Builder	CONSTRUCTION TASK	MONTH 1				
			wk 1	wk 2	wk 3	wk 4	
		Clearing, stump removal					
		Rough grading, driveway					
		Well					
		Basement excavation					
		Temporary utilities					
		Foundation footings					
		Other:					
		Inspection: footings					
		Foundation walls					
		Septic system installed					
		Inspection: well, septic					
		Foundation drainage, dampproofing					
		Other:					
		Inspection: foundation, drainage, dampproofing					
		Backfill foundation					
		Basement floor					
		Framing and sheathing: floors, walls, and roof					
		Fireplace, chimney					
		Roofing, soffit and fascia					
total:	total:						

MONTH 2				MONTH 3				MONTH 4				MONTH 5				MONTH 6			
wk 1	wk 2	wk 3	wk 4	wk 1	wk 2	wk 3	wk 4	wk 1	wk 2	wk 3	wk 4	wk 1	wk 2	wk 3	wk 4	wk 1	wk 2	wk 3	wk 4

No. & Amt of Loan Draw	No. & Amt of Payment to Builder	CONSTRUCTION TASK	MONTH 1				
			wk 1	wk 2	wk 3	wk 4	
		Inspection: framing					
		Rough-in of plumbing, wiring, HVAC					
		Windows, exterior doors					
		Siding, exterior finish					
		Decks, porches					
		Other:					
		Inspection: plumbing, wiring, HVAC, framing					
		Insulation (plus inspection)					
		Interior wall finish; gypsum board, plaster, etc.					
		Interior doors and trim					
		Floors: wood, resilient, tile					
		Interior painting					
		Cabinets, appliances					
		Wood floor finishing, carpet					
		Finish grade, walks, driveway					
		Landscaping					
		Other:					
		Other:					
		Inspection: final, receive C.O.					
total:	total:						

	MONTH 2				MONTH 3				MONTH 4				MONTH 5				MONTH 6			
	wk 1	wk 2	wk 3	wk 4	wk 1	wk 2	wk 3	wk 4	wk 1	wk 2	wk 3	wk 4	wk 1	wk 2	wk 3	wk 4	wk 1	wk 2	wk 3	wk 4

By the conclusion of your preconstruction meeting, all the planning details should be addressed, the tasks assigned, and the procedures in place to make for smooth running. Of course, your project will encounter a rough patch or two; every project does. Here are some suggestions to help you through those bumpy times.

RELATING TO WORKERS

Remember, the workers are the people who will build your dream. In addition to following the Golden Rule (*Whatever you want others to do for you, you should do for others*), you would be well advised to keep the following things in mind when interacting with your workers:

• Be prepared for meetings. Everybody's time is precious and you should recognize and respect this by preparing ahead for your regular construction meetings. Make sure that you know the subject of the meetings, gather any information that's your responsibility, and have your questions written out. It's also a good idea to take brief notes of each meeting for future reference.

• Avoid arguing in "public." By this I do not mean you and your partner, I'm referring to you and your builder. A much better tactic is to ask the builder to meet with you in private if you feel a need to disagree.

• Avoid blaming as a first response. If you or someone else discovers a construction error—a stairway that won't fit or a wall in the wrong place—don't immediately search for someone to blame. First, ascertain that a mistake has in fact been made; often things appear to be wrong when they're not. Next, hold a meeting with all the appropriate parties and work together to come up with the best possible solution. Then, try to determine whose *responsibility* (not fault) the mistake was and, if the solution costs money, figure out an equitable settlement. In construction, it is sometimes difficult to clearly assign the responsibility for mistakes to just one party, so it is often shared.

• Do not pester the workers. Idle chit-chat, casual conversation, or shooting the breeze with the workers may seem innocent enough, even polite, but it's really not. These interruptions slow down the pace of work and become an annoyance. In fact, a worker may be sufficiently distracted to cause an accident. You established the proper time for such conversation at the pre-construction conference, so try to stick to it.

• Do not withhold payments arbitrarily. If you and your builder don't see eye to eye about a portion of a bill or if you have some other disagreement, you may find it tempting to withhold payment to gain some leverage. This is not a good idea. Not only will you further aggravate the situation, but the builder may place a mechanic's lien on your property. First, try to work out the disagreement yourselves. If this cannot be done, consider paying the portion of the bill you believe to be correct and putting the disputed amount in an escrow account. Then, enlist some outside help and try to resolve your differences.

There are several tasks that must be completed before you make that final payment to your builder.

- The builder should finish all of the punch list items.

- You must obtain signed mechanic's lien releases from your builder (or general contractor) and all the subcontractors.

- You should receive a signed "house warranty" from your builder.

- You should obtain any warranties for items that are not covered by the builder's warranty, complete with instructions on how to follow up on any warranty claims.

- The lender's field representative should make a final inspection, verify that the project is completed, and release the final loan draw.

- The building inspector should make a final inspection, verify that the project is completed, and issue the certificate of occupancy (C.O.).

When you have received the C.O. and all the other items are completed, *then* you can make that final payment and the house is yours to inhabit.

SETTLING IN

Moving from your present home into your new one can be a major undertaking in and of itself. A little planning will make it less of an ordeal.

- Begin contacting and interviewing (by this time you should be a pro at this) moving companies several months ahead of the completion of construction. When you've settled on one, work out the logistics—truck size, packing, responsibilities, and estimated moving day.

- Several weeks before the scheduled moving day start notifying magazines, credit car companies, schools, post office, and other appropriate parties about your impending address change.

- As the moving date draws nearer, sort through your belongings and decide what you want to keep, give away, tag sale, or throw away; and start packing.

- Begin packing seldom-used items and then, a few days before the move, pack it all. Do an inventory of your possessions and make a photographic record of all your fragile or valuable items to help with the claims process should anything be damaged during the move.

- Mark the boxes and tag the larger items with the names of the room to which they should be moved when you unpack in your new home. Make extra copies of your floor plans to give to the movers on moving day.

- Take care of your financial (close bank accounts or cancel car and house insurance), medical, and other personal matters.

- A couple of weeks before the move, verify that your new house is on schedule and confirm your reservation with the moving company. Revise the date if you have to. If you are going to have to pay the movers the day of the move, verify the type of payment—bank check, certified check, credit card—that's required.

- If it's appropriate, arrange to have the utilities turned off at your old home.

- Cancel the newspaper or make arrangements to have it delivered to your new address.

- A day or two before the move pack up everything that's left inside and outside your house. Clean your old house; don't forget to defrost the freezer.

- On moving day empty out the house completely—check the closets, cabinets, basement, and attic for forgotten items. Leave your address so that the new owner can contact you with any questions.

As you move into your new home:
- Have one person available to answer questions and direct the movers. Give the movers the floor plans and a tour of the house.

- Protect the new home—floors, walls, trim—to avoid damage that might be done during the moving.

- Try to put furniture, boxes, and other items in the rooms where they will "live."

- If you are moving yourself, get help with any heavy or bulky items. You don't want to do any damage—to yourself or your possessions.

- If you discover any items were damaged in transit, immediately point them out to the movers and make the appropriate written documentation.

- Have refreshments on hand to quench the thirst and lift the spirits of everyone helping.

- When everything is moved, relax, sit back, and put your feet up on the nearest packing box.

MARK THE EXPERIENCE

Watching the construction of your house or addition is akin to watching your children grow; if you don't take the time to mark the experience you're apt to forget a lot of it. So take the time to think about how you would like to acknowledge and record the transformation of your project from a hole in the ground to a house, to a home. Here are some suggestions.

- Photograph or videotape every stage of construction and put them in the family album or video collection. Take pictures of the foundation, the framing, the mechanical systems, of everything. Not only will they be fun to look at through the years, someday they may play a very practical role. These pictures can act like x-rays, revealing the likely location of future problems. Photos are a must.

- Leave your mark on the structure itself. Put your hand imprints in fresh concrete, write names or messages to future owners on the framing. When I was a carpenter, remodeling an old home built in the early 1800's, I opened up a wall and found a message from the carpenter who originally built the house. It really gave me a sense of connection with the past.

- Speaking of connecting with the past, how about filling a time capsule with items from your everyday life and sealing it up inside a wall? Choose a wall—the kitchen or a bathroom—that has a good chance of being opened up during a future renovation. If you don't open it, just think of the people one hundred years from now who do.

- Perhaps one of the most significant things you can do is to have celebrations to signify notable moments during construction. Hold a "ceremonial groundbreaking" just before the cellar hole is dug. Have a champagne toast to celebrate the day your building is made "tight to the weather." Attach a pine bough to the top of the newly framed rafters.

The pine tree ritual is another connection with the past. The early houses and barns in this country had frames constructed of heavy timbers. These timbers were joined together into sections, called "bents," that formed the building's profile. To frame a building these bents were raised and secured, evenly spaced, on the floor deck. This "raising" was hard and dangerous work and couldn't be done by the carpenters alone. Many hands were needed to complete a successful raising and they typically became community-wide events. When the last bent was in place and the frame finally finished, a pine bough was attached to the peak of the building. The pine bough signified a safe and successful raising and showed respect to the wood that formed the frame. Sometimes a few lines of verse were written or read.

There was another part to this ceremony—and that was the party. The end of the work signaled the beginning of the celebration. Not just celebration for the fun of it, but celebration of a new beginning. Our ancestors knew the value and power of these rituals and you might try to find that same power for yourself. Given modern construction convention, perhaps a better time for such a celebration is after you've received your certificate of occupancy. Gather all the people who worked so hard, from the early planning stages, to the final driven nail, and give thanks to this community of people. Remember, these people have worked with you and helped to shepherd you from your dreams to a place where you can live, and dream of even better things to come.

blank

Appendices

Recommended Reading

BOOKS

DESIGN AND CONSTRUCTION

Alexander, Christopher. *A Pattern Language.* New York: Oxford University Press, 1977.

Alexander, Christopher. *The Timeless Way of Building.* New York: Oxford University Press, 1977.

Axelrod, Jerold L. *Architectural Plans for Adding On or Remodeling.* New York: McGraw-Hill, 1992.

Bianchina, Paul. *Illustrated Dictionary of Building Materials and Techniques.* New York: John Wiley & Sons, 1993.

Brand, Stewart. *How Buildings Learn: What Happens After They're Built.* New York: Viking Penguin, 1994.

Kilpatrick, John A. *Understanding House Construction.* 2nd ed. rev. Washington, DC: Home Builder Press, NAHB, 1993.

LeGwin, J. Hardy, & Associates. *Minispec: Residential Construction Specifications.* West Newton, MA: J. Hardy LeGwin & Associates, 1993.

Locke, Jim. *Apple Corps Guide to the Well-Built House.* Boston: Houghton Mifflin Co., 1988.

McHarg, Ian L. *Design with Nature.* Garden City, NY: Doubleday/Natural History Press, 1969.

Metz, Don. *New Compact House Designs: 27 Award-Winning Plans, 1,250 Square Feet or Less.* Pownal, VT: Story Communications Inc., 1991.

Moore, Charles, Gerald Allen, and Donlyn Lyndon. *The Place of Houses.* New York: Holt Reinhart Winston, 1974.

NAHB. *Quality Standards for the Professional Remodeler.* 2nd ed. Washington, DC: Home Builder Press, NAHB, 1991.

Olgay, Victor. *Design with Climate.* New York: Van Nostrand Reinhold, 1992.

GENERAL INTEREST

Coomer, Joe. *Dream House, On Building a House by a Pond.* Winchester, MA: Faber and Faber, 1992.

Foley, Mary Mix. *The American Home.* New York: Harper & Row, 1980.

Kidder, Tracy. *House.* Boston: Houghton Mifflin, 1985.

Manning, Richard. *A Good House.* New York: Penguin Books, 1993.

McCamant, Kathryn, and Charles Durrett. *Cohousing; A Contemporary Approach to Housing Ourselves.* Berkeley: Habit Press/Ten Speed Press, 1988.

Wright, Gwendolyn. *Building The Dream, A Social History of Housing in America.* New York, Pantheon Books, 1981.

GREEN BUILDING
(ENERGY EFFICIENCY, HEALTHY HOUSE, AND RESOURCE EFFICIENCY)

Barnett, Dianna Lopez, and William D. Browning. *A Primer on Sustainable Building.* Snowmass, CO: Rocky Mountain Institute, 1995.

Bower, John. *Healthy House.* New York: Carol Publishing Group, 1991.

Bower, John. *Healthy House: A Design and Construction Guide.* Unionville, IN: Healthy House, 1993.

Heede, Richard, and Staff of Rocky Mountain Institute. *Homemade Money: How to Save Energy and Money in Your Home.* Snowmass, CO: Rocky Mountain Institute, 1995.

Hubbard, Alice, and Clay Fong. *Community Energy Workbook.* Snowmass, CO: Rocky Mountain Institute, 1995.

Pearson, David. *The Natural House Book.* New York: Simon and Schuster/Fireside, 1989.

Pilatowicz, Grazyna. *Eco-Interiors.* New York: John Wiley and Sons, 1995.

HOME MORTGAGES, FINANCE, LEGAL

Anderson, Peter J. *A Consumer's Guide to Home Buying and Mortgage Financing.* Ascoda, MI: Anderson Distributing, 1991.

Bell, W. Frazier. *How to Get the Best Home Loan.* New York: Wiley, 1992.

Dorfman, John R. *The Mortgage Book.* Yonkers, NY: Consumer Reports Books, 1992.

Irwin, Robert. *Tips and Traps When Mortgage Hunting.* New York: McGraw-Hill, 1992.

Lenz, Sidney. *Your Money and Your Home; a Step-by-Step Guide to Financing or Refinancing Your Home.* Burbank, CA: Casa Graphics, 1992.

Lewis, Ralph. *Land Buying Checklist.* Washington, DC: Home Builder Press, NAHB, 1994.

Miller, Peter G. *The Common Sense Mortgage.* New York: Harper Collins, 1992.

NAHB. *Contracts and Liability for Builders and Remodelers.* 3rd ed. Washington, DC: Home Builder Press, NAHB, 1993.

Tobias, Andrew. *The Only Other Investment Guide You'll Ever Need.* New York: Bantam, 1987.

Steinmetz, Thomas C. *The Mortage Kit: How to Save Thousands of Dollars Financing Your Home.* Chicago: Dearborn Finan., 1991.

INSURANCE

Abromovitz, Les. *Family Insurance Handbook.* New York: McGraw-Hill, 1992.

Abromovitz, Les. *Family Insurance Handbook: The Complete Guide for the 1990's.* Blue Ridge Summit, PA: Tab Books, 1990.

Baldwin, Ben G. *The Complete Book of Insurance: Protecting Your Life, Health, Property and Income.* Chicago: Probus Publishing Co., 1991.

LAND PLANNING

Babize, Molly, and Walter Cudnohufsky. *Designing Your Corner of Vermont: Protecting Your Property Investment through Good Site Design.* Williston, VT: Village Press, 1991.

Brabec, Elizabeth A., Harry L. Dodson, Christine Reid, and Robert D. Yaro. *Rural by Design: Maintaining Small Town Character.* Chicago/Washington, DC: Planners Press, American Planning Association, 1994.

Lynch, Kevin. *Site Planning.* Cambridge, MA: MIT Press, 1971.

Yaro, Robert D., Randal G. Arendt, Harry L. Dodson, and Elizabeth A. Brabee. Dealing with Change In the Connecticut River Valley: A Design Manual for Conservation and Development. Amherst, MA: Center for Rural Massachusetts, University of Massachusetts, 1988.

PERIODICALS

Better Homes and Gardens
Meredith Corp.
1716 Locust St.
Des Moines, IA 50309-3023

Colonial Homes
The Hearst Corp.
959 Eighth Ave.
New York, NY 10019

Environ
P.O. Box 2204
Fort Collins, CO 80522

Fine Homebuilding
Taunton Press
Box 355
Newtown, CT 06470

Good House Keeping
The Hearst Corp.
959 Eighth Ave.
New York, NY 10019

Home Magazine
Hachette Filipacchi USA, Inc.
P.O. Box 53969
Boulder, CO 80323-3969

House Beautiful
P.O. Box 7024
Red Oak, IA 51591-0024

The Journal of Light Construction
RR#2, Box 146
Richmond, VT 05477

New Shelter
Rodale Press
33 E. Minor St.
Emmas, PA 18049

Old-House Interiors
Dove Tail Publishers
Blackburn Tavern, 2 Main St.
Gloucester, MA 01930

Old-House Journal
Dove Tail Publishers
Blackburn Tavern, 2 Main St.
Gloucester, MA 01930

Whole Earth Review
POINT
27 Gate Five Rd.
Sausalito, CA 94945

Woman's Day
Hachette Filipacchi
1633 Broadway
New York, NY 10019

Many periodicals, including *Better Homes and Gardens, House Beautiful, Good Housekeeping,* and *Woman's Day,* have special home building issues or sister magazines.

SOURCES FOR BOOKS ABOUT CONSTRUCTION

Home Builder Book Store
National Association of Home Builders
1201 15th St., NW
Washington, DC 20005
(800) 223-2665

Journal of Light Construction Bookstore
RR#2, Box 146
Richmond, VT 05477
(802) 434-5241

National Construction Book Catalog
BNi Building News
77 Wexford St.
Needham Heights, MA 02194
(800) 873-6379

Taunton Press
63 Main St., Box 355
Newton, CT 06470
(800) 243-7252

BUSINESS AND GOVERNMENT ASSISTANCE ORGANIZATIONS

Federal Consumer Product Safety Commission
800-638-2772

Federal Savings and Loan Association
Office of Thrift Supervision
800-253-2128

Council of Better Business Bureaus
4200 Wilson Blvd., Ste. 800
Arlington, VA 22203
703-276-0100

U.S. Chamber of Commerce
1615 H St., NW
Washington, DC 20062
202-659-6000

Your local phone book may be another good source of information. For example, many phone companies include a self-help guide that lists local phone numbers such as the Better Business Bureau, consumer protection office, and the offices of state and federally chartered lending agencies.

CREDIT REPORTING AGENCIES

For a good article on credit reporting agencies, see the May 1991 issue of *Consumer Reports*, page 356. The following is a list of the three major national credit bureaus. For a listing of local offices and/or phone numbers (including 800 numbers) check the yellow pages of your phone book. When you call be sure to inquire about the cost of the report. Costs vary depending on the reporting bureau and some states regulate the amount of the fee, so if you're not asked where you live, tell them. TRW will provide you with one free copy of your report each year. The information contained in one agency's report might be different from that in another, so you might want to get a report from each to make sure they're *all* correct.

Equifax
P.O. Box 4081
Atlanta, GA 30302
(404) 885-8000
(800) 685-1111

Trans Union
East:
P.O. Box 360
Philadelphia, PA 19105
(215) 569-4582

Midwest:
Consumer Relations
222 S. First St., Ste. 201
Louisville, KY 40202
(502) 584-0121

West:
P.O. Box 3110
Fullerton, CA 92634
714-738-3800

TRW Credit Data
National Consumer Relations Center
12606 Greenville Ave.
P.O. Box 749029
Dallas, TX 75374-9029
(214) 235-1200, ext. 251
(800) 422-4879

ENERGY EFFICIENCY PROGRAMS AND RATING SYSTEMS

There are many public and private energy efficiency programs and energy rating systems available to assist with residential energy conservation. These programs are typically regional in nature and you will have to do a little investigation to learn about the programs in your area.

To learn about public programs, such as home energy rating systems, weatherization programs, or state housing finance agencies, contact your state energy office or:

The National Assoc. of State Energy Officials
1615 M St., NW
Ste. 810
Washington, DC 20036
(202) 546-2200

Energy Star Homes
U.S. EPA (6202J)
410 M St., SW
Washington, DC 20460
(202) 775-6650

An example of one such program is:

NY-STAR, Inc.
41 State St., Ste. 1011
Albany, NY 12207
(518) 465-3115

To learn about privately sponsored energy conservation programs, contact your local utility—your electric or gas company. An example of one such program that's active in certain areas of Massachusetts, New Hampshire, and Rhode Island is:

The Energy Crafted Home Program
441 Stuart St., 5th floor
Boston, MA 02116
(800) 628-8413

FEDERAL GOVERNMENT AND RELATED PUBLICATIONS

Many of these are available directly from a bank, savings and loan, or other lending agency near you.

"Fannie Mae's Consumer Guide to Adustable Rate Mortgages" and other publications are available from:

Federal National Mortgage Association
Fannie Mae Fulfillment Center
Box 341
Annapolis, MD 20701-0341
(800) 471-5554

Consumer Handbook—What You Should Know About Home Equity Lines of Credit, Consumer Handbook on Adjustable Rate Mortgages, and other publications are available from:

Federal Reserve Board
Publications Services
Mail Stop 127
Board of Governors of the Federal Reserve System
Washington, DC 20551
(202) 452-3000

Settlement Costs Guide [HUD-398-H(3)] and other publications are available from:

The U.S. Department of Housing and Urban Development
Publications Office
Room 237
451 Seventh St., SW
Washington, DC 20410
202-708-4374
The Mortgage Money Guide [135-T] and a catalog of federal publications are available from:

U. S. Government Consumer Information Center
Pueblo, CO 81009
719-948-3334

Green building covers a number of topics including resource-efficient building materials, healthy-house construction, and energy-efficient building materials and methods. The following is a list of references and organizations that the homeowner might find useful, although some are geared more toward the professional builder.

COMPREHENSIVE SOURCES THAT COVER ALL THE GREEN-BUILDING ISSUES

Building with Nature
Carol Venolia
P.O. Box 369
Gualala, CA 95445
(707) 884-4513
A newsletter that attempts to link building professionals across the country, although it's weighted toward the West Coast. It consists mainly of philosophical discussions of green building issues.

Environmental Building News
RR1, Box 161
Brattleboro, VT 05301
(802) 257-7300
A newsletter that provides in-depth articles on materials, contruction methods and general news concerning all green-building issues.

Environmental by Design
Archemy Consulting Ltd.
1662 West 75th Ave.
Vancouver, BC V6P 6G2
(604) 266-7721
A sourcebook that focuses mainly on materials to be used on the interiors of buildings. Through the use of concise summaries, this resource provides information and guidance for choosing a wide variety of low-toxic, resource-efficient interior products.

Green Living
Dover Rd., HCR 63 Box 39
South Newfane, VT 05351
A quarterly journal distributed free of charge throughout southeastern Vermont, southwestern New Hampshire, and northern Massachusetts and available through subscriptions.
Northeast Sustainable Energy Association
23 Ames St.
Greenfield, MA 01301
(413) 774-6051
This professional organization concentrates on educating builders and designers about green-building concerns. It sponsors a yearly Quality Building Conference.

ENERGY-EFFICIENT AND RESOURCE-EFFICIENT DESIGN AND CONSTRUCTION

American Council for an Energy-Efficient Economy
1001 Connecticut Ave., NW, Ste. 801
Washington, DC 20036
(202) 429-8873
The ACEEE is a nonprofit lobbying group that promotes awareness of the need for energy efficiency. It has a catalog of books and publications, including *Residential Indoor Air Quality and Energy Efficiency*, an excellent overview of the concepts and methods for building healthy, energy-efficient houses, and the *Consumer Guide to Home Energy Savings*, a guide to insulating techniques and energy-efficient lighting and appliances.

Center for Resourceful Building Technology
P.O. Box 3413
Missoula, MT 59806
(406) 549-7678
This nonprofit organization focuses on educating builders and the general public about innovative building technologies. CRBT publishes the *Guide to Resource Efficient Building Elements*, a reference listing over 100 manufacturers of resource-efficient building products.

Energy-Efficient Building Association
Northcentral Technical College
100 Campus Dr.
Wausau, WI 54401-1899
(715) 675-6331
This trade association is dedicated to educating builders about the concepts and techniques required to build safe, energy-efficient buildings. EEBA hosts a yearly conference and publishes the proceedings, as well as other technical publications.

Rocky Mountain Institute
1739 Snowmass Creek Rd.
Snowmass, CO 81654-9199
(303) 927-3851
RMI publishes the *Efficient House Sourcebook*, a well-rounded collection of green building information, including in-depth reviews of books, periodicals, catalogs, information services, and associations.

Underground Space Center
790 Civil and Mineral Engineering Building
500 Pillsbury Dr., S.E.
University of Minnesota
Minneapolis, MN 55455
This research center is this country's major source for information on earth-sheltered housing and has published a number of books on the subject.

GOVERNMENT AND NATIONAL TRADE ASSOCIATIONS

National Appropriate Technology Assistance Service (NATAS)
P.O. Box 2525
Butte, MT 59702-2525
(800) 428-2525 (in Montana: 800-494-4572)
This agency of the U.S. Department of Energy provides assistance in locating technical and resource information on efficient and renewable energy and technology.

National Center for Appropriate Technology (NCAT)
U.S. Department of Energy
P.O. Box 3838
Butte, MT 59702
(406) 494-4572
NCAT is the research arm of the U.S. Department of Energy and publishes its findings on topics such as enginered wetlands, composting toilets, and solar water heaters in small booklets.

National Research Center (NRC)
National Association of Home Builders
400 Prince George Blvd.
Upper Marlboro, MD 20772-8731
(301) 249-4000
This research center publishes reports on specialized building materials and technology and has recently completed the Resource Conservation House, a demostration home built with resource-efficient materials.

Oak Ridge National Laboratory (ORNL)
Oak Ridge, TN 37831
(615) 576-5454
Managed under contract to the U.S. Department of Energy by Marin Marietta Energy Systems, the ORNL is a laboratory for building science. The laboratory's technical findings are published and available for sale to the public. Recent publications include the *Building Foundation Handbook* and the *Moisture Control Handbook*.

HEALTHY HOUSE

Safe Home Digest
Lloyd Publishing
24 East Ave., Ste. 1300
New Canaan, CT 06840
(203) 966-2099
SHD publishes the *Healthy House Building Resource Guide*, a comprehensive resource directory of publications, products, and services needed to build and maintain a healthy house, as well as a bimonthly newsletter.

Healthy House Institute
7471 North Shiloh Rd.
Unionville, IN 47468
(812) 332-5073
HHI is an independent resource center dedicated to sharing information and solutions to the problems caused by toxic materials in the home. HHI has its roots in a book by John Bower, *Healthy House Building, A Design and Construction Manual,* and publishes periodic reports on relevant topics.

PROFESSIONAL ASSOCIATIONS

American Institute of Architects (AIA)
1735 New York Ave., NW
Washington, DC 20006
(202) 626-7300

American Institute of Building Design (AIBD)
16 Wilton Rd, Bldg. D
Westport, CT 06880
(800) 366-2423

American Society of Interior Desigers (ASID)
608 Massachusetts Ave., NE
Washington, DC 20002
(202) 546-3480

National Association of Home Builders (NAHB)
15th and M Streets, NW
Washington, DC 20005
(202) 822-0200 (800) 368-5242

National Association of the Remodeling Industry (NARI)
1901 N. Moore St., Ste. 808
Arlington, VA 22209
For names of remodelers in your area call: (800) 440-6274

For information on systems-built housing:
NAHB Building Systems Councils
1201 15th St., NW
Washington, DC 20005
(800) 368-5242

OFFICE-SUPPLY CATALOGS

Charrette   (800) 367-3729
Dataprint Corp.   (800) 227-6191
Staples   (800) 333-3330
Viking Office Products   (800) 421-1222

HOME PLANNING SERVICES

Many planning tools and resources are available to people interested in building and renovating a home. You should take advantage of as many as you have the time to pursue! As mentioned in Step 2, many independently owned lumber yards have on-site planning and design centers. Some of these centers specialize in computer-aided kitchen design or other specific areas, and some offer assistance in planning an entire building project.

Lumber yards, building-materials suppliers and related businesses often sponsor clinics and workshops for homeowners. Examples of these programs are paint selection and application, deck construction, siding and gutter installation, window design and selection, and tool demonstrations. Local builders, lending agencies, and real estate companies also hold open houses and run seminars designed to provide planning and building information to the general public. These services and special programs are generally advertised in local media. If you do not see or hear of something, do not assume it is not offered! Call these businesses and ask what they have available. You should also check the local papers to see if there is a regular listing or schedule for home building and planning seminars. These services, seminars, and demonstrations are almost always free to consumers.

HOMEWORK SEMINARS

The seminar I have developed is a specific example of the programs that are available in communities. Like this book my HOMEWORK Seminar offers an education in planning the home-building and remodeling processes. The seminar also gives prospective home builders a chance to meet local building industry professionals and to hear what they have to say.

At a HOMEWORK Seminar, I (or someone I've trained) leads participants through the entire planning process. HOMEWORK Seminars are offered free to participants. Each attendee receives (also free of charge) a seminar manual and other valuable printed materials. The seminars are typically sponsored by two or three local businesses. The main sponsor, most often a lumber yard, is joined by other complimentary professionals—typically product manufacturers and lending institutions. All of the sponsors are on hand to contribute their expertise and answer questions. Participants get a good working knowledge of the planning process as well as a manual full of useful tips, worksheets, techniques, and strategies—essentially everything they need to thoroughly plan their building project from inception to completion. Participants enjoy learning and sharing information in the seminars' informal environment. To learn more about HOMEWORK Seminars, call (800) 736-1293.

MONTHLY MORTGAGE TABLES

The following tables show monthly payments on mortgages at interest rates from 5% to 8% and 9% to 12%. Remember, the payments shown here cover only interest and principal and that your actual pay-

15-YEAR MORTGAGES   **RATES**

AMOUNTS	5.000%	5.500%	6.000%	6.500%	7.000%	7.500%	8.000%
50,000.00	395.40	408.54	421.93	435.55	449.41	463.51	477.83
60,000.00	474.48	490.25	506.31	522.66	539.30	556.21	573.39
70,000.00	553.56	571.96	590.70	609.78	629.18	648.91	668.96
80,000.00	632.64	653.67	675.09	696.89	719.06	741.61	764.52
90,000.00	711.71	735.38	759.47	784.00	808.95	834.31	860.09
100,000.00	790.79	817.08	843.86	871.11	898.03	927.01	955.65
110,000.00	869.87	898.79	928.24	958.22	988.71	1,019.71	1,051.22
120,000.00	948.95	980.50	1,012.63	1,045.33	1,078.59	1,112.41	1,146.78
130,000.00	1,208.03	1,062.21	1,097.01	1,132.44	1,168.48	1,205.12	1,242.35
140,000.00	1,107.11	1,143.92	1,181.40	1,219.55	1,258.36	1,297.82	1,337.91
150,000.00	1,186.19	1,225.63	1,265.79	1,306.66	1,348.24	1,390.52	1,433.48
160,000.00	1,265.27	1,307.33	1,350.17	1,393.77	1,438.13	1,483.22	1,529.04
170,000.00	1,344.35	1,389.04	1,434.56	1,480.88	1,528.01	1,575.92	1,624.61
180,000.00	1,423.43	1,470.75	1,518.94	1,567.99	1,617.89	1,668.62	1,720.17
190,000.00	1,502.51	1,552.46	1,603.33	1,655.10	1,707.77	1,761.32	1,815.74
200,000.00	1,581.59	1,634.17	1,687.71	1,742.21	1,797.66	1,854.02	1,911.30
210,000.00	1,660.67	1,715.88	1,772.10	1,829.33	1,887.54	1,946.73	2,006.87
220,000.00	1,739.75	1,797.58	1,856.49	1,916.44	1,977.42	2,039.43	2,102.43
230,000.00	1,818.83	1,879.29	1,940.87	2,003.55	2,067.31	2,132.13	2,198.00
240,000.00	1,897.90	1,961.00	2,025.26	2,090.66	2,157.19	2,224.83	2,293.57
250,000.00	1,976.98	2,042.71	2,109.64	2,177.77	2,247.07	2,317.53	2,389.13
260,000.00	2,056.06	2,124.42	2,194.03	2,264.88	2,336.95	2,410.23	2,484.70
270,000.00	2,135.14	2,206.13	2,278.41	2,351.99	2,426.04	2,502.93	2,580.26
280,000.00	2,214.22	2,287.83	2,362.80	2,439.10	2,516.72	2,595.63	2,675.83
290,000.00	2,293.30	2,369.54	2,447.18	2,526.21	2,606.60	2,688.34	2,771.39

ments would probably include tax and home insurance payments and, as a result, be higher. Contact a local lender to learn what the exact rates would be for your area.

				RATES			
	9.000%	9.500%	10.000%	10.500%	11.000%	11.500%	12.000%
AMOUNTS							
50,000.00	507.13	522.11	537.30	552.70	568.30	584.10	600.08
60,000.00	608.56	626.53	644.76	663.24	681.96	700.91	720.10
70,000.00	709.99	730.96	752.22	773.78	795.62	817.73	840.12
80,000.00	811.41	835.38	859.68	884.32	909.28	934.55	960.13
90,000.00	912.84	939.80	967.14	994.86	1,022.94	1,051.37	1,080.15
100,000.00	1,104.27	1,044.22	1,074.61	1,105.40	1,136.60	1,168.19	1,200.17
110,000.00	1,115.69	1,148.65	1,182.07	1,215.94	1,250.26	1,285.01	1,320.18
120,000.00	1,217.12	1,253.07	1,289.53	1,326.48	1,363.92	1,401.83	1,440.20
130,000.00	1,318.55	1,357.49	1,396.99	1,437.02	1,477.58	1,518.65	1,560.22
140,000.00	1,419.97	1,461.91	1,504.45	1,547.56	1,591.24	1,635.47	1,680.24
150,000.00	1,521.40	1,566.34	1,611.91	1,658.10	1,704.90	1,752.28	1,800.25
160,000.00	1,622.83	1,670.76	1,719.37	1,768.64	1,818.56	1,869.10	1,920.27
170,000.00	1,724.25	1,775.18	1,826.83	1,879.18	1,932.21	1,985.92	2,040.29
180,000.00	1,825.68	1,879.60	1,934.29	1,989.72	2,045.87	2,102.74	2,160.30
190,000.00	1,927.11	1,984.03	2,041.75	2,100.26	2,159.53	2,219.56	2,280.32
200,000.00	2,028.53	2,088.45	2,149.21	2,210.80	2,273.19	2,336.38	2,400.34
210,000.00	2,129.96	2,192.87	2,256.67	2,321.34	2,386.85	2,453.20	2,520.35
220,000.00	2,231.39	2,297.29	2,364.13	2,431.88	2,500.51	2,570.02	2,640.37
230,000.00	2,332.81	2,401.72	2,471.59	2,542.42	2,614.17	2,686.84	2,760.39
240,000.00	2,434.24	2,506.14	2,579.05	2,652.96	2,727.83	2,803.66	2,880.40
250,000.00	2,535.67	2,610.56	2,686.51	2,763.50	2,841.49	2,920.47	3,000.42
260,000.00	2,637.09	2,714.98	2,793.97	2,874.04	2,955.15	3,037.29	3,120.44
270,000.00	2,738.52	2,819.41	2,901.43	2,984.58	3,068.81	3,154.11	3,240.45
280,000.00	2,839.95	2,923.83	3,008.89	3,095.12	3,182.47	3,270.93	3,360.47
290,000.00	2,941.37	3,028.25	3,116.36	3,205.66	3,296.13	3,387.75	3,480.49

AMOUNTS	5.000%	5.500%	6.000%	6.500%	7.000%	7.500%	8.000%	8.500%
50,000.00	329.98	343.94	358.22	372.79	387.65	402.80	418.22	433.91
60,000.00	395.97	412.73	429.86	447.34	465.18	483.36	501.86	520.69
70,000.00	461.97	481.52	501.50	521.90	542.71	563.92	585.51	607.48
80,000.00	527.96	550.31	573.14	596.46	620.24	644.47	669.15	694.26
90,000.00	593.96	619.10	644.79	671.02	697.77	725.03	752.80	781.04
100,000.00	659.96	687.89	716.43	745.57	775.30	805.59	836.44	867.82
110,000.00	725.95	756.68	788.07	820.13	852.83	886.15	920.08	954.61
120,000.00	791.95	825.46	859.72	894.69	930.36	966.71	1,003.73	1,041.39
130,000.00	857.94	894.25	931.36	969.25	1,007.89	1,047.27	1,087.37	1,128.17
140,000.00	923.94	963.04	1,003.00	1,043.80	1,085.42	1,127.83	1,171.02	1,214.95
150,000.00	989.93	1,031.83	1,074.65	1,118.36	1,162.95	1,208.39	1,254.66	1,301.73
160,000.00	1,055.93	1,100.62	1,146.29	1,192.92	1,240.48	1,288.95	1,338.30	1,388.52
170,000.00	1,121.92	1,169.41	1,217.93	1,267.47	1,318.01	1,369.51	1,421.95	1,475.30
180,000.00	1,187.92	1,238.20	1,289.58	1,342.03	1,395.54	1,450.07	1,505.59	1,562.08
190,000.00	1,253.92	1,306.99	1,361.22	1,416.59	1,473.07	1,530.63	1,589.24	1,648.86
200,000.00	1,319.91	1,375.77	1,432.86	1,491.15	1,550.60	1,611.19	1,672.88	1,735.65
210,000.00	1,385.91	1,444.56	1,504.51	1,565.70	1,628.13	1,691.75	1,756.52	1,822.43
220,000.00	1,451.90	1,513.35	1,576.15	1,640.26	1,705.66	1,772.31	1,840.17	1,909.21
230,000.00	1,517.90	1,582.14	1,647.79	1,714.82	1,783.19	1,852.06	1,923.81	1,995.99
240,000.00	1,583.89	1,650.93	1,719.43	1,789.38	1,860.72	1,933.42	2,007.46	2,082.78
250,000.00	1,649.89	1,719.72	1,791.08	1,863.93	1,938.25	2,013.98	2,091.10	2,169.56
260,000.00	1,715.89	1,788.51	1,862.72	1,938.49	2,015.78	2,094.54	2,174.74	2,256.34
270,000.00	1,781.88	1,857.30	1,934.36	2,013.05	2,093.31	2,175.10	2,258.39	2,343.12
280,000.00	1,847.88	1,926.00	2,006.01	2,087.60	2,170.84	2,255.66	2,342.03	2,429.91
290,000.00	1,913.87	1,994.87	2,077.65	2,162.16	2,248.37	2,336.22	2,425.68	2,516.69

AMOUNTS	9.000%	9.500%	10.000%	10.500%	11.000%	11.500%	12.000%	12.500%
50,000.00	449.86	466.074	82.51	499.19	516.09	533.21	550.54	568.07
60,000.00	539.84	559.28	579.01	599.03	619.31	639.86	660.65	681.68
70,000.00	629.81	652.49	675.52	698.87	722.53	746.50	770.76	795.30
80,000.00	719.78	745.71	772.02	798.70	825.75	853.14	880.87	908.91
90,000.00	809.75	838.92	868.52	898.54	928.97	959.79	990.98	1,022.53
100,000.00	899.73	932.13	965.02	998.38	1,032.19	1,066.43	1,101.09	1,136.14
110,000.00	989.70	1,205.34	1,061.52	1,098.22	1,135.41	1,173.07	1,211.19	1,249.75
120,000.00	1,079.67	1,118.56	1,158.03	1,198.22	1,238.63	1,279.72	1,321.30	1,363.37
130,000.00	1,169.64	1,211.77	1,254.53	1,297.89	1,341.84	1,386.36	1,431.41	1,476.98
140,000.00	1,259.62	1,304.98	1,351.03	1,397.73	1,445.06	1,493.00	1,541.52	1,590.60
150,000.00	1,349.59	1,398.20	1,447.53	1,497.57	1,548.28	1,599.64	1,651.63	1,704.21
160,000.00	1,439.56	1,491.41	1,544.03	1,597.41	1,651.50	1,706.29	1,761.74	1,817.83
170,000.00	1,529.53	1,584.62	1,640.54	1,697.25	1,754.72	1,812.93	1,871.85	1,931.44
180,000.00	1,619.51	1,677.84	1,737.04	1,797.08	1,857.94	1,919.57	1,981.96	2,045.05
190,000.00	1,709.48	1,771.05	1,833.54	1,896.92	1,961.16	2,026.22	2,092.06	2,158.67
200,000.00	1,799.45	1,864.26	1,930.04	1,996.76	2,064.38	2,132.86	2,202.17	2,272.28
210,000.00	1,889.42	1,957.48	2,026.55	2,096.60	2,167.60	2,239.50	2,312.28	2,385.90
220,000.00	1,979.40	2,050.69	2,123.05	2,196.44	2,270.81	2,346.15	2,422.39	2,499.51
230,000.00	2,069.37	2,143.90	2,219.55	2,296.27	2,374.03	2,452.79	2,532.50	2,613.12
240,000.00	2,159.34	2,237.11	2,316.05	2,396.11	2,477.25	2,559.43	2,642.61	2,726.74
250,000.00	2,249.31	2,330.33	2,412.55	2,495.95	2,580.47	2,666.07	2,752.72	2,840.35
260,000.00	2,339.29	2,423.54	2,509.06	2,595.79	2,683.69	2,772.72	2,862.82	2,953.97
270,000.00	2,429.26	2,516.75	2,605.56	2,695.63	2,786.91	2,879.36	2,972.93	3,067.58
280,000.00	2,519.23	2,609.97	2,702.06	2,795.46	2,890.13	2,986.00	3,083.04	3,181.19
290,000.00	2,609.21	2,703.18	2,798.56	2,895.30	2,993.35	3,092.65	3,193.15	3,294.81

AMOUNTS	5.000%	5.500%	6.000%	6.500%	7.000%	7.500%	8.000%	8.500%
50,000.00	292.30	307.04	322.15	337.60	353.39	369.50	385.91	402.61
60,000.00	350.75	368.45	386.58	405.12	424.07	443.39	463.09	483.14
70,000.00	409.21	429.86	451.01	472.65	494.75	517.29	540.27	563.66
80,000.00	467.67	491.27	515.44	540.17	565.42	591.19	617.45	644.18
90,000.00	526.13	552.68	579.87	607.69	636.10	665.09	694.63	724.70
100,000.00	584.59	614.09	644.30	675.21	706.78	738.99	771.82	805.23
110,000.00	643.05	675.05	708.73	742.73	777.46	812.89	849.00	885.75
120,000.00	701.51	736.91	773.16	810.25	848.14	886.79	926.18	966.27
130,000.00	759.97	798.31	837.59	877.77	918.81	960.69	1,003.36	1,046.80
140,000.00	818.43	859.72	902.02	945.29	989.49	1,034.59	1,080.54	1,127.32
150,000.00	876.89	921.13	966.45	1,012.81	1,060.17	1,108.49	1,157.72	1,207.84
160,000.00	935.34	982.54	1,030.88	1,080.33	1,130.85	1,182.39	1,234.91	1,288.36
170,000.00	993.80	1,043.95	1,095.31	1,147.85	1,201.52	1,256.29	1,312.09	1,368.89
180,000.00	1,052.26	1,105.36	1,159.74	1,215.37	1,272.20	1,330.18	1,389.27	1,449.41
190,000.00	1,110.72	1,166.77	1,224.17	1,282.89	1,342.88	1,404.08	1,446.45	1,529.93
200,000.00	1,169.18	1,228.18	1,288.60	1,350.41	1,413.56	1,447.98	1,543.63	1,610.45
210,000.00	1,227.64	1,289.58	1,353.03	1,417.94	1,484.24	1,551.88	1,620.81	1,690.98
220,000.00	1,286.10	1,350.99	1,417.46	1,485.46	1,554.91	1,625.78	1,698.00	1,771.50
230,000.00	1,344.56	1,412.40	1,481.89	1,552.98	1,625.59	1,699.68	1,775.18	1,852.02
240,000.00	1,403.02	1,473.81	1,546.32	1,620.50	1,696.27	1,773.58	1,852.36	1,932.55
250,000.00	1,461.48	1,535.22	1,610.75	1,688.02	1,766.95	1,847.48	1,929.54	2,013.07
260,000.00	1,519.93	1,596.63	1,675.18	1,755.54	1,837.63	1,921.38	2,006.72	2,093.59
270,000.00	1,578.39	1,658.04	1,739.61	1,823.06	1,908.30	1,995.28	2,083.90	2,174.11
280,000.00	1,636.85	1,719.45	1,804.04	1,890.58	1,978.98	2,069.18	2,161.09	2,254.64
290,000.00	1,695.31	1,780.85	1,868.47	1,958.10	2,049.66	2,143.07	2,238.27	2,335.16

AMOUNTS	9.000%	9.500%	10.000%	10.500%	11.000%	11.500%	12.000%	12.500%
50,000.00	419.60	436.85	454.35	472.09	490.06	508.23	526.61	545.18
60,000.00	503.52	524.22	545.22	566.51	588.07	609.88	631.93	654.21
70,000.00	587.44	611.59	636.09	660.93	686.08	711.53	737.26	763.25
80,000.00	671.36	698.96	726.96	755.35	784.09	813.18	842.58	872.28
90,000.00	755.28	786.33	817.83	849.76	882.10	914.82	947.90	981.32
100,000.00	839.20	873.70	908.70	944.18	980.11	1,016.47	1,053.22	1,090.35
110,000.00	923.12	961.07	999.57	1,038.60	1,078.12	1,118.12	1,158.55	1,199.39
120,000.00	1,007.04	1,048.44	1,090.44	1,133.02	1,176.14	1,219.76	1,263.87	1,308.43
130,000.00	1,090.96	1,135.81	1,181.31	1,227.44	1,274.15	1,321.41	1,369.19	1,417.46
140,000.00	1,174.87	1,223.18	1,272.18	1,321.85	1,372.16	1,423.06	1,474.51	1,526.50
150,000.00	1,258.79	1,310.55	1,363.05	1,416.27	1,470.17	1,524.70	1,579.84	1,635.53
160,000.00	1,342.71	1,397.91	1,453.92	1,510.69	1,568.18	1,626.35	1,685.16	1,744.57
170,000.00	1,426.63	1,485.28	1,544.79	1,605.11	1,666.19	1,728.00	1,790.48	1,853.60
180,000.00	1,510.55	1,572.65	1,635.66	1,699.53	1,764.20	1,829.64	1,895.80	1,962.64
190,000.00	1,594.47	1,660.02	1,726.53	1,793.95	1,862.21	1,931.29	2,001.13	2,071.67
200,000.00	1,678.39	1,747.39	1,817.40	1,888.36	1,960.23	2,032.94	2,106.45	2,180.71
210,000.00	1,762.31	1,834.76	1,908.27	1,982.78	2,058.24	2,134.58	2,211.77	2,289.74
220,000.00	1,846.23	1,922.13	1,999.14	2,077.20	2,156.25	2,236.23	2,317.09	2,398.78
230,000.00	1,930.15	2,009.50	2,090.01	2,171.62	2,254.26	2,337.88	2,422.42	2,507.81
240,000.00	2,014.07	2,096.87	2,180.88	2,266.04	2,352.27	2,439.53	2,527.74	2,616.85
250,000.00	2,097.99	2,184.24	2,271.75	2,360.45	2,450.28	2,541.17	2,633.06	2,725.89
260,000.00	2,181.91	2,271.61	2,362.62	2,454.87	2,548.29	2,642.82	2,738.38	2,834.92
270,000.00	2,265.83	2,358.98	2,453.49	2,549.29	2,646.31	2,744.47	2,843.71	2,943.96
280,000.00	2,349.75	2,446.35	2,544.36	2,643.71	2,744.32	2,846.11	2,949.03	3,052.99
290,000.00	2,433.67	2,533.72	2,635.23	2,738.13	2,842.33	2,947.76	3,054.35	3,162.03

AMOUNTS	5.000%	5.500%	6.000%	6.500%	7.000%	7.500%	8.000%	8.500%
50,000.00	268.41	283.89	299.78	316.03	332.65	349.61	366.88	384.46
60,000.00	322.09	340.67	359.73	379.24	399.18	419.53	440.26	461.35
70,000.00	375.78	397.45	419.69	442.45	465.71	489.45	513.64	538.24
80,000.00	429.46	454.23	479.64	505.65	532.24	559.37	587.01	615.13
90,000.00	483.14	511.01	539.60	568.86	598.77	629.29	660.39	692.02
100,000.00	536.82	567.79	599.55	632.07	645.30	699.21	733.76	768.91
110,000.00	590.50	624.57	659.51	695.27	731.83	769.14	807.14	845.80
120,000.00	644.19	681.35	719.46	758.48	798.36	839.06	880.52	922.70
130,000.00	697.87	738.13	779.42	821.69	864.89	908.98	953.89	999.59
140,000.00	751.55	794.90	839.37	884.90	931.42	978.90	1,027.27	1,076.48
150,000.00	805.23	851.68	899.33	948.10	997.95	1,048.82	1,100.65	1,153.37
160,000.00	858.91	908.46	959.28	1,011.31	1,064.48	1,118.74	1,174.02	1,230.26
170,000.00	912.60	965.24	1,019.24	1,074.52	1,131.01	1,188.66	1,247.40	1,307.15
180,000.00	966.28	1,022.02	1,079.19	1,137.72	1,197.54	1,258.59	1,320.78	1,384.04
190,000.00	1,019.96	1,078.80	1,139.15	1,200.93	1,264.07	1,328.51	1,394.15	1,460.94
200,000.00	1,073.64	1,135.58	1,199.10	1,264.14	1,330.61	1,398.43	1,467.53	1,537.83
210,000.00	1,127.33	1,192.36	1,259.06	1,327.34	1,397.14	1,468.35	1,540.91	1,614.72
220,000.00	1,181.01	1,249.14	1,319.01	1,390.55	1,463.67	1,538.27	1,614.28	1,691.61
230,000.00	1,234.69	1,305.91	1,378.97	1,453.76	1,530.20	1,608.19	1,687.66	1,768.50
240,000.00	1,288.37	1,362.69	1,438.92	1,516.96	1,596.73	1,678.11	1,761.04	1,845.39
250,000.00	1,342.05	1,419.47	1,498.88	1,580.17	1,663.26	1,748.04	1,834.41	1,922.28
260,000.00	1,395.74	1,476.25	1,558.83	1,643.38	1,729.79	1,817.96	1,907.79	1,999.18
270,000.00	1,449.42	1,533.03	1,618.79	1,706.58	1,796.32	1,887.88	1,981.16	2,076.07
280,000.00	1,503.10	1,589.81	1,678.74	1,769.79	1,862.85	1,957.80	2,054.54	2,152.96
290,000.00	1,556.78	1,646.59	1,738.70	1,833.00	1,929.38	2,027.72	2,127.92	2,229.85

AMOUNTS	9.000%	9.500%	10.000%	10.500%	11.000%	11.500%	12.000%	12.500%
50,000.00	402.31	420.43	438.79	457.37	476.16	495.15	514.31	533.63
60,000.00	482.77	504.51	526.54	548.84	571.39	594.17	617.17	640.35
70,000.00	563.24	588.60	614.30	640.32	666.63	693.20	720.03	747.08
80,000.00	643.70	672.68	702.06	731.79	761.86	792.23	822.89	853.81
90,000.00	724.16	756.77	789.81	823.27	857.09	891.26	925.75	960.53
100,000.00	804.62	840.85	877.57	914.74	952.32	990.29	1,028.61	1,067.26
110,000.00	885.08	924.94	956.33	1,006.21	1,047.56	1,089.32	1,131.47	1,173.98
120,000.00	965.55	1,009.03	1,053.09	1,097.69	1,142.79	1,188.35	1,234.34	1,280.71
130,000.00	1,046.01	1,093.11	1,140.84	1,189.16	1,238.02	1,287.38	1,337.20	1,387.44
140,000.00	1,126.47	1,177.20	1,228.60	1,280.64	1,333.25	1,386.41	1,440.06	1,494.16
150,000.00	1,206.93	1,261.28	1,316.36	1,372.11	1,428.49	1,485.44	1,542.92	1,600.89
160,000.00	1,287.40	1,345.37	1,404.11	1,463.58	1,523.72	1,584.47	1,645.78	1,707.61
170,000.00	1,367.86	1,429.45	1,491.87	1,555.06	1,618.95	1,683.50	1,748.64	1,814.34
180,000.00	1,448.32	1,513.54	1,579.63	1,646.53	1,714.18	1,782.52	1,851.50	1,921.06
190,000.00	1,528.78	1,597.62	1,667.39	1,738.00	1,809.41	1,881.55	1,954.36	2,027.79
200,000.00	1,609.25	1,681.71	1,755.14	1,829.48	1,904.65	1,980.58	2,057.23	2,134.52
210,000.00	1,689.71	1,765.79	1,842.90	1,920.95	1,999.88	2,079.61	2,160.09	2,241.24
220,000.00	1,770.17	1,849.88	1,930.66	2,012.43	2,095.11	2,178.64	2,262.95	2,347.97
230,000.00	1,850.63	1,933.96	2,018.41	2,103.90	2,190.34	2,277.67	2,365.81	2,454.69
240,000.00	1,931.09	2,018.05	2,106.17	2,195.37	2,285.58	2,376.70	2,468.67	2,561.42
250,000.00	2,011.56	2,102.14	2,193.93	2,286.85	2,380.81	2,475.73	2,571.53	2,668.14
260,000.00	2,092.02	2,186.22	2,281.69	2,378.32	2,476.04	2,574.76	2,674.39	2,774.87
270,000.00	2,172.48	2,270.31	2,369.44	2,469.90	2,571.27	2,673.79	2,777.25	2,881.60
280,000.00	2,252.94	2,354.39	2,457.20	2,561.27	2,666.51	2,772.82	2,880.12	2,988.32
290,000.00	2,333.41	2,438.48	2,544.96	2,652.74	2,761.74	2,871.85	2,982.98	3,095.05

Sample Owner-Designer Contract

Here's a basic contract I offer my clients. The designer you hire will probably have his or her own contract, but this one will serve as a good reference.

Agreement made this day of August, 199 _____ , between _____ (insert designer's name), hereafter called the Designer, of _____ (insert city and state) and _____ (insert owner's name), hereafter called the Owner.

Project Information

Owner's Address:

_____

_____

Project Location:

_____

_____

Project Description:

_____

_____

I. THE DESIGNER AGREES TO PERFORM THE FOLLOWING SERVICES:

1. Schematic Design Phase   The Designer will assess the Owner's needs and requirements and prepare preliminary, schematic design documents for the Owner's approval.

2. Design Development Phase   Based on the approved Schematic Design Documents and Owner-authorized changes, the Designer will prepare Design Development Documentsconsisting of drawings and other documentation that describe the size and character of the project.

3. Construction Document Phase   Based on the approved Design Development Documents and any further Owner-authorized changes, the designer shall prepare Construction Documents consisting of drawings and specifications of sufficient detail to obtain fixed bids/estimates for the construction project.

4. Estimating/Bidding/Negotiation Phase After approval of the Construction Documents, the Designer shall assist the Owners in obtaining bids/estimates and in selecting a contractor.

5. Construction Phase During the construction of the project, the designer will visit the site and be in contact with the builder and owners as necessary to keep updated about the progress of the work and will be available to discuss and answer questions about the project. The Designer is not responsible for the quantity, quality, schedule, or any other aspect of the work being performed by the contractor and/or his/her subcontractors because they are the sole responsibilities of the contractor and/or his/her subcontractors.

6. Completion of Services The Designer's responsibility to provide services shall end fifteen days after substantial completion of the work.

II. THE OWNER'S RESPONSIBILITY SHALL INCLUDE AND THE OWNER AGREES TO:

1. Provide full information regarding the requirements for the project.

2. Establish an overall budget for the project.

3. Furnish information describing the physical characteristics and legal limitations of the project site, as applicable, including, but not limited to, rights of way, easements, boundaries, zoning restrictions, deed restrictions, percolation tests, and wetland areas.

4. Pay the Designer's fees and reimbursable expenses as set forth in Section IV of this contract.

5. Review and approve the various phases in a timely fashion as to permit the orderly progress of the project.

III. CONTRACT TERMINATION

1. This Agreement may be terminated by either party upon not less than seven days written notice should the other party fail substantially to perform in accordance with the terms of this Agreement through no fault of the party initiating the termination.

2. Upon termination of the Agreement, the Owner(s) agree to pay the Designer within seven days for the work done to that date, plus all reimbursable expenses.

3. If work on the project is suspended by the Owner(s) for more than thirty consecutive days, the Designer shall be compensated in full, forthwith, for the services that he performed prior to such suspension (excluding any services performed after receiving a written request to suspend work).

IV. BASIS OF COMPENSATION

1. Bid Design Package/Estimate Design Package

Phase	Part #	Fee

a. Schematic Design Phase

(Attach detailed description of services)	1.	_____
	2.	_____
	3.	_____

Design Development Phase

(Attach detailed description of services)	1.	_____
	2.	_____
	3.	_____

Construction Document Phase

(Attach detailed description of services)	1.	_____
	2.	_____

Bidding/Estimating Phase

(Attach detailed description of services)	1.	_____

Construction Phase

(Attach detailed description of services)	1.	_____
	2.	_____

TOTAL FEE

1. Payments are due within 10 days of receipt of an invoice, which indicates the completion of that phase. A phase or part of a phase is typically completed with a meeting between the Designer and Owner.

2. If during the course of the project the Designer is required by the Owner(s) to make significant changes in the scope or size of the project or major revisions on approved design phases, additional compensation will be paid as a fixed fee to be determined for each change or revision.

3. Reimbursable expenses will be billed with each phase and include such items as prints, photocopies, photos, drafting papers, model supplies, and shipping.

4. Any additional services which might be required, such as structural engineering, civil engineering, interior design, landscape design, etc., are not included in the Designer's fee and shall be contracted for and billed separately. Before contracting for any such services, the Designer shall consult with the Owner(s) and get their approval and authorization.

5. Claims, disputes, or other matters in question between the parties to this Agreement arising out of or relating to this Agreement or breach thereof shall be subject to and decided by arbitration in accordance with the Construction Industry Association currently in effect unless the parties mutually agree otherwise. The award rendered by the arbitrator or arbitrators shall be final, and judgment may be entered upon it in accordance with applicable law in any court having jurisdiction thereof.

6. This Agreement represents the entire agreement between the Owner(s) and Designer and any changes shall be in writing and signed by both parties.

_____

Peter Jeswald, Designer

_____   _____
Owner   Witness

_____   _____
Owner   Witness

Index

liability, 247
mortgage, 215
performance bond, 247
private mortgage, 215
recommended reading, 266
for remodeling, 246
workers compensation, 246–47
International Conference of Building Officials, 233
Interviews, 86–90
building professionals worksheets, 91–117
lenders worksheets, 220–21
stock plans worksheets, 100–105
warning signs, 90
worksheet, 222–25

J

Joist, 14

L

Land planning, recommended reading, 266
Liability insurance, 247
Line of credit, 212
Loans, see Financing
Loan-to-value ratio, 39–40, 211, 215
LTV, see Loan-to-value ratio

M

Maggie Mae (MGIC), see Mortgage Guaranty
Insurance Corporation
Masonry work, 187
Mechanics liens, 121
MGIC (Maggie Mae), see Mortgage Guaranty
Insurance Corporation
Mistakes, handling, 258
Moisture protection, 188
Mortgage, 205
Mortgage Guaranty Insurance Corporation, 220

N

NARI, see National Association of the Remodeling
Industry
National Association of the Remodeling Industry, 86

O

On center (O.C.), 13
Oversights, in remodeling, 175

P

Payment schedule, 249–50, 253
Performance bond, 247
Periodicals, 266–67
Permits, see Permitting process
Permitting process
approvals, 190, 235–36
approvals checklist, 242–44

building codes, 233–35
building permit, 232–34
starting, 230
well approval and drilling worksheet, 239–41
who to see, 230–31
zoning application worksheet, 237–38
zoning board of appeals, 231–32
zoning regulations, 231
Pitch, 14
PITI, see Financing, principle, interest, taxes, and
insurance
Planning and development board, 231, 235
Planning process, 1–5
construction industry, 5
decisions, 4
emotional support, 4–5
the family, 2–3
principles, 18–20
time and money, 3
Plans
services, 13, 29
terminology, 11–13
PMI, see Private mortgage insurance
Pre-construction
conference, 248–50
planning, see Planning process
Pricing methods, 191–93
Principles, 18–20
Private mortgage insurance, 215
Professional associations, 274
Program, 13
Project designer, viii
role of, 10
Project designer, see Designer(s)
Project manager, viii
defined, 8–9
role of, 8–10
Project planner, viii
Publications, 22. See also Recommended reading
Public works, department of, 231, 235

R

Radon gas, 62, 251
Rafter, 14
Recommended reading
construction books, 267–68
credit reporting agencies, 268–69
design, 264
energy efficiency, 265, 271–72
financing, 265, 270
general interest, 264–65
green building, 265, 271–72
house systems, 273
insurance, 266
land planning, 266legal, 265
periodicals, 266–67
trade associations, 273

Before You Build...
HOMEWORK Seminars cover:

• How to interview and hire a designer, builder, and other professionals
• Practical tips for setting a budget, writing a contract, and working with lenders
• How to organize your building project to:
>   •minimize hassles
>   • maximize the creative joy of the building process
>   • set realistic expectations for your timeline
>   • avoid problem relationships throughout the building process
>   • maximize efficiency and cost savings
>   • avoid the pitfalls of the permitting process
>   • plan for energy-efficient construction

For more information, call Peter Jeswald at ODT, Inc.: (800) 786-1293.

Dealer inquiries are invited.

Before You Build...
HOMEWORK CONSULT

Peter Jeswald has designed a program for individuals who want to work one on one with a home-planning professional. During a HOMEWORK consult session, your project is analyzed and assessed using the ten-step process presented in this book. Specific strategies are developed to make your project run smoothly and successfully. Afterward, you are given a written report that recaps your meeting and reaffirms your planning strategies. You also receive an hour's worth of follow-up phone consultation time that you can use to ask questions and help resolve planning issues that might arise during your project.

In addition, you are supplied with support materials you can use throughout your building project. These include: a HOMEWORK-ITINERARY Checklist, a 250-page manual, a copy of this book, and an audiotape of your itinerary consultation.

To learn more about HOMEWORK-ITINERARY consultations, call (800) 736-1293.